"OPEN THE SKY"

The Story of Missionary Pilot Dwayne King

*We prayed that as God had broken down
the wall, He will open up the sky.*
—"Kostya" Rudoy,
Russian flight student

By Mark Winheld

"Open the Sky"
The Story of Missionary Pilot Dwayne King
by Mark Winheld

Printed in the United States of America

ISBN 9781612154268

Unless otherwise indicated, Bible quotations are taken from the New International Version (NIV). Copyright © 1973, 1978, 1984 by International Bible Society. Zondervan. Other versions, noted in text, are The King James Version (KJV); The New American Standard Bible (NASB), copyright © 1960, 1962, 1963, 1968, 1971, 1972, 1973, 1975, 1977, 1995 by The Lockman Foundation; and The Revised Standard Version (RSV), copyright © 1946, 1952 by the National Council of Churches of Christ in the USA. Thomas Nelson & Sons.

www.xulonpress.com

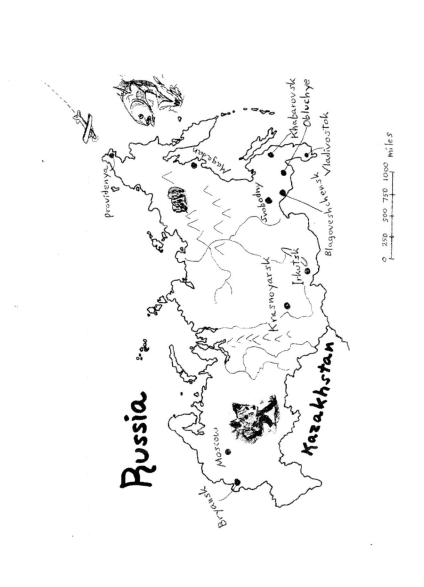

Russia

Kazakhstan

Providenya

Magadan

Khabarovsk
Obluchye

Svobodny

Blagoveshchensk
Vladivostok

Krasnoyarsk

Irkutsk

Moscow

Bryansk

0   250 500 750 1000 miles

Russia

Providenya

Bering Strait

Nome

Arctic Circle

Bettles

Yukon River

Anchorage

King Ranch

Tok

Canada

Glennallen

Whitehorse

Teslin

Soldotna

Bristol Bay

Aleutian Islands

Alaska

N

0 100 200 300 400 500 Miles

"OPEN THE SKY"

Adventure is enticing. Adventure with purpose is intoxicating—it's only sad that so few people experience it, and so many Christ followers think they can't have it. Dwayne King's life proves that fulfilling God's purpose is the highest adventure. Serving Him is life's great reward ... and airplanes! Let's not forget about airplanes!

> **—Stephen Saint,**
> son of martyred missionary Nate Saint
> and author of *End of the Spear*

... the most contagious, infectious, enthusiastic Christian I have ever known. Dwayne has been a bush pilot and church planter in the wilds of Alaska, a pioneer in taking the Gospel to Far East Russia after the fall of the Iron Curtain and then on to Kazakhstan, and the founder of Kingdom Air Corps—training and inspiring others to use the airplane for ministry to remote regions of the world. Dwayne's life is filled with rich and often humorous stories of how God has used this servant to inspire all. His faith and actions have blessed me as his friend.

> **—Alvin O. "Bud Austin, Ph.D.,**
> president emeritus, LeTourneau University

As a pilot who owns a home in Alaska, I know many people who have crossed paths with Dwayne King, and I understand the difficulty of flying in the remote bush. He and I share a love for the Alaskan frontier. The advance of the Gospel in much of the State of Alaska today is due to men like Dwayne King and others who have sacrificed to take the Good News to the ends of the earth. He has lived a fascinating life.

> **—Franklin Graham,**
> president and CEO, Billy Graham
> Evangelistic Association, Samaritan's Purse

When God wants to do something special, he gives special gifts to special people. Dwayne King is such a man. An outstanding bush pilot, an excellent church planter, a passionate soul-winner, a gifted recruiter and an accomplished fund-raiser are just some of the gifts God has blessed him with.

—Leander Rempel,
former SEND Alaska director

... I thought I knew Dwayne well. Mark Winheld's collection of anecdotes and insights sheds additional light on this remarkable man, and now, knowing him better, I admire him even more. Thanks, Mark, for capturing the essence of a man who has impacted the Kingdom of God more than anyone I can call a personal friend.

—Rev. Paul Blasko,
pastor emeritus, Twin Orchards Baptist Church

This account of the life of Dwayne King—bush pilot, entrepreneur, visionary and warm-hearted evangelist—will stir your heart with his missionary adventures. Here is a story of a real person who desired to bring glory to God through reaching the peoples of the far north in North America and Russia with the good news of salvation through faith in Jesus Christ.

—Frank M. Severn,
general director emeritus, SEND International

Davis College has been training missionaries for over one hundred years. It is our privilege that Dwayne King is a distinguished alumnus from the class of 1963. God has greatly used him in mission work, and it is the honor of our college to bestow upon him the honorary Doctorate of Divinity degree. Dwayne King is an example of a godly missionary and is a missionary's missionary. It is our prayer that "Open the Sky" *would challenge many to the mission field.*

—Dino Pedrone, D.Min.,
president, Davis College

DEDICATION

Ann Lewis, mission team "mother," who
nagged me until I agreed to write it;

and the usual suspects:

Pastor Paul Blasko, who midwifed
me into God's family;
SEND International, which sent me to the
land of my fathers, where I found
Russian brothers and sisters, whose faith
and courage model His fullness;

and in memory of

Lt. Col. Franklin B. Resseguie, USAF (Ret.),
my other pilot friend and first publisher; and
Bible scholar Floyd Barackman, whose holiness
and friendship drew me deeper into the family.

On earth they encouraged me, and still do.

ACKNOWLEDGMENTS

BECAUSE I BELIEVE that thanking everyone in general thanks no one in particular, and that singling out only a few helpers relegates the others to chicken-liver status, I want this to be as complete as possible—in the spirit of the search order issued by the federal marshal played by Tommy Lee Jones in *The Fugitive*: "... every henhouse, outhouse ... and doghouse!"

So, thanks—in no particular order—to:

Those who responded to requests for advice, endorsements or interviews: Frank Severn, Dr. Alvin O. "Bud" Austin, Franklin Graham, Stephen Saint, Roger A. Krenzin, Leander and Louise Rempel, Rev. Paul Blasko, Dave and Liz Givens, Carl Kresge, Vernon ("Steve") and Dorris Stevenson, Vladimir Trossavitch Lebedev, Win and Gracia Stiefel, Lydia Fairchild, Phil and Glenna Dufresne, Dick Camp, Bill Berkheiser, Lew Parks, Elsie Livers, Rev. Gennady Abramov, Lena Sidenko, Rev. Yuri Sipko, Oleg and Tanya Vasin, Nicolai and Tatiana Koshelupov, Durland "Dur" Vining, Don and Ann Lewis, J.C. Harder, Dr. Dino J. Pedrone, Marla McCrorie, and Herbert Paul;

Helpers in the mechanics of writing, graphics, publicity, travel arrangements and, later, navigating the scary thunderheads of publishing: Red Barn Computers of Binghamton (especially their Remote Rescue service, which kept my technologically-challenged brain from melting down when my word processor got cranky); Marcie Williamson, June Adamek, Emily Gelser, Mike and Ana Palmiter, and Craig Hall;

Editor Beth K. Vogt, publisher Xulon Press, copyright attorney Mark Levy, and map designer Makaela Davis, Dwayne's great-granddaughter;

The late Russell T. Hitt, whose *Jungle Pilot*—the Nate Saint story—inspired Dwayne to fly for God, and inspired me with an ideal model of a missionary aviator biography; and Hitt's son, David A. Hitt, for his friendship and encouragement;

Twin Orchards Baptist Church, SEND International, LeTourneau University, Davis College, Kingdom Air Corps, Southern Tier Christian Writers' Fellowship, and Friends of the George F. Johnson Memorial Library;

Lorraine Hillborn, for special permission to use the song, "Missionary Pilot," by her late husband, Ruben Hillborn; and Hal Farrar, for permission to use Hal's poem, also titled "Missionary Pilot";

The King family, of course;

and finally,

Everyone who prayed, whom I could not begin to name; and others I should name, but whom—despite my best efforts—I've overlooked.

CONTENTS

Part 1

MEET DWAYNE

"A Real Piece of Work"

Author's note: *Most definitions of "a real piece of work" have negative or derisive connotations, but also refer to being colorful and attention-getting. It is these latter qualities that describe Dwayne—these, as well as the first famous use of the phrase, in Shakespeare's* Hamlet: *"What a piece of work is man! How noble in reason! How infinite in faculty! In form and moving how . . . admirable!"*

God loves you, and Dwayne has a wonderful plan for your life.
—Dwayne King,
recruiting missionaries

1. MY FRIEND, the shameless opportunist

I am part of the fellowship of the unashamed ...

I ... live by faith, lean on His presence, walk by patience, am uplifted by prayer, and labor by power.

My face is set, my gait is fast, my goal is heaven. My road is narrow, my way rough, my Guide reliable, my mission clear. I cannot be bought, compromised, detoured, lured away, turned back, deluded, or delayed. I will not give up, shut up, or let up. I will go on until He comes, and work until He stops me.

I am a disciple of Jesus.

— attributed to Bob Moorehead,
as quoted in *Run With the Vision*,
Sjogren and Stearns, 1995

CROCODILE DUNDEE star Paul Hogan, playing a fictional super-hunter in the wilds of the Australian Outback, sees a pretty reporter approaching. He quickly hides his safety razor and resumes shaving with a twelve-inch Bowie knife.

Cut to the wilds of Alaska. In a garage cluttered with communications gear, hunting supplies and moose antlers, Dwayne King, a real missionary playing himself, is doing his own romantic impression. He gleefully appropriates a suggestion by another reporter to rename the staging area of his next mission—which he has already named the Command Center—the "Situation Room."

Dwayne in "Situation Room," 2006

Dwayne's shameless willingness to piggyback on CNN's Wolf Blitzer (or anyone else famous) is aimed at a different seduction. The hotrodder-turned-bushpilot-turned-missionary uses any opportunity to woo the lost for Christ. "Sometimes," he observes, "you have to let the image produce the fruit for the Kingdom."

In March 2005, he expressed happiness that I planned to write his biography, quickly adding that it should glorify God, not him. Fair enough. But God's power usually works through people, and Dwayne is a real piece of work.

Power is unleashed when God's purposes, human gifts and historic opportunities come together. God's purpose is to enlarge the Kingdom of His love. Dwayne's gift is encouragement, maximized by wilderness-honed aviation skills and a jack-of-all-trades knack for working cheerfully under extreme conditions. The opportunity was the collapse of the Soviet Union. Dwayne seized the opportunity in 1991, becoming one of the first missionary pilots to fly into Russia after the melting of the "Ice Curtain," as the Iron Curtain was known in Siberia and the Far East. His Alaskan ministry, and later role in strengthening the Russian evangelical church, became legendary.

For years, scattered "Dwayne stories" from assorted Alaska Airlines flight crews, missionaries and church workers signaled that an extraordinary life of faith was being lived among us. Here's how a friend, Marla McCrorie, describes his fame: "It wasn't until my car crossed into Alaska that I understood who Dwayne was. I called ahead to ask directions, and the answer was, 'just drive to Glennallen and ask anybody.' In truth, everyone for two hundred miles around knew where to find Dwayne."

It's easy to see why. He brings zest and zeal to whatever he's doing: wrestling blocks of stone into the foundations of a new church ... inspiring a Russian pastor to win a nose-to-nose shouting match with the not-quite-defunct KGB ... juggling endless crises ranging from yanked visas to fouled-up construction logistics ... sharing a dream of fishing where Christ's disciples fished in Galilee ... training his Kingdom Air Corps students to fly small planes over Alaskan mountains and glaciers.

It's easy to chuckle when this ordinary-looking guy with the contagious grin goes into action, whether haggling with cabbies about rides for American church-building volunteers or trying to interest a couple of Aeroflot officials in an aviation training deal that could help missionary pilots. Hands wave, eyes light up, and enthusiastic but fractured Russian gallops several sentences ahead of the interpreter. It's even easier to be moved by his urgency to satisfy the spiritual hunger of the Russians he loves while there is still light between the dawn of freedom and the approach of new darkness. The merry heart gives way to a purpose as unshakable as the rock on which his faith stands.

Marla sums up the earthly source of his staying power—his wife, Carolyn: "It takes a Carolyn to make a complete Dwayne. Carolyn is the rescuer, the teleprompter, the keeper of correspondence, nutrition and sanity. Without Carolyn, he would have bled or starved to death, quadruple-booked himself and forgotten everyone's name." According to another friend, Ann Lewis, "Carolyn tries to keep him on an even keel, or he'd be trying to fly somewhere without a plane."

He's not the easiest interview to pin down, either, although he's happy to talk when cornered. Older brother Dave suggests helpfully, "Of course, you could go to Kazakhstan and try to nail his feet to the floor. Ha!"

More than six strenuous decades and a bout of prostate cancer have not appreciably slowed him down, as he proved on Thanksgiving 2007. "We play a family football game we call the Turkey Bowl," said younger sister Carole King-Rhinevault. "Dwayne added a bit of excitement when he ran from the sidelines to tackle the other team's ball carrier to the ground. Only then did he realize he had just tackled his niece, Addie, who was at that moment wondering when he might release the neck hold he had on her." He claimed later he didn't know it was supposed to be *touch* football. Still later, however, Carolyn noted: "He is finding out his 66-year-old body cannot keep up with his 26-year-old brain that tells him he can jump and run eighteen hours a day!"

Dwayne's adventure and the life story behind it will be told as much as possible in his own words, and by others, including the author, whose lives he has touched. This book is about him, not me, but there are reasons besides friendship for a few personal thoughts here.

As a former reporter, I know that complete objectivity is unattainable, especially in religion, politics, and relationships. It's more honest for a writer to simply disclose up front the baggage being brought to the story. My baggage includes a mostly secular Jewish upbringing and Russian family roots, combined with an adventurous streak and—until relatively recently—a highly opinionated political faith that humanity could achieve social justice unaided by any higher power.

At first, Dwayne and I found each other a little strange. I had never met a Christian missionary before and was leery of anyone who seemed too enthusiastic or spontaneous. I thought, *This guy must be a used-car salesman or game show host!* Dwayne, for his part, embodied the mission-ary's proverbial readiness to preach, pray or die at a moment's notice—he liked my spiritual testimony, but couldn't understand why I had to write it down before sharing it. I also had never picked up the practical skills his ministries depend on. During mission construction trips, I often half-joked, "I had a fine liberal arts education, so I don't actually know how to *do* anything."

Our differences were no bar to friendship. In Far East Russia I once heard a wise Korean missionary observe, "Traditions don't bond people. Christ bonds people."

I had come to Christ relatively late in life. Far from cutting me off from my childhood ideals, conversion made me appreciate them even more by giving them a rock to stand on and a love that gave them meaning. I was soon attracted to Dwayne's vision of divine justice in Russia and the gusto with which he plunged into that forbidding, wounded land. Our paths crossed several times when I volunteered for church-building missions. On one journey, he delivered me from arrogance by reminding me that certain people I criticized must answer to God, not me. On that trip, his expert piloting of a sputtering Cessna high above the Canadian Rockies also delivered me from my own ultimate interview—which, I fervently felt, would be highly premature!

So I'm no neutral observer, but sympathetic bias sometimes allows a clearer view. In defense of subjectivity, C.S. Lewis says personal experi-ence is obviously the best way to understand anything that affects one's self. My understanding of Dwayne's influence on others comes from his influence on me; that's why some of the narrative is from my viewpoint.

If he inspired this late-blooming believer, how much more must he inspire those with whole lifetimes ahead of them to follow in his prop wash! He surely knows how to jump-start inspiration. In 1997, in Vladivostok, he explained how he recruits workers for the harvest: "Take them to the uttermost ends of the earth, let them experience pioneer ministry, and they won't ever be the same."

Catching the vision beyond day-to-day obstacles, beyond all the threats, doubts and shortcomings, beyond the construction debris on a Vladivostok hilltop, he makes Russian believers and their foreign brothers and sisters see what he sees: "Jesus will build his church. No Iron Curtain will stop that. No police or army will stop that. That's the purpose of God. We are with God and He is with us."

Dwayne's modeling was an important lesson in a lifetime of learning how Christianity "works." When I met him I was a baby Christian, ripe to be molded by good shepherds or deconstructed by bad ones. The Christians at my new church were *Christianity*. My pastor was *The Clergy*. My new missionary friend was *Missionaries*. The (purely hypothetical!) discovery of a spiritual mentor with one arm in the collection plate and the other around someone else's spouse would now do no more than sadden me, but might have derailed my faith then.

The baggage I brought to the Cross included the secular culture's usual semi-comic, semi-sinister stereotype of missionaries as repressed, puritanical fanatics who generally ended up in gigantic cast-iron stewpots tended by hungry cannibals.

I quickly discarded that image when I learned more about Dwayne and other real missionaries. My attitude changed to awe. Raised on World War II stories from my parents' generation, images indelibly evoked for later generations by such tributes as *Saving Private Ryan* and *Band of Brothers*, I had grown up worshipping righteous warriors. Then I realized missionaries, too, were often heroic. Not only that, they routinely shouldered additional burdens in the field: Family responsibilities. Financial uncertainty. Foreign languages. Unarmed vulnerability to unpredictable danger. A lifetime hitch, if burnout didn't strike first.

This realization introduced a second stereotype, harder to shake because it was partly true: Missionaries must be superhuman giants! It's easy to counter that missionaries are simply ordinary people empowered to live extraordinary lives. As Dwayne puts it, "We're just people who say, *Here we are—God's frozen chosen*," acknowledging with Martin Luther that God's power is what makes the difference:

Did we in our own strength confide, our striving would be losing.

But simply knowing something isn't the same as understanding it. Any knowledge of God's truth must remain dim until we are in His presence, when faith will become sight. Secular ways of thinking yield slowly to the emotional reality He grants as we approach Him. I still struggle to understand how missionaries, accomplishing what they do, can remain normal, joy-filled people. That's because I have not yet reached, and might never reach, that level of readiness—which is really a depth of love—to seek God's glory without counting the cost.

Clues to this love appear in Dwayne's journeys in Alaska and Eurasia to cold landscapes of remote places and unkindled hearts; journeys through dark nights of self-doubt, following the light. Clues appear in the letters of an earlier missionary pilot, Nate Saint, martyred in Ecuador, whose life story inspired Dwayne to fly for God. Both men learned that the daily tasks of wilderness survival could be transformed from time-consuming barriers to ministry into ministry itself.

That makes life an act of worship. If that doesn't glorify God, I don't know what does.

2. SEPT. 1-2, 1991: Into the Unknown

As we came in and landed I was very, very nervous. Very scared.
Our bags were packed with Bibles. We didn't know whether that
was going to be legal or not.

—Dwayne King

The jailer ... fell trembling ... and asked, "Sirs, what must I do to
be saved?" ... Then they spoke the word of the Lord to him and to
all the others in his house.

—Acts 16: 29-30, 32

MONDAY, SEPTEMBER 2, 1991 — The Piper Navajo was inside
Soviet airspace and starting to descend toward the military airstrip
in Far East Russia. Copilot and team leader Dwayne King had no clue to
the outcome of the flight his whole life had been aimed at and which would
change it forever. The 48-year-old Alaska bush pilot and missionary was
focused on a more immediate issue: forbidden fruit. Twenty minutes to
touchdown, losing altitude over the Bering Sea with Providenya in sight,
he remembered it was illegal to bring in fresh produce.

"You better eat it, and eat it fast," Dwayne told the others on board.
They obediently stuffed their faces with about a dozen apples, oranges
and bananas, and handed him the cores and peels. Minutes before final
approach, he opened a side window and tossed out the scraps—all but one
of which disappeared.

The Piper's wheels hit the potholed gravel runway between the mountains on the tip of the rocky, desolate Chukotka Peninsula. The plane
bounced and settled, taxiing past red-starred helicopters and cargo trans-

ports toward the weathered, concrete-slab airport terminal. A banana peel was draped over the tail, flapping in the breeze.

Pilot Tim Harold kicked the rudder, trying to shake off the incriminating peel. Providenya—"Providence"—lived up to its name: The peel dropped to the runway and nobody noticed it, including a squad of soldiers armed with AK-47 assault rifles who quickly surrounded the plane. As for the quick-chewing, hard-swallowing passengers, "Nobody got sick," Dwayne recalls.

"The butterflies in my stomach were just churning," but for other reasons, he explained at a missions conference later that year at Twin Orchards Baptist Church in Vestal, New York.

"As we came in and landed, I was very, very nervous. Very scared. Our bags were packed with Bibles. We didn't know whether that was going to be legal or not... We were landing in the middle of a military base. Acres of tanks and armored personnel carriers, rocket launchers, anti-aircraft guns, and ammunition stacked twenty feet high... There was a whole contingent of KGB and police and military people. They were probably just as scared about us. Who knows what we were bringing in? We shut down the engines and let the stair down, and there was a guard standing right there at the bottom."

Maybe, Dwayne thought, the people would be friendlier than the display of military hardware. It was a short-lived hope. "I thought, *Well, I'll just smile.* So I gave him a big old smile and he just glared right through me. I thought, *I'll shake his hand.* So I reached down to grab his hand, and he wouldn't even extend his hand."

He just barked, "Documenti! Pahssport!" He glanced at the papers and jerked a thumb in the direction of the terminal. "You come, me!"

"We went," said Dwayne.

The seemingly ill-fated journey wasn't some spur-of-the-moment lark, soon to be forgotten. From the long process of plowing through bureaucratic paperwork to a nearly unbelievable meeting that night, "We were breaking new ground for ourselves and for missions," Dwayne said. An American-led mission had been launched two years earlier in western Russia to help revive the tiny network of Evangelical and Baptist churches that had survived seventy years of official atheism. But the effort had not yet reached Russia's remote Far East—until the flight to Providenya opened the back door. To Dwayne, already a veteran pilot, it seemed miraculous that the flight ever got off the ground at all. More than a year earlier, Soviet officials had flatly refused his request. He prayed continuously that they would relent—which they finally did, but with strict conditions.

On Saturday, August 31, at Glennallen, Alaska, the team climbed aboard the twin-engine, propeller-driven business aircraft: Tim and Dwayne, the pilots; Vernon "Steve" Stevenson, Alaska director for SEND International, the Detroit-based mission that had begun working in Russia in 1989; Gary Ridley, Alaska Bible College president; and Robert Crane, SEND church department head.

They flew to Nome, checked weather reports and filed a flight plan.

"We had the frequencies to contact the Russian air traffic controllers at a precise point inside a ten-minute window, at an IFR [instrument flight rules] intersection where Russian airspace starts," Dwayne said. "We knew we had to approach the border within a few minutes of our ETA [estimated time of arrival]. We had the code number to identify us, to stop the MIGs from scrambling after us."

The next day, Sunday, they took off. "Everything was in place and we headed out. It was a beautiful day."

Two hundred ten miles, seventy-five minutes and one day later (they had crossed the International Date Line), the plane, loaded with Bibles, Christian literature and presents, reached the intersection "right on." Dwayne called the Providenya control tower. Static filled the cockpit. Then the Russian controller's voice, sounding like it was coming down a hollow concrete pipe, crackled from the radio: "Ve read you."

"Request permission to enter Soviet air space."

"Stond by!"

In broken but understandable English, the controller broadcast the required course heading and altitude changes, which had to be translated from meters into feet, then added, "Seex Charlie-Charlie. *Come to Russia.*" A cheer broke out among the team members. They were making history.

After the ominous reception on landing, the next stop was the terminal. That's where Dwayne began to find out what was missing.

"We had to fill out all these forms. Not only did we have to fill out the forms, we had to *make* the forms. There were no copiers in Providenya. They had one form, hand-written, so we had to take that form, hand-write our own form, and then fill in all the information—our names and addresses, why we were there, what we had, how much we had, when we came and when we were to leave ... You talk about red tape! No pun intended."

Dwayne and Bob Crane led the way into the customs room. A stern young agent confronted them.

"Vut is purpose of your coming?" she demanded in heavily accented English.

"Religious business," Dwayne answered, as instructed in a previous briefing.

"Vut in baggage?"

"Clothes, personal belongings, gifts, printed materials."

"Take out."

Dwayne and the others had each brought only a few pounds of clothing and toiletries, to make room for nearly two hundred Russian-language New Testaments. He started unpacking them.

"Zese not allowed!"

"But we're not selling them. We're going to give them to people."

"You give me vun!"

"I'll give you two!"

She took the Bibles and, with a hint of a smile, said, "Go!"

In thankfulness, Dwayne silently asked a question usually asked in despair: *God! Why me? I don't deserve this!* A few more guards and customs agents asked for and received Bibles. Moments later, in the terminal hallway, the Americans were mobbed by a crowd of people who had gotten wind of the visit and begged for Bibles and Gospel literature. The team was discovering what else was missing.

"They didn't have Bibles over there," Dwayne recalls. "In the Providenya region there was no Evangelical or Baptist church. There was no underground church. There was no above-ground church. There was one Russian Orthodox church."

After clearing customs, they were startled by a friendly voice: "You stay my house. Ve speak English." It was Nicolai Gustagushn, the control tower operator who had cleared them to land. After a short, bone-jarring ride on unpaved streets, Dwayne and Tim Harold walked toward one of the tall, drab cement buildings overlooking the base. Their host opened a rusting steel door and led them into a foyer with a cracked stone floor smelling of dog feces and urine. They stepped haltingly in the darkness— someone had stolen the entryway's single light bulb—and climbed four or five flights of stairs, bypassing the broken elevator.

Nicolai unlocked another steel door in a dark corridor and welcomed them into a tiny, neat apartment. They shared a meal with him, his wife Natalia and their 16-year-old daughter, Maria, who interpreted. Maria had learned about Christ from a pastor who had visited the year before from Nome. She told Dwayne and Tim she wanted to attend Alaska Bible College in 1992.

Nicolai practiced his English with a few minutes of small talk— "You know John Vayne?" Later he said, "Tell me about ze God." He said he did not believe in God but was only curious, and asked Dwayne to read Scripture to him. Using a Russian-English Bible, Dwayne and Tim recounted how God had created the world for a purpose, and how man had corrupted it, and himself. The discussion went on into the early hours of the morning.

Then Nicolai asked, "What must I do to be saved?"

Dwayne and Tim sat stunned. The Book of Acts was coming to life before their eyes with words first spoken nearly two thousand years earlier by a prison warden to another pair of missionaries in another far country. Those missionaries, Paul and Silas, had been stripped, beaten and shackled in darkness, but had passed the night singing hymns of praise. Then they saved the Philippian jailer's life, but the jailer wanted a different kind of saving.

So did Nicolai.

"I couldn't believe it," Dwayne recalls. "I immediately took him to Romans 10: 9-10. I told him what he needed to believe in his heart. What he needed to express with his mouth. What he needed to say to God."

He showed Nicolai a prayer of repentance in the back of his Bible: *"Lord Jesus, I need you. Thank you for dying on the cross for my sins. I open the door of my life and receive you as my Savior and Lord. Thank you for forgiving my sins and giving me eternal life. Take control of the throne of my life. Make me the kind of person you want me to be."*

Nicolai read it aloud.

"I said to his daughter, 'Maria, ask your father if he understands what he really did.' Maria asked him and he looked at me and said in broken English, 'I pray, I pray,' and he pointed to that prayer. I asked him, 'Do you want to say this to God?'"

"*Da* [yes]," he replied, standing stiffly at attention and shaking as he approached the God he had denied all his life. He wept as he read it again.

For the next four days the team walked around the city of about four thousand, sharing their faith openly in schools and on the streets, with Maria interpreting. They gave Bibles and Gospel tracts to passersby and people waiting in lines at shops. Most of the recipients hesitated before accepting the literature, but when the team members looked back, they saw the townspeople reading intently. The Americans also met with the town council and a Russian Orthodox priest—a Soviet military veteran— who had shortly before started the first church in the region.

Among those initially hesitant about receiving Bibles was one of the approximately sixteen hundred Eskimo and Chukchi people living in Providenya.

"She really didn't reach out to take it," Dwayne recalls. "I said, *Gift ... Gift*, and she took that Bible and just clutched it to herself. I've never seen people love God's word so much. She took my arm and kissed my hand. And she immediately went to her pocketbook and started digging through it, and the first thing she pulled out was one of these car pine-scent things with two almost bare-naked women on both sides of it, and she gave it to me."

The audience at the missions conference was dissolving in laughter. "Here I was, hanging on to this thing," he said, recounting a quick succession of schemes to hide it from the other missionaries.

"I put it in my Bible. And then fear struck me, and I says, *That's no place for that*, and I took it out of there and stuck it in my camera bag. And I thought, *Oh, no, I hope I don't die tonight. The word will get back. What do I do with this thing?*"

He continued, and the laughter died.

"That was a prized possession. That's what she thought an American would really love. She began to dig deeper in her pocketbook, and came out with old, junky earrings and a stone ... just a stone. She gave me whatever she had."

Dwayne and Nicolai taught each other Dwayne's favorite phrase of encouragement, "Bless your heart," in their respective languages.

The plane had come to Providenya with five men aboard, but left with six—reflecting a journey almost as amazing as the flight itself. SEND planner Robert Provost, who was to link up with Dwayne's team days earlier for the flight back to Alaska, was in Moscow when the coup against the reform government erupted. He escaped from the turmoil on whatever planes and trains he could find. After a week-long trip full of halts and delays, and no communication with the team, he made it to Providenya the day they left.

"On our last day, we took off from the field there and banked the plane east, for the United States and Nome," said Dwayne, who was the pilot in command on the flight home. "I called our position back to the Providenya tower, and Nicolai's very last words, just as we approached the border, were, 'May God bless you. Please come back.' When we heard a Russian air traffic controller mentioning God, most of us wept."

Dwayne asked those at the missions conference to pray that the doors to Russia would stay open. He had planned to return soon after that first flight, but visas were delayed—possibly, he believes, because of objections from Orthodox leaders. Ironically, it was the presumably Communist officials who had the last word—and it was a highly favorable one. At the conference, Dwayne shared a letter, written in halting but heartfelt English, from the Providenya town council.

The letter termed "useful" and "promising" the American team's proposals to start Bible courses. The letter said, "The people of Providenya like all Soviet people were for seventy years period deprived of possibility to have Bibles, to educated [*sic*] their kids as Christians, especially in the remoted [*sic*] areas." Religion had been rooted out by "cruel and bloody methods" since 1917, so restoration of its important role in human life would be difficult, the letter went on. "And you are going to do a gratifying, blessed and worthwhile labor ... Let the God help you ... We are waiting for you to come."

"Beloved," Dwayne asked those at the conference, "who would have ever thought just months ago that a field of 300 million people would be opened up to us? *To go in and plant churches? In the Communist nation of Russia? Who would have ever thought it?*"

To Dwayne, the pleas from the Providenya officials and Nicolai were as compelling as another two thousand-year-old echo from Acts: Paul's vision in the night of a man of Macedonia calling for help. From that time forward, he would continue to obey the call—in the sky and on the ground, in the snows of Siberia and the deserts of Central Asia, in sickness and in health, pushing out the perimeter of the Kingdom and training the next generation of missionary pilots to follow, and go beyond.

Part 2

EARLY YEARS

Reeling in a Hot–Rodder

I loved hot cars. All I wanted was a '32 Ford street rod. I had to have a car that sounded good and looked good.

—Dwayne King

Therefore, since we are surrounded by such a great cloud of witnesses, let us throw off everything that hinders ... and let us run with perseverance the race marked out for us.

—Hebrews 12: 1, 2

3. BOYHOOD: Speed Dreams and a Heart for God

I always loved to go fast when I was a kid. I wanted to be a hot-rodder. To me, the greatest thing was if I could work for Gault Chevrolet the rest of my life as a mechanic, and I could build hot rods on weekends, and I could drive them down there at Five Mile Point Speedway in Kirkwood. Oh, man, that was the greatest!

—Dwayne King

DWAYNE NEVER LOST his love of speed and sense of fun. The road from "motorhead" to a life of serving the Godhead did not so much transform him as channel, expand and discipline what was already there.

The road began on September 17, 1942, in upstate New York. The second of four children, Dwayne was born in Ideal Hospital in the village of Endicott to Paul and Margaret King, who lived in the neighboring Town of Vestal, a rural suburb of Binghamton. Childhood in the two-story brick house at 116 Lewis Street was a happy, conventional blend of family life, sports, school and church. His older brother, David, offers an iconic image that could have been a snapshot in millions of American family albums: "I can still see Dwayne riding his tricycle, wearing his cowboy outfit."

The youngest boy, Rick—eleven years Dwayne's junior—got along well with his brothers, but the two older boys, closer in age, spent more time together. Dave recalls: "Dwayne and I shared everything from our bedroom to bicycles, Dad's cars to Grandpa's tools... We played together every day and enjoyed the neighborhood boys as well." They also enjoyed their younger sister, Carole, but the feeling was not always reciprocated, she recalls with mock bitterness.

They lived to bring unhappiness to their only sister, and doing so brought them much pleasure. My brothers once tied me to a tree ... so that I

31

could not follow them on an adventure into the nearby woods. When I was approximately 3 years old Dwayne gave me my first haircut. My mother appeared as a huge clump of blonde curly locks hit the floor. He was in big trouble for that one, but I do not remember the punishment he received or if he talked his way out of the situation.

Dwayne quickly showed athletic skills and was a good team player in neighborhood games of whiffle ball. He enjoyed speed, even when it wasn't on wheels or in the sky—he was a star outfielder on the Vestal Little League traveling team, and ran track and cross-country for Vestal Central High School. Mechanical ability and thrifty self-reliance also developed early, thanks in part to his father, a machinist at IBM in Endicott. He learned to work with his hands in the welding and blacksmithing shop at his maternal grandfather's home on George Street in Vestal. "I wasn't afraid of dirt and power machinery," Dwayne recalls.

His mother clerked at McLean's department store on Endicott's Washington Avenue ("The Ave"). While he and his father waited in the car for her to get off work, his father would make up detailed stories about people walking by. "I was so intrigued by them," Dwayne said.

Win it, Race it, Repair it

Dwayne absorbed a strong work ethic from both parents. The boys kept busy, Dave recalls.

Dwayne later became the family mechanic and kept our bicycles running smooth, repaired the family radio and everything else that needed fixing. We both delivered newspapers to earn money. I remember one day asking my father for a bicycle. He told me that when he had asked his dad for a bicycle, his father told him to earn the money and then he could have one. So Dwayne and I both learned very young that if we wanted something, we were going to earn it ourselves. That was one of the best lessons our dad could have taught us. So I got a job delivering newspapers with Dwayne's help, and he earned his bike in a contest collecting old shoes for a radio station [WENE].

It was no surprise to Carole that Dwayne's deluge of shoes won him the brand-new Schwinn. "The garage was full, the basement was full," she said. "Whatever was the radio station going to do with all those smelly shoes?" When Dwayne was sick, Carole had to deliver papers on what she described as his very long route, which included customers for the weekly

32

Vestal News and two dailies, the *Endicott Bulletin* and the *Binghamton Press*. "There was much grumbling on my part. I do not remember my brother David helping. I am not sure how he escaped this activity. Maybe he didn't, and I just have a poor memory."

Ultimately, however, she left no doubt about her true feelings toward Dwayne: "I am blessed to have him as a brother."

In his teen years, Dwayne graduated from fixing Dave's bicycles to rebuilding his brother's '55 Chevy engine. "I loved hot cars. All I wanted was a '32 Ford street rod," Dwayne recalls. "I had to have a car that sounded good and looked good." Dave's Chevy sounded fine to Dwayne, but not to Endicott village police. They frequently ticketed him for a noisy muffler.

Dwayne's work experience included collecting garbage for Ed Flipse, who was also his Sunday School teacher. The main attraction of that job was Ed's big, warm shop where he could work on cars. He sharpened his skills further as a mechanic's helper at Gault Chevrolet, then on Grant Avenue in Endicott. Ed Cregan, his future wife's uncle, got him that job—his first regular, paid position doing something he loved.

In most ways, Dwayne was like any other car-minded kid starting out on the grease rack and changing oil, recalls co-worker Lew J. Parks, who specialized in automatic transmissions and repairing Corvairs. But even then, he added, "Dwayne kind of caught my attention. He marched to his own drummer." Lew, who later became a mechanic for racing legend A.J. Foyt, said Dwayne seemed more interested in his surroundings than most young men. They went their separate ways, but reconnected years later in a setting Lew never would have predicted.

Repair skills were especially useful for someone whose treatment of cars guaranteed they would need frequent repairs. "Dwayne was always going through transmissions," recalls Durland W. "Dur" Vining, a church friend and later partner in missions. He reluctantly let Dwayne drive his red, two-seater Austin-Healey roadster on Vestal's winding, hilly roads. "It was the pride of my life. I thought he was gonna wreck it!" He credited the roadster's survival—and Dwayne's, years later, in the skies over Alaska—to "God-given natural ability."

Faith and Family Roots

The family regularly attended "Cal Tab"—Calvary Tabernacle—in Vestal. Dwayne was active in the youth group, but he was all boy and no saint. "He was the reason I was always in trouble, but he would tell you different," said cousin Bill Berkheiser. "I think the turning point in

Dwayne's life, as in all of us, was when he received Christ as his savior." That occurred in 1954 at Lake Arrowhead Bible Camp in nearby Brackney, Pennsylvania, when Dwayne was 11.

Dwayne credits his family as the "circle of influence" that led him not only to the Lord, but to later turning points in deciding what to do with his salvation—and how to do it. The lifeline that fed the circle began two generations earlier with his maternal grandparents, William Berkheiser Sr. and his wife Emily. Dwayne described Emily as the family's major link to Bible-believing, fundamental churches, saying, "She was rock-solid as the anchor of Christian influence." It was her prayers that led her grown children to salvation and eventually resulted in three generations of Christian workers, among them Dwayne and Dave, recalls her son—Dwayne's uncle—William H. Berkheiser. Uncle Bill, like Grandma Emily, had a burning desire to see everyone in the family saved and serving the Lord. Dwayne described him as the major dynamic in "getting everyone squared around spiritually—he made it his mission to have his family get right with God." He credits his uncle with being his strongest spiritual motivator during his teens: "He made the difference."

Two other uncles inspired Dwayne with stories of their World War II service and strengthened his impulse to serve God in some concrete way.

Bob Oris, his mother's sister's husband, built bridges across the Rhine with the U.S. Army Corps of Engineers. Uncle Bob, a machinist at IBM, and Aunt Marion, a housewife, were an important spiritual influence on the King kids, bringing them into a family musical team that sang at Cal Tab and other churches. Bob and Marion later played a major part in encouraging Dwayne's ministry plans and supporting his and Carolyn's missionary careers.

Lloyd King, Dwayne's father's brother, was a decorated Air Force veteran. Dwayne remembers him as a "gung-ho" airman who tackled "gutsy, dangerous" missions, such as ferrying supplies to China over the notorious "Hump"—the Himalayas—in World War II. He also flew in Korea, and later in Vietnam with the "Dirty Thirty." The nickname came from the grimy Vietnamese Air Force coveralls the elite American pilots wore constantly on twenty-four hour duty shifts while sharing combat, supply, and training missions with their South Vietnamese counterparts. He flew C-119 "Flying Boxcars" and—in all three wars—venerable C-47 "Gooney Birds," military versions of 1930s-era DC-3 civilian passenger planes.

Lloyd died in the spring of 2006 and was buried with full honors at Arlington National Cemetery. He was, said Dwayne, a man who served his country with great passion and great love, adding, "It spoke to something within me that sparked the inspiration to serve the Lord the same way." Lloyd, in turn, had seen in his nephew a similar passion and love that went beyond mere preoccupation with hot-rodding or even a conventional religious career. "He told my parents I ought to be fixing or flying airplanes for God, rather than being some kind of preacher," Dwayne recalls.

Voices from the Darkness

Meanwhile, in the early 1950s, faraway events were beginning to focus Dwayne's vision of service toward a particular people and place. Vestal residents and other Americans were hearing stories of suffering and heroism for Christ's sake. However, to a nation basking in the afterglow of World War II victory, flush with prosperity and not overly traumatized by the Cold War and the Korean conflict, the news was little more than distant thunder on the horizon of a safe, sunny world. In Endicott, the late George F. Johnson's footwear empire—Endicott-Johnson—was a few years into its long decline. But the legacy of a benevolent industry that anticipated the Millennial Kingdom was still strong. It was hard to imagine that in Russia, former ally Josef Stalin was subjecting a much larger empire to horrors of Tribulation proportions.

However, the impact of the news got through. In 1953—the year Stalin died—a Russian pastor visited Cal Tab, accompanied by interpreter Peter Deyneka, the Russian-born American evangelist who founded the Slavic Gospel Association. They told of Siberian churches burned and pastors hung or crucified. They told of church members, charged with the crime of owning Bibles, shipped to slave labor camps where they and millions of other Russians died. They showed pictures of midnight baptisms and worship services in caves and forests. They later mailed photographs of Christians with eyes blacked out to prevent identification by Soviet police. They brought one message: "Please pray." Cal Tab worshippers did. Church youth kept images of the grim historical reality alive with skits depicting Russian Christians being lined up and shot for refusing to renounce their faith.

After 1961, the congregation also prayed that the newly erected Berlin Wall would come down. "How crazy is that?" Dwayne deadpanned to a chuckling audience in 2007. Another seemingly far-fetched prediction came from Dwayne's mother in the 1950s. Like many American parents then, Margaret King told her mischievous son that if he continued misbehaving, she would send him to Siberia.

"I credit this time as God planting the seed of Russian ministry in my heart," Dwayne said.

God soon planted more seeds in his mind about how he would eventually get there, and in his heart about the companion who would go with him.

4. A CALL From the Sky

... my work in coming years will be the marrying of the possibilities of aviation to the needs of missionaries.
—Missionary Nate Saint

I N 1959 DWAYNE READ *Jungle Pilot*, Christian journalist Russell T. Hitt's book about the life and martyrdom of Nate Saint. In 1956, Nate and four other American missionaries were speared to death in Ecuador by the Waodani Indians they had been trying to contact. Dwayne identified with Nate's humor and daring. He was deeply moved by what had moved the martyred pilot: the conviction that the "Auca savages" were people for whom Christ had died, but who would never receive His gift unless others reached them with the good news. The shadowy "they" in Romans 10: 14-15 suddenly became visible and present to him:

> How, then, can they call on the one they have not believed in? And how can they believe in the one of whom they have not heard? And how can they hear without someone preaching to them? And how can they preach unless they are sent?

He was also excited by the possibilities of mission aviation, a challenge toward which his love of mechanics and speed were already drawing him. Again, God touched his heart. "*Jungle Pilot* was probably the first book I ever read cover to cover," Dwayne said. "I began to struggle between hot rods and ministry for God." This time, however, God seemed to point a way that would satisfy both loves: wings.

The aviation seed was falling on prepared ground. Dwayne had a flight school in mind even before reading *Jungle Pilot*. In the mid-1950s, he was already admiring photographs of Christian pilot/mechanics—some planning mission careers—in his grandfather's copies of *Now*, the magazine of LeTourneau Technical Institute (now LeTourneau University). R.G. LeTourneau, founder of the nondenominational Christian school in Longview, Texas, was a builder of heavy machinery, a generous philanthropist and a supporter of missions in South America and Africa. Dwayne looked at photos of Nate repairing planes and thought, *I can do that!*

Dwayne's growing call to missions was further reinforced by a missionary to India who visited Cal Tab in 1959, the year he read *Jungle Pilot*. "Both were significant events that challenged me to make some decision on God's eternal purpose for my life," he wrote years later in a request for mission support from his wife's home church, Twin Orchards Community (later Twin Orchards Baptist) Church in Vestal. "I just realized He put me here for the exclusive purpose of glorifying Him. His purpose was clear to me: *Go*." This referred to Christ's last words to His disciples in Matthew 28:19, the Great Commission: ... *go and make disciples of all nations ...*

Take This Life

Dwayne's mother, Margaret, was the clincher: "God used many people to influence me, but my mother had the greatest impact." He was running upstairs one day when he overheard her praying aloud in her room. "I heard her say my name," he recalls. He knew she was troubled and fearful about some aspects of his life—chasing girls, hot-rodding and poor school performance.

"It dawned on me—she was before the Throne, petitioning God to do something with me. When I heard her cry out to God and offer up her son to be His servant, I was moved to give my life."

Serving God in missions wasn't the only life-changing decision the 17-year-old high school senior made in 1959. By then, he and Carolyn Pfaff realized they wanted to be married. They could not have been more different.

Carolyn was born on January 31, 1943, to Frank and Helen Pfaff. She spent her early childhood in Endicott near close relatives, many of whom worked for IBM, and attended a Methodist church. Her father died when she was 4, a loss she said contributed to her fearful shyness—"Birthday parties were a nightmare." Frank's death left a wound that would not be healed until years later, in Russia. Her mother married Richard Merritt when she was 11, and the family moved to Vestal. She and Dwayne met in high school at Bible Club meetings and began dating steadily.

As Dwayne and Carolyn remember it, there was something unreal about their courtship. Carolyn didn't know what she wanted to be, but she knew what she didn't want to be: a nurse or a missionary. Dwayne was not a missionary and had never been in a plane, but—inspired by *Jungle Pilot*—he asked her if she wanted to be a missionary pilot's wife. Carolyn, without a clue about what that might involve, said "Yes." So she became a missionary pilot's wife ... and a nurse. She was, and is, a private, quiet person for whom order, neatness and predictability were, and are, important. He wasn't, and isn't.

Stronger than their differences, however, was the bond they shared. She, like Dwayne, had accepted the Lord at Lake Arrowhead at age 11. Both worked at Christian summer camps and knew by their mid-teens that they wanted to serve God. Carolyn, working at a camp for handicapped children from New York City, was moved to dedicate her life by the words chosen for the camp's theme one summer: "... ourselves your servants for Jesus' sake."

In 1960, during his senior year at Vestal, Dwayne applied to flight schools at LeTourneau and Moody Bible Institute in Chicago. LeTourneau accepted him, but Moody turned him down because of poor grades—"I was a C and D student, except for A's in Auto Mechanics." However, Moody said he could attend the Bible program for a chance to pull his grades high enough for the school's flight training program.

Dwayne was ready for college, but his bank account wasn't. Headers, glasspack mufflers, rebuilt transmissions and other hot-rod expenses had seen to that. Dave came to the rescue by urging his younger brother to join him at Practical Bible Training School (now Davis College), in Johnson City, New York, where Dave was in his second year. The rest of the family agreed. They knew Dwayne was strong in his commitment to ministry and didn't want him to waste a year earning money for LeTourneau or Moody. He could start at Practical in the fall and save money on the school's lower fees.

Monkeyshines, Music and Marriage

So Practical was the practical solution. But, like many transitions in Dwayne's life, it wasn't smooth and quiet. "I was on academic probation, financial probation and social probation," he admitted cheerfully to a crowd of laughing Davis students years later. "But these people just accepted me and encouraged me." The first two probations were for starting school a few days late, with no money. The third was not long in coming.

In the first semester we were doing "chicken fights" upstairs in the dorm. I was on one guy's shoulders, wrestling with another guy, and we knocked the fire extinguisher off the wall, setting it off. We filled the hallway with powder from the extinguisher and were caught by the dean of men, Mr. Kirk. That put me on social probation. That year I barely stayed ahead of the probation board.

Hot rods, he recalls, also figured prominently in his freshman antics—which, if not always tolerated by the authorities, sometimes amused them.

"I had that old '39 Cadillac LaSalle, the four-door, and I had written 'The Untouchables' on the back of it—remember that program?—and we bought some of these old brimmed hats and toy tommy guns, y'know? And it was just so tempting!"

What was so tempting, he explained years later, was terrorizing "poor Mr. Kirk and some of the gracious older people" relaxing in their rocking chairs on the porch of the main building next to the school's circular drive. The fun depended on the good-natured victims—teachers and school officials—being in on the gag and obligingly playing their parts. "We used to come around the corner, throw open the suicide doors and just riddle the front row, and they would dive for cover! We had so much fun in those days in that car."

The drive with the tall pine tree in the middle was an irresistible magnet not only for the LaSalle, but for some of Dwayne's other souped-up but street-legal creations, including a 1948 Ford coupe with an Oldsmobile Rocket 88 V-8 powerplant shoehorned under the hood. "I used to love to see if I could get all the way around the circle on two wheels," he recalls. "The two outside ones!"

Dwayne roomed with Dave for a year and was a quartet member and song leader. He gained ministry experience singing and preaching with the group on weekend road trips to more than twenty states, and to Britain on a longer engagement. Meanwhile, Carolyn enrolled in the Registered Nurse program at Wilson hospital in Johnson City, but hazing of new students (their dorm rooms were torn up), plus homesickness, nearly ended her nursing education the day it began. "After three hours I called Dwayne and told him to come and get me. I was *not* staying," she recalls. "Of course, he made me." After a year at Wilson, she switched to—and completed—Licensed Practical Nurse training at Binghamton General Hospital.

Dwayne graduated with a Bible diploma in the spring of 1963, and they were married on August 17 at Twin Orchards. Best man Tom Kelly was a fellow Practical Bible student, and maid of honor Penny Henneman was Carolyn's best friend in high school. The usher was Ron Hawkins, another Practical student, whose friendship with Dwayne had an unlikely beginning. He had sent Dwayne to Wilson hospital with a concussion resulting from what Dwayne called a "friendly fight" shortly after the chicken-fight incident. Years later, Practical decided Dwayne's missionary achievements far outweighed any undergraduate disturbances, and named him a Distinguished Alumnus and honorary Doctor of Divinity.

With Carolyn by his side, LeTourneau's acceptance letter in his luggage and the predictable world of Vestal shrinking in his rear-view mirror, the long road west beckoned Dwayne skyward.

5. TEXAS: Lessons in Flying and Faith

Dwayne learned the power of prayer, faith and holiness from Fay.

— Dorothy Fisher,
on Dwayne's mentor, Fay Livers

TWO WEEKS AFTER the wedding, Carolyn recalls, "He carried me off to Texas, crying all the way." They headed for LeTourneau in the infamous '48 Ford coupe. On the rear of their homemade trailer, Dwayne's father-in-law had painted, in DayGlo orange, "Texas or Bust." The hot rod accomplished both—the latter frequently, Dwayne recalls. "We busted in Ohio, Indiana and Texarkana, and limped into Texas without a floorboard," which had been removed to allow easier access for repairs en route.

The ministry he wanted to learn at LeTourneau was limited. "I just wanted to be a missionary pilot, just turn wrenches and drive airplanes," he said. The college taught him that, and more. Teacher J.C. Harder, a Native Alaskan, took care of much of the aviation training and became a lifelong friend. Carolyn said J.C. did something else for Dwayne, too: "He kept whispering *Alaska* in his ear." J.C. recalls that when he met Dwayne in November 1964,

> I had just returned from Vietnam and was hired by LeTourneau as an aviation mechanic instructor... We started out as a student-instructor relationship and shortly became good friends. He happened to be the first student I signed off to take his private pilot check ride. I wasn't his instructor for all of his training toward his private pilot certificate, but was privileged to finish him up and then work with him on some of his other certificates and ratings... I kept encouraging him to think about being a missionary pilot in my home state of Alaska. We also did some

aircraft rebuild projects together, for Dwayne to gain mechanic experience and to hopefully supplement both our incomes.

Perhaps with Alaska in mind, J.C. taught Dwayne some maneuvers for a flying environment that would be less forgiving than flat East Texas. These included "tree-hopping": flying low and pulling up and over obstacles at the last moment. He also helped him overcome his dislike and limited understanding of electricity. "I warned him, as I had done many times with other students, that the course you disliked most ... was the subject the Lord allowed you to work on most in the field," J.C. recalls. "Dwayne was no exception. He gained the respect of the [Alaskan] village people and won many to the Lord by helping them fix their aircraft electrical problems."

Dwayne has never pretended to be fearless or superhuman, and is probably incapable of being humorless, as J.C.'s memories attest:

> ... during our church's Thanksgiving dinner, Dwayne and another fellow came in late ... he was white as a sheet and very subdued, for Dwayne. He said he needed to confide in me about his latest escapade. He and a friend [LeTourneau student Bill Lawrence] had been rebuilding a little two-place Culver Cadet airplane. A lot of important parts had not yet been installed, but they figured they had enough to give it a "taxi" test down the little runway. Before they knew it, they found themselves in the air. Neither of them had ever flown a Culver Cadet, and besides, they only put enough gas in the tank for about one time around the [flight] pattern. It took them numerous times around the pattern, but they finally got it down in one piece. Dwayne said, "Even though the cockpit is extremely small, you *can* get on your knees in a Culver Cadet!"
>
> Another time Dwayne and I laugh about... Late one night we were on Dwayne's motorcycle, driving home from working on one of our aircraft rebuilding projects. All of a sudden Dwayne slammed on the brakes, screeched to a stop, jumped off the cycle, ran over to the edge of the road and started throwing up. I figured he had been hit with the twenty-four hour flu bug that was going around. It turned out he had been hit by a great big Texas June bug right in the mouth, and the juice from the mashed bug was straining through his teeth. The more he thought about it the sicker he got, until he couldn't take it any longer, and had to stop and throw up.

Friendship with Dwayne could be a frustrating, unnerving, amusing, but ultimately inspirational roller-coaster ride, J.C. suggests.

You can get to know a person quite well while riveting sheet metal together or installing fabric on an aircraft. My first impression of Dwayne was of a person with an overabundance of zest for life—maybe a little bit of "Ready-Fire-Aim" attitude. He would start projects with what seemed to me like very little planning. For the most part, they always seemed to turn out all right. Maybe they had more planning than I knew of, or maybe the Lord was directing, unbeknown to me. Dwayne was a real encouragement to me. Whenever I was "low" or discouraged because of finances, instructing challenges, students, administration, etcetera, Dwayne would always understand and pray for me. With his attitude toward life, who could be around him and be discouraged? We have had many good times together and enjoy each other's company.

J.C. fondly recalls Dwayne's well-known expression of excitement: "Whenever he would hear something exciting he would always respond by hollering, 'Wowee! Wowee!' You then knew you had Dwayne's attention. Sometimes I think he is slowing down—until I observe him watching a NASCAR race on TV. Nobody close to him is safe as he jumps up and down, swings his arms and hollers at the TV, rooting for his favorite drivers."

Dwayne's tinkering expertise was sometimes the source of new experiences Carolyn faced as his bride. Here's an excerpt from the Fall 2000 issue of *NOW* magazine in which Contributing Editor Dorothy Fisher describes a 1965 incident involving the '48 Ford in downtown Longview:

> It had an Oldsmobile engine, two chrome scavenger [exhaust pipes] and painted [wheels]. The engine was so big there was no room for the fuel pump, so Dwayne mounted an electric fuel pump inside the fender well ...
>
> It was the hot rod that Carolyn was driving when it stopped cold. She called her husband. "The car won't go and I'm stuck in the middle of the street ..."

It didn't help, Carolyn recalls, that she was nine months pregnant with their first child and wearing her clean, white nurse's uniform, trying to get to her hospital job. Curious bystanders gawked as she followed Dwayne's telephoned instructions.

> "Kick the back part of the left front fender," he instructed. "Kick it really hard with the switch on. Then listen for the tick, tick, tick and that

will mean the fuel pump is working." She threw the switch on, gave the fender a mighty kick and heard the sweet sound of a ticking fuel pump.

She was able to start the car.

Enthusiasm Meets Holiness

Dwayne's employer and greatest spiritual mentor at Longview was welder Fay Livers, a LeTourneau graduate and former trustee. His life hammered home in Dwayne the conviction planted a few years earlier by Nate Saint's story: The ordinary tasks and obstacles of life, regardless of their nature, could be transformed into a ministry. However, as Dorothy Fisher writes, that wasn't Dwayne's initial reaction when he saw Longview Welding Co. "with Scripture verses on a big marquee in front."

> He recalled, "The first time I saw the shop, I thought this guy must really be a fanatic." But after he worked there for a while he came to love and respect Fay. An unabashed love for his Lord just naturally spilled out in everything Livers did. "The customers would come in and see the mechanics down on their knees in this messy old office and hear us praying." Dwayne learned the power of prayer, faith and holiness from Fay.

Dwayne may have felt at first that the big marquee out front was excessive, but it expressed what he eventually realized was Fay's most important teaching: "the effect of a bold witness. Everybody got some word of witness in his shop." The admiration was mutual. "We love him dearly," Elsie Livers said of Dwayne, who flew to Longview in 2000 to speak at Fay's funeral. "He was the most enthusiastic Christian that we had ever known. We loved him from the first time that we met." His activities at LeTourneau included song leading—"Victory in Jesus" quickly became his crowd-rousing theme song.

Elsie recalls Dwayne's flair for drama:

> He was in parades to spread the Gospel. If my memory is correct, a brewery was coming to Longview. [Dwayne and others] took an old wrecked car, put a make-believe-looking man in the car, hanging out the door with red all over him, and pulled it on a trailer [behind Fay's Gospel-emblazoned Model T] with signs that this is the work of the devil.

1965 was a year of milestones. Dwayne finished his studies at LeTourneau with his FAA airframe and powerplant mechanic ratings and private pilot's license. Their first child, David William, was born on August 2, and the young family soon headed for Ellsworth, Maine. Dwayne started work at Bar Harbor Airways, gaining more flying and repair experience. They also joined Emmanuel Baptist Church, where Dwayne became a youth leader and continued his song-leading ministry.

"The church there accepted us as family—not normal for New Englanders," Carolyn recalls. Several men of the church chipped in and bought Dwayne a Cessna 120, a single-engine two-seater, to sharpen his piloting skills. Emmanuel, as well as Dwayne and Carolyn's home churches and several others, still support their mission careers.

Meanwhile, Dwayne's brother Dave and his wife Joan were living in Livermore, Maine, where they had started a new church. The families visited frequently.

In the late 1960s, Dwayne and Carolyn began a series of moves that would position them for service in the Kingdom to which they had pledged their lives. In 1967 they applied to join Arctic Missions Inc. (AMI), a non-denominational group organized to bring the Gospel to Alaskan Indian, Aleut and Inuit peoples. AMI asked them to attend a missionary internship in Farmington, Michigan. Their second child, Jonathan Richard, was born there on December 13. AMI eventually accepted the Kings' application, but by then, Dwayne had found another job. In the spring of 1968 they moved again, this time to Soldotna, Alaska, where Dwayne went to work for the Missionary Aviation Repair Center (MARC).

Before leaving Vestal, they attended a commissioning service at Cal Tab. Dur Vining and the other deacons laid their hands on Dwayne and Carolyn, asked God's blessing and launched them into the adventure of a lifetime.

Part 3

ALASKA

Beauty and Dry Bones

It's really very safe to fly through the narrow canyon near Valdez or through the tiny notch in Gunsight Mountain. The odds are next to nothing that anybody else is coming the other way.

—Dwayne King

... the moment one definitely commits oneself, then Providence moves too. All sorts of things occur to help one that would never otherwise have occurred.

—W.H. Murray,
The Scottish Himalayan Expedition

6. SOLDOTNA: Finding the Groove

The hand of the LORD was upon me, and ... set me out in the middle of a valley; it was full of bones ... He asked me, "Son of man, can these bones live?"

I said, "O Sovereign LORD, you alone know."

Then he said to me, "Prophesy to these bones and say to them, 'Dry bones, hear the word of the LORD! ... I will make breath enter you, and you will come to life... Then you will know that I am the LORD.'"

So I prophesied as I was commanded. And as I was prophesying, there was a noise, a rattling sound, and the bones came together, bone to bone ...

Then he said to me, "Prophesy to the breath; prophesy, son of man, and say to it ... 'Come from the four winds, O breath, and breathe into these slain, that they may live.'"

So I prophesied as he commanded me, and breath entered them; they came to life and stood up on their feet—a vast army.

—Ezekiel 37: 1-10

THE KINGS' FIRST home in Alaska was a two-room log cabin on the Kenai Peninsula, an appropriate introduction to life in the ruggedly beautiful 49th state hyped by its promoters as America's last frontier. The cabin was on the "Gaede 80," an eighty-acre tract in Soldotna homesteaded by medical bush pilot Elmer Gaede. Amenities were few—water came from a hand-operated pump (thankfully indoors)—but Dr. Gaede let them live there rent-free.

As a pilot-mechanic with MARC, Dwayne was focused more on plane innards than human hearts. But his own heart was soon touched by a wound so deep it forced him to relegate his first love to second place. From then on, aviation would be only the means, not the end, in his call to serve God. He was wounded by a vision of beauty and death seen three decades earlier by missionaries Vince and Becky Joy, founders of Central Alaska Mission (CAM).

Dwayne and Carolyn revisiting their first Alaska home

"God was speaking to the prophet Ezekiel, but he could have spoken similar words to Vince Joy," Dwayne said at the 1991 missions conference in Vestal. "When the Joys first went to Alaska in 1937, it was a vast and beautiful land, but a land of spiritual dry bones. The Copper River Valley, where they settled, had only the traces of a dying Russian Orthodox Church. No life. No breath. And no living presence of the Gospel of Christ." Nearly fifty-five years later, Dwayne spoke of hope, his new neighbors, and their problems as he saw them in 1991:

> Today the bones are showing life. The church of Jesus Christ is evident in small groups of believers—fellowships in villages and towns across central Alaska and northwestern Canada—but this land still presents the challenge of Ezekiel: "Prophesy, son of man, that these bones may live!" Who are these dry bones? What kind of person lives in the Far North? Eighty percent of Alaska's population is white. Some were born in Alaska and some have chosen to settle... Many are very independent

people who moved north to be on their own. Twenty percent of the population is native. Many of the people, like the Athabaskan Indians of the Copper River Basin, have been born in the twentieth century.

A great rift exists between the old folks who knew the old ways and the young people who want to be part of modern society. Whites and natives, young and old, both need to be reached. Both are dry bones in these lands. Isolation and the stress of the wilderness bring out the best and the worst in people. Many turn to alcohol to cover their wounds, problems and hurts. Teens struggle with life meaning. Marriages collapse and family problems are not uncommon.

During their first winter in Alaska, Dwayne was gone for weeks on end with MARC while Carolyn, expecting again, stayed in the cabin with David, 3, and Jonathan, 1. Becky was born in Soldotna on April 16, 1969. "God's word had always been important to me," Carolyn wrote in her testimony. "Now it became my lifeline. I repeated, *What time I am afraid I will trust in the Lord*, [Psalm 56:3] over and over." Meanwhile, with the help of "Doc" Gaede and other mentors, Dwayne gained firsthand knowledge of Alaskan flying and missions.

Flying the MARC Cessna 180 to the villages, and spending time with Dave Penz of Arctic Missions, opened my eyes to village missions with natives. I often stayed in these villages with them. Flying for the Evangelical Covenant Church under Roald Amundson's leadership at MARC really opened the way for experience in the Alaskan bush. Flying the Cessna 180—and Piper Cub bush planes and twin-engine Cessnas— really broadened my experience. Living in Unalakleet, Nome and Bethel for weeks at a time, knowing Carolyn was at home in a log cabin, was difficult. But I fell in love with the native people, and came to realize we needed to go to the villages.

Strengthening Home Ties

Dwayne kept close ties with his older brother and continued expanding his aviation experience during extended visits to the Lower 48. The family stayed for a few months in Montpelier, Vermont, with Dave and Joan, who had started another new church. Dave felt the same way about maintaining ties, saying, "It was time to reconnect with my little brother." In Montpelier, Dwayne worked for Vermont International Airways. The family then returned to Ellsworth, Maine, where Dwayne again went to work for Bar Harbor Airways and began raising support for missions while earning a commercial license.

"From the very beginning, he wanted to make his flying useful to other people," recalls the Rev. Paul Blasko. He and Dwayne met in 1967, Paul's first year at Twin Orchards Baptist Church, and the young pastor's first impression never changed. "This is a guy I'd like to have for a friend," Paul said, ticking off the qualities that he and many others would see for more than four decades: "energetic ... upbeat ... down-to-earth ... honest ... fun-loving ... "

Especially fun-loving.

During visits to Twin Orchards to report on Alaska activities, Dwayne would treat winners of Vacation Bible School contests to plane rides. After one flight with Paul and several young Bible students aboard, Dwayne landed at Tri-Cities Airport in Endicott. He turned to his passengers and announced with a straight face, "This really worked out good! We just ran out of gas."

Paul Blasko and Dwayne

Paul himself is not above deadpan one-liners and has had his share of wilderness adventures, but that's where the similarities end. His home on a quiet, tree-lined street in Vestal testifies to this. He sits in his living room, a neat, organized nest where memories and relics have their assigned places, and talks of his friend—a force of nature who crashes into lives and scatters the neatness in peals of laughter, leaving uplifted spirits in his wake. Paul's long friendship with Dwayne, like Dwayne's marriage to Carolyn, is typical of Dwayne's relationships in which serving God trumps differences in personality.

A Bus Breaks Down, a Mission Begins

A bus breakdown in August 1969 put Dwayne on the road to a better fit between his passion for flying, his hands-on skills and his growing desire to reach out personally to isolated Alaskans. He and his dad were driving a school bus to Alaska for the Soldotna school district when they broke down in Glennallen. Two workers from Central Alaska Mission (CAM)— Merritt Tegler and Jim Johnson—put them up overnight and helped repair the bus. The next day, Dwayne signed up with CAM.

Dwayne was growing, but CAM wasn't. Foundering for lack of leadership since Vince Joy's death, it could have put him on a sinking ship. Fortunately, the organization merged in 1970 with Far Eastern Gospel Crusade, founded soon after World War II by American servicemen and women burdened for the spiritual needs of people in Asia. Combining operations was easier than agreeing on the new name—SEND International— recalls missionary Leander Rempel, who, as Alaska director, played a major role in developing new leadership.

> Have you ever tried to find a new name for a Christian organization? Everybody wants to appear more spiritual than the next person, so the name has to come from the Bible and must have at least ten proof texts attached to it. By the time you are done, you have a name so cumbersome that it is almost impossible to use. It took ten years. The name came from John 20:21 (KJV)—*as my Father hath sent me, even so send I you.*

Still later, it occurred to the Detroit-based nondenominational mission that the title could be a catchy acronym: "Start churches, Evangelize the unreached, Nurture disciples, Develop leaders."

At the 1991 missions conference, Dwayne traced the common threads of the merged groups that were so appealing to him: ministry as a way of life, patiently building spiritual credibility by developing real relationships with people and sharing the conditions under which they lived, while meeting their physical and psychological needs:

> Very early, missionaries found people asking for help when there was a medical emergency. People in pain search for relief, so Faith Hospital was started to meet medical needs. The staff . . . reached beyond the physical needs to touch deeper emotional and spiritual pain. New,

enlarged facilities served the local community, and many would come from a distance by plane or helicopter, ambulance or car.

The wilderness separates men, but radio can penetrate the isolation. Radio station KCAM was started to meet the needs of the wilderness, where distance, long dark winters, and isolated days on the job, away from home, make life lonely and uncertain. Another SEND station, KRSA, performed a similar function in southeast Alaska, broadcasting to loggers and fishermen, Native villagers and settlers in remote, sea-locked areas along the coast.

SEND's first missionaries were pioneers committed to meet people's needs no matter what the personal cost. Today, Alaska is vastly changed, but meeting people and impacting lives still takes time and endurance. SEND missionaries live where they work, and live what they believe, under the scrutiny of their community. Relationships are built over a wood pile, a cup of coffee, berry-picking, hunting and fishing. There are planes to fix, roads to build, houses to finish, joys and sorrows to be shared. Friendships are nurtured, not created in an instant. The long, dark hours of winter are perfect for getting close to people. Many have shorter working hours in winter, and are free to investigate and study the Bible. Discipleship is a slow, careful process of listening and teaching, as a group of believers becomes a church of Jesus Christ.

Dwayne's first SEND posting would plunge him and Carolyn into that world of wilderness bonding and service. His aviation ministry began, their last child was born—Joel Paul, on January 16, 1973—and some discipline was added to Dwayne's free-form work habits. It was an arena where some who became lifelong friends first saw him in action, loving him through his weaknesses and encouraging his strengths, setting the pattern for him to love and encourage others. It was the valley where Carolyn hit a low point and let God lead her upward again.

7. TOK: Getting Serious

In Alaska I have a handle ... people know me as the Faster Pastor. And I hear it on Channel 19 on the CB coming across loud and clear, "Hey, Faster Pastor, you copy?" And so we'll share back and forth with the truckers and the other pilots and the Eskimos in the villages ... and I love to go fast.

It's easier to get forgiveness than permission.

—Dwayne King

TOK, "GATEWAY TO ALASKA," was Dwayne's gateway to a nine-year ministry: creating and leading the local church, flying to surrounding Indian villages and supporting missionaries in Canada's Yukon Territory. In the summer of 1971, however, the southeastern settlement of about seven hundred along the Alaska Highway looked like a gateway to nowhere. The immediate problem was the negative mindset of some mission and local church people. Without the friendship and support of Leander and Louise Rempel, it could have stopped Dwayne's work before it started.

Rempels and Kings, 1995

During the previous winter, Leander—SEND's Alaska director—and his wife had driven up from Glennallen on weekends to run the Tok ministry, a duty the Kings were to take over. Their relationship, Louise recalls, got off to a good, if hectic, start: "My first memory is seeing them driving their van into our yard in Glennallen... They were there with their three children—tired, sort of dirty from the trip up the highway. Dwayne was *noisy*, the kids were restless, and Carolyn and I were trying to keep the peace. But it was a 'fit' between us right from the start."

Louise described Dwayne as a "funny, likeable guy, an awesome pilot, a picky eater, always in a rush—trotted or ran instead of walking, seemingly never tired, and willing to do anything—but not perfect!" He became almost a member of the Rempel family.

Starting Wasn't Easy

Dwayne would need all his resilience to overcome the problems he faced at the outset. He already knew about some of them, and Leander gave him a heads-up about the others. Here's how Leander remembers it:

> ... the negative element in the mission had already bent Dwayne's ear to convey that there was no hope of saving the mission after Vince Joy died. They knew that Dwayne was interested in flying, so they were quick to point out that there was no hope of fulfilling that dream, since the mission had voted some years previously that there would be no flying ministry in Central Alaska Mission.
>
> Beside the problems in the mission, there were many problems in Tok... The negative element bent my ear, telling me I would have to deal with Dwayne and Carolyn with regard to how they disciplined their children. I don't think Dwayne and I ever discussed that issue, since I felt I had my hands full disciplining my own children without tackling theirs!
>
> This whole scenario confirmed a statement Phil Armstrong, mission general director at that time, made many times. He said the negative element ... always got to the new missionaries long before the people who had a positive attitude ever got around to voicing their opinion—if they said anything at all.

Leander, who calls Dwayne "possibly my closest friend," left no doubt in 1971 about his own attitude and plans for his new worker:

> My first impression of him was that here was a breath of fresh air. Here was what we needed. . . . He was bigger than the mission. The mission had a man with a tremendous entrepreneurial spirit in the person of Vince

Joy. Here was another man cut from the same mold. The mission had attempted to contain Vince with a whole series of committees that put up roadblock after roadblock... The old mission would have attempted to contain [Dwayne]. The new mission was going to encourage him and free him for ministry.

Leander's first priority for Dwayne was to create a church in Tok. Not a building—that already existed—but a body of believers.

"My advice to Dwayne was to disregard the problems in the church and build the church with new converts. Which is exactly what he did. He not only built the ministry in Tok, but in Tanacross and Tetlin as well," Leander said of Dwayne's work in small settlements nearby.

In 1972 at Glennallen, Dwayne met another colleague who became a lifelong friend. Summer missionary Richard A. Camp, now retired as both adjunct professor of Bible at Davis College and SEND's Northeast representative, recalls his first interaction: "Dwayne needed a haircut and I gave him one, and that's the last one he ever asked for." Dwayne said it was a bad haircut, and Dick Camp admitted it may have been too short. "I was still thinking U.S. Navy," he said. God's payback, perhaps, for the disastrous haircut Dwayne had inflicted on his younger sister Carole when they were children.

Another interaction alerted Dick to a more serious problem: a lack of discipline that threatened to limit Dwayne's spiritual growth. When Dwayne asked to borrow his sermon notes, Dick realized formal Bible study wasn't Dwayne's strong suit—he was focused on flying planes for evangelism, but was "flying by the seat of his pants" in preparing worship services.

A figure from Dwayne's past came to the rescue. Uncle William H. Berkheiser, who had put him on track spiritually in his teens, helped get him back on track in Alaska. Dwayne had asked his uncle, a retired mission director and church planter in the Lower 48, to evaluate the Tok ministry. Rev. and Mrs. Berkheiser spent three weeks in Tok, culminating in two days of teaching the fine points of church planting and local church organization.

The visit was a wake-up call—on one occasion, literally. Early one morning, Uncle Bill pounded on Dwayne's door and yelled, "Hey! Time to get up!" He made it clear to his sleepy nephew that if he planned to be a pastor, he would have to rise early and spend time with God, Dick recalls. "That made an impression on Dwayne. There was a serious change in his spiritual life at that point." Dwayne realized he couldn't feed his flock on the spur of the moment or with someone else's sermon notes.

"I think that was pivotal," said Dick.

Leander described another problem, one that went deeper than irregular scheduling.

> Dwayne has tremendous highs, and on the flip side, gets lower than a snail's belly. I have been with him in many celebrations but have also scraped him off the floor on countless occasions as well ... his love for people and his desire to please them has gotten him into trouble... When we placed him in Tok, we felt that Tok would become a hub for evangelism and church planting. Dwayne was to be the leader of the band. In almost every case, a spirit of division flared up between the workers and Dwayne... [They focused on] his weakness of making promises he could not keep... Dwayne does not have a very high opinion of himself. When criticism flared up among his colleagues, he caved in and became extremely depressed and would not defend himself.

When several families left the church, Faith Chapel, over doctrinal differences, "this hurt Dwayne terribly," said Gracia Stiefel, a congregation member and lifelong friend.

Leander and others with whom Dwayne worked focused on his strengths. First and always among those who enabled him to use those strengths was Carolyn. Leander described her as a "quiet, unassuming, godly mother to her children, and a faithful wife to a man who, though he is a tremendous soul winner, an excellent missionary, an outstanding pilot and a great man of God, is nonetheless an extremely difficult man to live with."

> There are very few women who would have stuck it out. He has dragged her from one continent to another despite the fact that she doesn't like to be uprooted ... despite the fact that she hates the dirt they have shoveled out of these living quarters, and despite the fact that she likes nice things. She has made every hovel into a home that Dwayne could navigate out of.

Tok was a crisis for Carolyn as well as Dwayne:

> What did I know about being a pastor's wife? *Nothing!* Being on the highway, we got lots of people coming through. I used to beg, "Please, Lord, no more." And He would say, "Just one more." But the church was

young and it became a real family to us. God really worked in my life there. Through depression and an identity crisis, when I could no longer live up to my expectations and those of others, He rebuilt my life through His word. I clung to Jeremiah 29: 11-14—*I know the plans I have for you ... plans to prosper you and not to harm you, plans to give you hope and a future. Then you will call upon me and come and pray to me, and I will listen to you. You will seek me and find me when you seek me with all your heart. I will be found by you ... and will bring you back from captivity.*

I knew that I had to start working out what God had worked in. The year we were in Soldotna, I had gone to my first women's Bible study. Now, in Tok, I had a real burden for these women. God helped me overcome my fear of opening my mouth, and I started two Bible studies. Life was great. I could have been content there forever.

There would be other crises through the years, and help would come from the same source.

Faith Chapel: Growing Together

Between crises there was ministry, vividly experienced by two couples who grew with it almost from the beginning: Philip and Glenna Dufresne, recent arrivals in Tok, and Win and Gracia Stiefel, then teachers in the nearby Athabaskan village of Northway. The Steifels met Dwayne when he came to Northway to show an old 16mm Billy Graham film. "To say it was a memorable evening would be an understatement," Gracia recalls.

The film kept breaking, and when it did, an area character named Yukon Ben would wander up to the front of the hall and begin to imitate Billy Graham. Yukon Ben ... was half Norwegian and half Indian, and he had a full gray beard and often wore a shabby gray suit. He hardly looked like the famous evangelist, but he did give an interesting performance. When the film would break, Dwayne would jump up and try to fix it as fast as possible. This jack-in-the-box performance between Yukon and Dwayne-The-Technician kept us all in stitches... Another memory of that evening was of Dwayne, who was sitting near us, slumping down farther and farther in his seat and looking very young and vulnerable.

The Stiefels loved the music at Faith Chapel. "Dwayne loved to lead singing, and only Carolyn could accompany his timing and antics," Gracia recalls. "We often raised the roof, and singing in church has never been more fun than in those early years in Tok." However, she added, it took a bit longer for the diverse congregation to accept the rest of Dwayne's ministry.

> The church was an interesting mix of Lutherans, Catholics, Presbyterians, Methodists and so on. To make it even more interesting, several of us had graduated from pretty liberal church colleges or state universities. We all thought individually that we would straighten out that young Baptist on doctrinal and various other issues. Poor Dwayne! I can't imagine how he survived those early years.

A case in point was Glenna Dufresne, who, with her husband and two young sons, had moved to Tok a few weeks after the Kings. An ad for vacation Bible school on the grocery store bulletin board caught her eye.

> I was a self-defined intellectual, raised going to church (Presbyterian) but not knowing Jesus Christ. I had rejected all my upbringing, and was studying all the New Age philosophies and "true science": evolution. I went and knocked on the door of the [Kings'] trailer and asked what would be taught to the children. I didn't want my babies exposed to any life-after-death talk or miraculous events. Carolyn assured me that all the teaching would be age-appropriate and what was in the Bible.

Uncle Bill Berkheiser's rescue mission, combined with Dwayne's personality and the natural bonding between families, quickly transformed many in the congregation from skeptics to enthusiastic followers and friends of the Kings. Gracia recalls:

> Dwayne's devotional habits and sermon preparation made a big change, and we in the congregation benefited greatly... We respected Dwayne very much as pastor because of his care for all of us, but he never put himself up as a great authority. He was humble and very willing to ask for help and advice. The church seemed full of young families with young children, and we all grew up together... Dwayne had a way of making everyone ... feel like they were special.

Dwayne's improvement in "talking the talk" was matched by his and Carolyn's willingness to "walk the walk," inspiring Glenna and Gracia to do the same. Being made to feel special, of course, made it hard for them to refuse the Kings' requests to become teachers in the church. In the process of their involvement, they and their husbands found faith. Glenna describes how it happened:

> I knew better than to send my kids to church—bad parenting!— so I had to take them. While they were in Sunday school, I was in the Adult class. My boys quickly fell in love with Dwayne and Carolyn and [teachers] Ben and Daisy Gerdes, so that more and more I entrusted them to their care and influence. Plus I was being exposed to the Gospel, and arguing and challenging all the way. But, as I later found out, they were all praying [for me], and by March of 1972 I had accepted Jesus Christ as my Lord and Savior. Once I came to the Lord, the boys and I were in Faith Chapel every time the doors were open.
>
> During those eight or nine months, Dwayne and Carolyn encouraged me, loved me and accepted me. They always asked about my life and the things we were dealing with (moving in, getting utilities hooked up, clearing land). In short, they never lost patience with me, no matter how ornery I was... No one seemed to reject my ideas or ridicule my questions.
>
> They were dealing with the same things we were ... several small children; getting ready for winter and what that requires in the North... The Kings were people, just like me. They helped and needed help. Their house was often noisy and hectic.
>
> Yet in the midst of it all, Carolyn was stable and solid and consistent... In her wisdom—she is still the wisest woman I know, and the most knowledgeable in the Bible—she started having me teach Good News Club [a Child Evangelism Fellowship ministry], knowing that the teacher learns more than the students. Carolyn is a woman of few words, but you'd better pay attention, because every word is a jewel. I was a hungry, dry sponge for the Word of God, and I would call her and Dwayne at all hours of the day and night with my questions.
>
> ... By spring of 1974, my husband, Phil, had accepted Jesus Christ as his Lord and Savior. Dwayne and Carolyn had been reaching out to him, and Dwayne had started a one-to-one Bible study with him. Phil and Carolyn had a special relationship, both of them being people of few words and a similar sense of humor—dry, sarcastic, and teasing.

Recreation was as important as worship, teaching and mutual aid in bonding the young church families, Gracia recalls.

> No matter how old or young, birthdays were special, and we put our coins in the large, pink plastic birthday cake and listened while everyone sang to us... We would have gym nights that started with a potluck

supper, and then ... a rousing game of volleyball. Dwayne was always right in the middle, and always joking and encouraging. The church also had a lot of picnics during our short summer. Many in the church had an unsaved spouse, and these events would be "safe enough" to attend. I really think the fun we had was a great testimony to the unsaved, and there were several that did come to the Lord.

Dwayne often didn't do things halfway. He wanted his family to enjoy camping, as our family did, so we planned a two-family outing. It would have made sense to drive to a nice campsite and try a couple of nights. However, Dwayne had different ideas. He knew of a remote military airstrip quite a ways up from Northway, on the Nabesna River. We drove our vans to Northway, then Dwayne flew both families in three trips to our wilderness setting.

Our families were young. Joel [King] and our daughter Senya were under 2, and we had a four-month-old baby girl also. We surveyed our surroundings, which thrilled me because there was a herd of horses on the airfield.

We set up two tents, and we woke up with a start the next morning to a loud, high-powered rifle shot right outside. A large, formidable Athabaskan Indian had decided to see who was camping in his area. There were some tense moments, but Dwayne explained our visit. [The man] became friendly, and even provided me with a bridle for riding. We spent a few days there, but it wasn't Carolyn's idea of a family vacation. It was just one of the many times we saw Carolyn faithfully follow Dwayne out of her comfort zone.

A Time to Laugh

Tok wasn't the first place, and wouldn't be the last, where Dwayne saw—and often instigated—the funny side of life. Leander Rempel, who has a similar outlook, describes how Dwayne concocted some entertainment from ingredients not normally considered amusing: an empty gas tank, northern lights and a dignified clergyman.

On a bitterly cold night in the early 1970s, driving out for a pastoral visit, Leander asked Dwayne how long the fuel gauge had been on empty. "Only a few hours," was the reassuring reply. But as they started back to Tok after the visit, Dwayne asked innocently, "If we run out of gas, you'll push, won't you?" Leander shot back, "Not on your life!" But a few minutes later, Leander recalls,

Sure enough, the car started sucking air... At ten miles per hour Dwayne jumped out and began to push, urging me to do likewise... Well, I wasn't going to sit in the car while he was pushing, so reluctantly I got out and pushed... At that point it hit me. I should have known all along. I yelled out, "Dwayne, you knucklehead, you have a five-gallon can of gas in the back of the car!" He just roared with laughter. He had achieved his objective, which was to have the Alaska director push the car while he sat in the driver's seat.

On the ride home, Dwayne noticed how gorgeous the northern lights were and wondered if Dr. Sidney Kerr of Ontario, the speaker at a missionary retreat, had ever seen them. Dwayne and Leander decided he hadn't, and should. It was well past midnight. "The next question was, who would wake him? Dwayne figured since I was the area director, I would have to wake him."

I went into his bedroom and he was definitely sound asleep ... the fact that he was sound asleep could certainly be heard throughout the house trailer we were in, and more than likely all of Tok was aware of it. I called his name several times, to no avail. So I shook him. It had been years and years since he had slept in a bunk bed. He sat bolt upright and smashed his head on the bunk above. Well, now he was seeing more than northern lights. He was looking at the Milky Way in Technicolor, with several other galaxies thrown in besides. He said he had never seen northern lights, and yes, he wanted to see them.

So I went outside and waited with Dwayne. He appeared several minutes [later], dressed in a regal bathrobe and house slippers. All of the attire was great for Toronto. Where we were, long johns and bunny boots would have been more in keeping... He proceeded to look up in the sky, which caused him to lose his balance... Then he uttered a statement that just topped it off. In this low, growly voice, he said, "I'm deeply indebted to you boys." He forthwith staggered back to bed, and Dwayne and I split our sides laughing. I don't know when we got to bed.

A Time to Fly

Leander credits Dwayne with largely creating the mission's flying program. Given Alaska's vast distances and skeletal road network, aviation was the only approach that made sense—for administrators as well as missionary pastors. "God had not called me to Alaska to be a Christian car driver," Leander quipped. The program had modest beginnings, Mildred M. Morehouse writes in *Through Open Doors*, a history of SEND International.

King found a secondhand plane in Tok. He reported, "The engine was frozen up, and you could do chin-ups on the propeller." But the price was

right, and missionaries got the plane in working order. It was assigned to
Eagle, the northernmost church location in 1972.

The fledgling mission fleet also included some borrowed planes,
Leander recalls. He described a typical errand in one of them, a single-
engine Cessna 206, bringing supplies and workers to repair a missionary's home. Leander's account suggests that Dwayne's careful approach
to flying was not necessarily humorless:

> The road to Eagle was closed in the winter, but we had a missionary
> there, Dan Kees. The plane did not have a belly pod for cargo, so we
> had to fit all the humans and supplies into the cabin, plus the clothes and
> emergency gear for the five fellows traveling. The fellow in the back was
> jammed into the seat, with all the supplies piled around him. Loading
> had been accomplished with a great deal of joking and bantering, with
> Dwayne entering in to the nth degree. As an example, Dan had ordered
> a case of eggs. [Dwayne suggested] they would take up less room if we
> cracked all the eggs into a five-gallon bucket.
>
> The temperature was 30 degrees below zero, with a thirty-mile-per-
> hour wind... On the trip it suddenly got very quiet in the rear seat, which
> was very unusual for SEND mechanic Keith Daniels, who was sitting
> in that seat. Not long after it got quiet, we could smell what had taken
> place. [After they landed at the Eagle airstrip] Dan met us in his pickup
> truck and we hustled . . . a person didn't want to stay outside any longer
> than he had to! As we were unloading, Keith handed his paper bag to the
> missionary. Dan said, "What's this? What's this?" Just as he got it open
> and the whole mess was staring him in the face, Keith said, "Those are
> the three pancakes and caribou sausage I had for breakfast this morning."

On these errands, Dwayne always tried to pack in the maximum safe
number of mission workers to expose as many of them as possible to the
needs of the villages. When he returned after dark, church members would
drive to the airstrip and shine their headlights on the runway. The headlight
brigade included Phil Dufresne, who sometimes drag-raced Dwayne home
after he landed. "Phil and I were students in Dwayne's first Tok ground-
school class, and Dwayne taught many to fly," Glenna Dufresne recalls.
"Several of the local boys became pilots because of his involvement in
their lives."

Flying suited Dwayne's active style and was vital to his ministry,
recalls Gracia Stiefel.

Dwayne ... has always had the energy level of a kindergarten class. The mission kept him flying often. He used his mechanical abilities to help many local pilots, and met many locals that way. He flew in hunters to hunting grounds, and accident or medical patients to the Faith Hospital 140 miles away. He started a fly-in ministry to Tetlin, [an isolated] Indian village. He also started a ministry in Tanacross, an Indian village ten miles north of Tok. Dwayne genuinely loved and interacted with the native people in our area. He was comfortable in very humble homes.

She and Dwayne would fly to Tanacross on Mondays in what she described as a "difficult but wonderful ministry" with interior Athabaskan people.

We often had to go from house to house to get the people to come to the house we met in. When there was a lot of drinking going on in the village, people would lock their doors. The spiritual warfare was very evident on those evenings, but Dwayne would always carry on, and we'd have people from toddlers to elders singing and listening to stories, and a Bible lesson. The people loved Dwayne because he treated them with love and respect.

One of the men came to the Lord in Tanacross, but still battled with alcohol. I don't know how many times Dwayne ... brought him home or flew him to Glennallen to dry out. One of these times, he grabbed the controls and put the plane upside-down, but Dwayne got it flying level again. Dwayne would also go to wino camps in the woods, near bars in Tok, and he would take the people he knew out of them. Eventually, he had a little cabin built behind the church, where he could have his friends sleep off the effects of alcohol.

"This is some thirty-five plus years later," Gracia said in 2009, "and if I am at a potlatch in the Copper River Valley and there are visitors from the Upper Tanana, they always ask, 'Where's that Dwayne King now?'" Dwayne credits the success of that ministry to Paul Milanowski, a Wycliffe Bible translator who spent much of his life with the Athabaskan people. Dwayne said Paul taught him many of their words and phrases, and something even more important:

He taught me to love native people. Before, I wanted them to become Christians only because I pitied their need for Christ. But I learned to love them because of appreciation of who they were—their culture, their language. They were real people.

Dwayne may have had a sketchy approach to some tasks, but flying wasn't one of them. "One thing that stands out in my mind is the way he handles himself as a pilot," Louise Rempel said. "He can be joking, doing all kinds of unorthodox things, but as soon as there is an airplane waiting ... Dwayne becomes professional, thorough and careful. No goofing around when that part of his life comes to the fore!" He knew the risks of flying small planes over rough terrain in bad weather, and always insisted on well maintained, quality equipment—especially navigation equipment. Minimizing risk would allow him to log some fourteen thousand flight hours without an accident—far more than the average for bush pilots in Alaska.

"I keep the back door open," Dwayne said, summarizing what all pilots know but not all practice. "Keep Plan B ready. I always keep in mind where I can divert to a safe landing—a village, a gravel bar, a bush strip. I made a lot of strips myself. And, I plan for a safe reserve of daylight." Long runways help—takeoffs can be aborted even when airborne, and if problems surface later, it's easier to circle and land. But, he added, long runways are a luxury often unavailable in Alaska. Judgment is vital. Unlike technical knowledge and natural skill, judgment is developed by experience—and Dwayne would acquire nearly forty-five years of it, compensating for the inevitable erosion of reflexes. Knowledge can sense when a cylinder is about to fail, he said, but judgment is what aborts the takeoff, resisting pressures to *go.*

"We're as safe as we can be in the context of what we do," he added. The context is John 14: 6—*I am the way and the truth and the life*—and it was painted on the tail of the plane he flew on his first SEND mission in Alaska. "It's not a rabbit foot or a lucky charm or a crutch. It's our witness."

Planes used for mission business looked respectable, or at least reliable. "However," Leander recalls, "Dwayne always had his own planes for hunting and exploring, and these were a different story." They were the butt of many jokes, and they all had names. One was the notorious Piper PA-20 Pacer he called the "Piper Paper Spacer." The name was a deliberate garbling of the plane's model designation, inspired partly by his father-in-law, Dick Merritt, who dismissed the craft's fabric skin as "paper." It was the second Central Alaska Mission plane Dwayne cobbled together with pieces salvaged from various wrecks. To save time and money, and to be light enough to fly in and out of short mountain airstrips, it had no electrical system, no overall paint job, no springs in the front seats, and no rear seats at all. Passengers sat on sleeping bags. It had an ancient Narco Superhomer radio dubbed the "coffee grinder" because the tuning knob resembled a small crank.

According to Leander, the Paper Spacer had entertainment as well as practical value:

> Dwayne loved to take visitors for sight-seeing rides and would inevitably lead them to his bush plane, just to watch the looks of alarm as he started loading them into this airplane, which looked like it would fall apart before it got to the end of the runway. Really, the plane was in excellent mechanical condition. It just looked ragged because of all the different paint jobs that came from taking a wing from one plane, the fuselage from another, and the other wing from a third aircraft. After the visitors had registered shocked expressions, he would inform them with a roar of laughter that the plane they would be taking was parked nearby.

Sometimes he pushed the gag a little further, telling visitors the plane had no starter. He made them push it to the runway while he sat in the cockpit and pretended to pop the nonexistent clutch. Then he'd tell them, "Oh, we'll just take this [other] one, with the paint on it."

Dwayne's close friends and associates, however, got to ride in his personal bush planes. Louise Rempel describes an outing in the Paper Spacer:

> I remember a hot dog roast with Dwayne and Carolyn in Bettles, along a river bed in the dead of winter—Dwayne's idea. He flew us out one by one... When it was my turn, he climbed in first—there was only one door, on the passenger side—and then I got in. At that point he said: "Oh—that door doesn't shut. Just hang on to it. You'll be fine." And I was! And we flew off to the hot dog roast, and I felt I was like a bird in the sky! There was so little between us and the "air"—the freedom of a bird, flying in this thing with hardly anything you could call seats, except for the pilot's, but an engine that worked perfectly!

Louise recalls another flight that, she said, "typifies Dwayne's zest for life, fun, and, yes, caring!"

> To help us when we were moving back to Alaska, Dwayne set up a guard for us on the Glenn Highway to watch our big trailer while our truck was in Anchorage for repairs. But do you just get a person to watch your things for you? Oh, no—not with Dwayne. Why not get up in the morning, brew some fresh coffee and warm up some cinnamon

rolls, and fly—yes, fly, not drive—them out to the guy? And, yes, of course, land right on the highway and taxi up to the spot where the fellow is camped out!

The guard, Hal Farrar, became a lifelong friend.

Dwayne's joy in flight never got old. Giving a volunteer a ride over the Matanuska Glacier, he responded to the grandeur with song. On another occasion, he reminded a nervous passenger that the risks of wilderness aviation were outweighed by the adventure and fulfillment of mission work. During the Tok years, flying alone on his own time, his zest for fun apparently couldn't resist one challenge. "A story he won't want me to tell began surfacing," said Leander, who, of course, told it.

The story had it that Dwayne had crossed the Tok River bridge in his Paper Spacer. He didn't cross it the conventional way. He crossed it by flying under the bridge [an approximately 40-by-100-foot space]. I bided my time ... and when we were all alone, driving somewhere in a car, in the dark, I asked him about the accuracy of this story. He changed the subject and nothing more was said—he didn't need to say anything else.

"But the Greatest of These ..."

Fortunately for Dwayne's ministry and those at the receiving end of it, the zest and daring were also channeled into people. His achievements in Tok—enlarging the chapel, building a parsonage, greatly expanding the ministry and guiding people to Christ—were accomplished in this spirit, which itself flowed from a deeper quality: a practical love for people that stepped out on faith, leaving God and the home office to supply the details. Despite setbacks, some self-created and others beyond his control, it was a quality that would serve him well over the years in mission fields where the love of God seemed even more remote than in Tok. Leander wasn't the only mentor-turned-friend who recognized this quality early on—and let him unleash it, even if it created a bumpy ride for bureaucrats.

Dr. Alvin O. "Bud" Austin, former president of LeTourneau University, termed Dwayne "contagious," having a sympathetic but not pushy interest in anyone he met. This quality usually resulted in instant bonding. "Two of my grandsons spent just a few hours with him, and they talk about him like they would a close uncle," Bud said. Dwayne was especially effective in Alaska because he met people where they were and did what they did, recalls Frank M. Severn, SEND director emeritus. "He fixed things, built things, went hunting, flew a plane, and always did it with other people. He used every opportunity to talk about Christ or encourage people in their walk of faith."

Dwayne and "Bud" Austin

"He always seemed to light up whenever we showed up," Glenna Dufresne recalls. "That was, and is, his giftedness—to make whoever is in front of his face seem like the most important person on the world."

The home office might have been unsettled by Dwayne's habit of leading from the front, but it gave many people their first and most durable image of a follower of Christ. It was a style that worked, and he never changed it, recalls "Steve" Stevenson, SEND/Alaska director from 1988 to 1995.

> ... some colleagues came and complained because Dwayne was "not in his office" during certain hours when everyone else was. No one ever knew where he was. He didn't report in or out like others. My answer was, "I don't have to worry about where Dwayne is, because I know that wherever he is, he is in ministry."

Mentors and supervisors have tried with limited success to make Dwayne mesh more smoothly with organizational gears—and he, in turn, has rubbed off on them. Bud credits him with making his own personal witness more spontaneous. Frank called him an "an 'out-of-the-box' person who tends to drive administrators to distraction," but added, "Missions need a few Dwayne Kings!"

"I see Dwayne as a point man," Paul Blasko said. "People see his infectious involvement with the Lord, making Christianity believable." Two who believed—Win and Gracia Stiefel—did so after hearing Paul speak at the Tok church, but Paul gave the credit to Dwayne. "I told him, 'Your investment in this couple brought them to Jesus. I just happened to be here when it happened.'" Wherever the credit belongs, Gracia recalls, there were no egos involved. "No one could have been happier than Dwayne. He didn't seem jealous of the abilities of others if it brought people to the Lord... Some pastors are reluctant to have others preach or teach in 'their' church, but that could never be said of Dwayne."

Dwayne's influence inspired not only salvation decisions, but lifelong directions. Choices made later by the Stiefels and Dufresnes reflected that influence. The Stiefels served as missionaries for ten years in northern Siberia. The Dufresnes, who also came to Christ at Tok, later worked as cooks at Alaska Bible College and became active in SEND and other Christian ministries. Dwayne's influence continued through the years—he and Carolyn helped and encouraged the Stiefels when both couples served in Russia, and in 1990 he counseled them through a family crisis.

To Paul Blasko, Dwayne's love for people echoes the disciple Barnabas, "The Encourager." As told in Acts 15: 36-39, Barnabas wanted to give a second chance to John Mark, his young cousin who had deserted him and the Apostle Paul on a previous mission journey. The latter, understandably leery about taking John Mark on the next trip, refused. Paul and Barnabas separated over this disagreement, and Barnabas took John Mark with him on his next trip. The gamble paid off. John Mark became a valued and dependable worker (2 Timothy 4:11).

"Paul was concerned about the work. Barnabas was concerned about the worker," Paul Blasko said. "That's what Dwayne sees in so many people—possibilities. He's willing to work with raw material, with God, in bringing out the best in them."

Dwayne would spend the rest of his career working out the pattern that had been worked in at Tok: giving others the chances his mentors had given him. More immediately, the strengthening he received there would be tested over the next few years by tragedy, near-failure, frustration and joy, played out against a harsher, more remote backdrop.

8. BETTLES: Cold Crucible

Describe a "typical" day's or week's activities.
— missionary questionnaire,
Twin Orchards Baptist Church

... Immediately upon getting up, do whatever it takes to get warm. Start the fires, fix the stove, cut & split and haul wood, stuff all the cracks I can in this old shack. # 1 object in this ministry is Stay Warm. I am chronically unorganized & impulsive and constantly behind in fixing all the junk—chainsaw, airplane, truck, stove and all the Kids stuff. All this takes a tremendous amount of time... We try to use the activities of just existing as a ministry.
— Dwayne King,
February 1982

You think I'm doing this for my health? You think I like being cold?
— Dwayne King,

FROM 1981 TO 1984 the Kings lived in Bettles, thirty-five miles above the Arctic Circle—the farthest north of any SEND mission posting. Winter temperatures commonly dropped to 60 and 70 degrees below zero—one day was a record minus 84—with wind chills nearly twice that. The four growing kids were trying their wings. Dwayne was challenged as never before by his family's needs and the hardships of wilderness ministry in a place tourism promoters advertise more for the beauty of the northern lights than the weather.

Home was a rented, two-story log house, more than thirty years old, in adjoining Evansville, an Eskimo-Indian village of eighty-nine people. The

Kings had no running water or sewer, and used an outhouse in the summer and fall of the first year. With hand tools and power equipment, Dwayne and his older sons, Dave and Jon, sank a twenty-six foot shaft for water and dug a sewer. Both were "very shaky," Dwayne wrote in the missionary questionnaire: "... now only two feet of water in the well, [and] expect pump or water to quit any time."

Fresh fruits and vegetables were once-a-month luxuries purchased on flying shopping trips to Fairbanks, two hundred miles away, or Glennallen, four hundred miles distant. They hunted moose, fished for salmon, drank a lot of powdered milk and occasionally bought chicken, ham and pork. The kids attended a public school consisting of two rooms and three teachers.

Friends Lighten the Load

The cold of Bettles was tempered by the warmth of new friends who supported the Kings with inspiration and practical help.

David and Tamara Ketscher owned the Bettles Trading Post and Sourdough Outfitters, buying furs and selling dogsleds. Mick and Cece Manns owned a recreational gold mine for tourists, where they allowed the Ketschers—who had a heart for ministry—to set up the Brooks Range Bible Camp in 1978. When Dwayne and Carolyn came to Bettles and organized a church, Dave Ketscher called it an answer to prayer. Dwayne said the thanks should go to the Ketshers:

> It was their spirit—the call of the furthest-out and hard-to-reach—that challenged me to come to Bettles. They really had pioneered this ministry on the south slopes of the Brooks Range. I caught Dave's heart and vision for the villages. And every summer they welcome us back to bring the village kids together for Bible camp.

Dwayne called Tam a "rock-solid character of a woman you can trust to be ethical, straightforward, and smart." A Native Alaskan villager also praised Dave's choice of a wife. Watching Tam unload planes and tackle other strenuous tasks around the store while Dave was out flying, he pronounced her "big, strong, and good-looking." Dave memorialized the compliment in a vanity license plate he gave her: "BS & GL."

Mick and Cece, whose job was bulldozing snow from the local airstrip for state maintenance crews, opened their home to the Kings while Dwayne and his sons were refurbishing the Evansville house. They also gave SEND free use of the Bible camp.

Another friend was Postmistress Jeanie Stevens, one of those who met in the Ketshers' upstairs apartment for worship before Bettles Bible Church was built. After one service, they planned to fly to Fairbanks for some shopping—the Kings and Jeanie in Dwayne's plane, and the Ketschers in theirs. Tam prayed for safety. Dwayne, on the other hand, urged the group to pray for wisdom and good judgment instead. He explained, "If God wants to take us in a plane, He can. Good pilots die in good airplanes."

Jeanie said, "I'm going with Tam!"

Trust and Tragedy

Dwayne was hit by two major crises during the first year in Bettles, but neither one was caused by the harshness of the new location or occurred anywhere near it.

The first was his ordination examination in February at Cal Tab in Vestal, and it was Paul Blasko's faith that saved the day when Dwayne's usual eloquence failed him. "Dwayne is one of the finer missionary speakers who makes real what God has done," said Paul, who conducted the ordination council. "That was the only time I saw him not in command of a situation—he absolutely choked." Council members were growing increasingly concerned with Dwayne's inability to express doctrinal beliefs, so Paul rephrased the questions as if he were speaking to a fifth grader. "He still didn't get it," Paul said.

A consensus seemed to be looming: Postpone the decision for six months, then reconvene. At that point, Paul recalls, he said to the council: "I'd like to add something to the mix. I know what he believes, and it matches up with what we want in a candidate for ordination." He told the council that he had heard Dwayne preach and teach in Alaska and knew he was committed to the Lord and the Bible. Paul said he had no difficulty in recommending him. The council agreed. "When they ordained him," Paul said, "they were ordaining a proven servant of God."

Trust went both ways during their friendship. "He'd ask my opinion at times," Paul said. "This showed less about my expertise than about his desire for wide enough input to make a good decision." It also showed that although Dwayne never abandoned his point-man style, he was increasingly willing to seek counsel from others. He didn't always follow it. When Paul periodically told him he would live longer if he slowed down, "It'd just roll off his back." But when Dwayne learned years later that he had prostate cancer, he was deeply grateful for his friend's presence. Dwayne told him, "This is of God. I can't think of anyone I'd rather have with me at this time."

The next crisis was a tragedy that struck the entire SEND organization. On September 12, 1981, Philip E. Armstrong, one of the mission's founders, and four others died when SEND's twin-engine Beechcraft Bonanaza went down in bad weather off the coast of Cape Yakataga in the Gulf of Alaska. Phil, SEND's minister of missions, was a co-creator and former general director of Far Eastern Gospel Crusade, a forerunner of SEND International. The others were pilot Paul Backlund, an Alaska Bible College graduate and youth pastor; retired Sperry-Rand executive Paul Mortenson, a mission board member and leadership trainer; Wanda Ediger, recently appointed office manager of SEND's new radio station, KRSA; and Bill Ballou, mission business manager and coordinator of the KRSA project.

The plane was returning to Glennallen after a visit to the project site in Petersburg. KRSA station manager Jim Andrews and chief engineer John Hurni took the visitors to the Petersburg airport and saw them off.

"Their next stop was heaven," Jim said.

Louise Rempel recalls Dwayne's role in what she described as a "very difficult experience":

> After some days of searching [by military and local pilots], the mission carried out one final exercise. This was headed up by Dwayne: His mission was to get the exact coordinates last given to our plane on that fateful night and see just where that would have put it. Dwayne very accurately did that, and I will never forget him coming back to our home ... with his heart visibly broken and shattered. The coordinates had placed the plane in the water—and it, and our five people, were gone! He and Leander, as brothers in the Lord and friends, lay on our living room floor with the stereo turned up to a loud level, singing and finding comfort in the God they know and love so much, who, they knew, doesn't make any mistakes. That's Dwayne—who has experienced many hard things, but whose determination to serve his Lord has not been diminished!

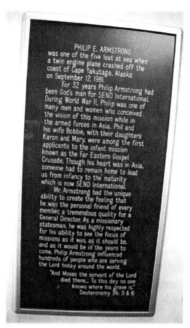

Memorial at SEND International headquarters

Fun is Where You Find it

Partners in grief and faith, Dwayne and Leander were also, as always, two of a kind in appreciating life's comedy—which often seemed to surface when they were showing around greenhorns from gentler places. In a story he calls "The Olive Touch," Leander tells of introducing a SEND official, whom he identifies only as "Gus," to the North.

"He was a good representative, though he had difficulty understanding how things were done in Alaska," Leander recalls. So Leander and Dwayne flew to Anchorage, picked up Gus and his wife Olive and flew them to Victory Bible Camp in the Talkeetna Mountains to visit a summer retreat for missionaries.

Dwayne, as a good pilot should, flew over the landing strip several times to make sure the runway was clear and that conditions had not changed since he last landed a plane there. It was a four-hazard strip: Hazard Number One was that it started on a high, solid rock bluff with about a thousand-foot drop-off. If you approached it too low, your propeller definitely started acting like a blender with the rock bluff. If you approached it too high, you couldn't take your wheels down in time to brake so you didn't hit Hazard Number Three, which was a lake at the end of the runway.

After you touched down, you had to deal with Hazard Number Four—the runway sloped down at a fairly steep angle. If you didn't "stick your wheels to the turf" the first time, the plane had a tendency to keep flying. That very quickly took you back to Hazard Number Two, which was that the runway, in addition to sloping down, was "not too long."

Let's get back to Gus and Olive—they had never flown in a small plane before. So when Dwayne did his several passes, they were sure there was something wrong with the plane or down on the ground that prevented him from landing. Well, the third pass over the strip, Dwayne decided it was time to "put her down." He banked the plane, made his final turn and headed straight for the rock wall—at the end of which, they had observed, was the lake. Gus figured he had met his end and he was glad it was in the service of the King.

Gus didn't meet his heavenly King that time. The other King landed them safely. "When the retreat was over," Leander added, "Gus and Olive opted to go to Glennallen by car." Olive stayed there while Dwayne and Leander gave Gus an informative tour. But, as Leander relates, they couldn't provide all the comforts of home he was accustomed to.

We flew Gus out to Bettles to experience, firsthand, "friendship evangelism" and "church planting" Alaskan style... The only place Gus and I could sleep was in the attic ... on two mattresses right in the corner where the eves came down; Gus and I slept head to head. Just before we fell asleep, Gus informed me that he sometimes snored, and the way to get him to stop was the method Olive used. She just gently patted his bald spot just above his eyebrows. Well, he fell asleep before I did. The soft rumble in his throat turned into a roar, and the roar gave way to a snarling chainsaw. So I proceeded to pat his bald spot—gently. Then a little harder—to no avail. I just didn't have the Olive touch. I finally gave up and went downstairs to sleep on the couch while Gus dreamed about Olive.

The next morning, Leander adds, Gus got his promised look at Alaska-style missionary work.

It started before breakfast was finished. There was a knock on the door. The fellow asked whether Dwayne had an altimeter for a Cessna 180. Dwayne said he thought he did, so they went out to Dwayne's shed and scrounged around... All morning and afternoon there was a steady stream of traffic to the Kings' spare parts shed, which Dwayne dragged with him wherever he went. While people approached Dwayne for spare parts for their airplanes or snow machines, he took the opportunity to speak to them about their relationship with the Lord. At the end of the day, Gus commented, "I thought I would see church planting!" It took several more visits before Gus realized how you started a church in Alaska.

Breaking Through the Ice

What Gus couldn't see in a brief visit was the day-to-day grind of existence that underlay the ministry, an existence continually threatened by a bleak mix of isolation, cold, depression and broken equipment. The winter of 1981-82 was the hardest, Dwayne indicated in February 1982, responding to questions in the Twin Orchards missionary questionnaire. With no existing church in the area to step into, the Kings were blazing a new trail—and the closest missionaries who might have helped were in Fairbanks, two hundred miles away. Dwayne described a never-ending contest between what had to be done and what could go wrong.

> There is very little resemblance of a schedule with me ... am spending a lot of time cutting down big logs for the new parsonage. This spring I will spend fifty to sixty hours a week pouring cement or building sewer system, drilling well, etc. Some weeks I will spend forty hours, more or less, on counseling, Bible teaching, discipling, etc. Some things are fixed and can be called a schedule. Church every Sunday. Monday night fly to Jim River Road Camp and teach Bible class. Tuesday Carolyn teaches Ladies' Bible Study in Bettles. Thursday, men's Bible study. . . . Each one of these takes preparation and study time, but when some of this junk around here quits (water pump lines freeze, sno-go [snowmobile] won't run, sled hitches break, oil stove goes out, and any number of other things) then there are adjustments to be made.

Asked to list the greatest obstacles to his work, he replied, "Ice, snow and 60 below... The Bettles syndrome, which is negativism, gossip and humanism," which he defined as the philosophy that people can successfully live their lives without the need for any outside help. Needs seemed overwhelming:

> I need to be more of a loving, forgiving, caring father and husband. To use my time wisely; to be more productive in ministry to people. I need to study more. I need gas for my airplane so I can get out to where the people are more. I need help from people who want to come up for short

periods and help build, fly, work on my plane. I need new dope and fabric, and a valve job on my Paper Spacer.

Asked to list special "wants," he replied: "A good oil stove instead of this borrowed piece of junk. Some tools ... to get jobs done faster and easier. A ham radio so I can communicate to the outside world (I'm just getting my ham license)." Before he could obtain the license, advancing technology made ham radio obsolete.

Tersely, he summed up a major obstacle to ministry: "the time it takes to just live." However, when time spent on daily tasks involved other people—whether helping or being helped by them—a mysterious transformation took place: Obstacles became opportunities. It was more than just helping people rummage through his spare parts shed.

"We try to use the activities of just existing as a ministry," he wrote. "...take someone out to cut wood with. Work on stove with someone else. Fix airplanes w/owners." The interaction was constant, even in subzero weather, recalls visitor Frank Severn.

> I listened as he counseled a couple in the bush that was having marriage difficulties, over a two-way radio. I saw the pure joy on Native American faces when Dwayne flew into their village. All the villagers gathered around him ... he took the chief for a ride in his two-seat Piper Cub. I am sure he allowed the chief to take the wheel during flight. He loved to teach flying to anyone.

Hardships were balanced by blessings, Dwayne indicated in the questionnaire. Dark winters were followed by summers that were "just great. Warm ... 60-70 ... daylight twenty-four hours." The Fairbanks missionaries were far away, but cooperative: "... they are a big help to us. We send some people to them."

He described the biggest blessing of all in relating where God had given him the most success and personal fulfillment: "When most of this junk is fixed, and I see God at work in the hearts of people we are teaching the Word to. We begin to see changes in people's lives. The men begin to take responsibility in the local church when they recognize the gifts God has given them, and they begin to use them for the building up of one another.

"This is what keeps me going."

Near the end of the missionary questionnaire, Dwayne urged the Twin Orchards congregation to continue supporting missions and to pray for his family. He concluded:

I have been very open and it almost seems like I've been light about some things. A missionary must have a sense of humor, right? We appreciate all that Twin Orchards has done for us through the years. You're the greatest church to have behind us... You have prayed and given sacrificially. What more can a missionary ask for?

Showers of Blessing

Carolyn answered that question in letters to friends and supporters. The winter of 1982-83 was loosening its grip, and prayers—some of which Dwayne had requested in the questionnaire—were being answered. Summer was a time of growth for the King children and renewed Bible Camp activity for the mission. Warmth and light strengthened the family for another long siege of cold and darkness, from which they would emerge into another spring that brought major changes on the horizon.

Her April 1983 letter gave thanks for "those unexpected people God puts in our lives to bless and be blessed by." Blessings from friends and strangers alike ranged from prayers to running errands to flying in supplies. Topping Carolyn's list was satisfaction in helping women find God's love, as she had found it in the darkness at Tok. The Seventh Annual Ladies' Retreat there was attended by one hundred women, whose testimonies showed "steady, quiet growth in those we've left ... we still have a place in their hearts." She described her work in Bettles as the "joy (and scary responsibility) of helping women put their lives back into perspective when they seem to be falling apart."

The blessings included:

My friend who prays very specific things for me every day ... Friends who run errands in town when we can't get in ... Old friend who came to wire the basement ... Jim River guys to do the plumbing ... A stranger (but not now) to help put the logs in place ... Dr. James Dobson's film series on video [for] all the areas Dwayne flies into with people who wouldn't normally come to a Bible study ... Gymnastics team that spent ten days teaching our kids not only gymnastics, but life values and control of their God-given bodies ... Being able to encourage and help some Christian miners hauling huge equipment over the ice trail ... The Cessna 206 to haul more "stuff" ... DC-4 to haul building supplies and appliances—including a dishwasher! . . . Tremendously supportive mission family ... Pure enjoyment of a deep, abiding friendship that won't end because we're separated by thousands of miles ... *You!*

She gave her letter the title of a popular Christian song, "Showers of Blessing," which includes the phrase: "Mercy drops 'round us are falling." However, she gave Bettles weather the last word: "Showers are still snow, but with a hint of spring appearing ... *mud*."

Summer saw the first of the King children getting ready to leave the nest, Carolyn wrote in her next letter. Dave, who had just turned 18, bought his own plane and was accepted at Columbia International University, a Christian school in South Carolina. He and Jon worked at gold mining camps, learning to operate and maintain heavy equipment, leaving Becky and Joel at home to help Dwayne build their new house.

Meanwhile, thirty-seven young children and teens attended three Bible camp sessions and had an exciting time panning for gold, catching twenty-inch graylings and watching lightning start forest fires. An extra bonus for Carolyn was caring for a 2-year-old and a 3-year-old, the children of one of the summer mission staffers. "A renewed experience after grown-up kids," she called it.

She continued, "By the time you read this, the roof should be on the new house and the inside all sanded, ready for log oil, some windows cut and the furnace in." She thanked members of an Arizona church and others who had come up to help, and requested two prayers: for Dave's new life at Columbia, and that the house would be far enough along to move into by November.

"Fall is here (mid-August)," she concluded. "Hunting season is imminent!" Dwayne's farewell to his college-bound son was dramatic.

One of the most memorable experiences with David was preparing his own Piper PA-20 Pacer for his long solo flight to Columbia, South Carolina. I in my Pacer, and Dave in his, took off in close formation from Bettles. At about the Arctic Circle, heading south, I waved my wings and he did the same, then I banked for home and let him go. It's a good thing I didn't have a radio—I couldn't talk. I cried like a baby all the way back. I was so proud of his adventurous spirit of heading for Bible College, so far away. He'd call along the way—bad spark plugs in White Horse, Yukon. Leaking fuel tank in Edmonton. Customs in Minnesota made him open up the whole airplane. What kind of crazy 18-year-old flies his own plane from the Arctic? And he made it, and went on to fly it all over America.

Winter darkness closed in, bringing reasons for joy amid frustration. Carolyn started her December 1983 letter with gratitude for faithful friends and supporters, letting Philippians 1:3-5 (NASB) speak for the family: *I thank God in all my remembrance of you, always offering prayer with joy ... in view of your participation in the gospel from the first day until now.* Using the image of the home they were building, she expressed not only thanks, but also showed her increasing strength and peace in bleak surroundings, and her continuing love and patience toward those she and Dwayne had come to serve.

It's a humbling experience to be always on the receiving end—able to give so little in return for the sacrifice you make to keep us here, not seeing much fruit for the labor. This is not only our very dark winter season, but also a dark winter season for the church, seeing little growth.

People are like these logs we've been working with... Each one presents its own difficulty . . . yet each has beauty. Each one has its own characteristics and has to be worked with as an individual. Some take much fitting, cutting and chiseling before they fit together—*For even as the body is one yet has many members ... though they are many, are one body, so also is Christ* (1 Corinthians 12:12, NASB)... *in whom the whole building, being fitted together, is growing into a holy temple ...* (Ephesians 2:21, NASB).

Even after the structure is up, it takes much work to make it livable. November 1 it looked impossible—yet with many people working together, it *was* possible to move in November 10. The church body is here, but not yet a holy temple ... there is still much fitting to be done, with each one working with the others in love until we all fit together.

But just as we cut windows to let in the light, there are bright spots: a few committed hearts, joys to work with, answers to *your* prayers ... David home from [college]—God is doing great things in his life ... a quite unfinished but very livable *warm* house—seems like a palace . . . meat left by two hunter friends . . . safety—only serious accident was Dwayne's broken thumb as a result of dropping the last log in the wrong place—didn't slow him down much.

—Thankfully yours, The Kings

Relocation was the theme of Carolyn's May 1984 letter: "moving things, people, etc., from place to place."

... moving one pile of snow to another before it relocates in our basement in liquid form. Do you know how difficult it is to write the word

"May" when there's three feet of snow (or more) and it's still coming down?

... moving the Kings from Bettles to Glennallen ... The high school situation here has become difficult—only three students, no sports or other activities, etc., due to the decreased enrollment as families have been transferred. We would like Becky and Jon to have the opportunity of being in a bigger school, with more extracurricular activities and Christian friends as well as a good basic education.

... Dwayne will be taking over the flying ministry for the mission for one year while our chief pilot, Richard Nalos, is on furlough. He will also be the director of development for Alaska Bible College, which involves extension schools, recruiting students, etc. I will be managing the college bookstore.

... Larry and Kathy Boone, who have already spent one summer in Bettles, are ready and anxious to take over the ministry here.

"Other movings around" mostly highlighted the activities of children no longer kids—a second son took to the sky, and Joel was the only pre-teen left.

... Jon has tried his wings and made his first solo flights, waiting anxiously for school to be out so he can get back to the gold mine.

... David flew his plane home from Columbia International University the long way to visit his birthplace—Longview, Texas, and LeTourneau College—and other friends in California. He's now on a commercial fishing boat out of Dillingham in the Bristol Bay area.

... Becky will be working at Victory Bible Camp and then helping with ours. Hard to think "camp" with all this snow.

... Joel has been invited to go sailing for three weeks in the Washington area with a local family—a great adventure for him ... Dwayne was able to take planeloads of people to our Tok retreats, Billy Graham Crusade in Anchorage and ... a Native New Life conference ...

—In His Care,
The Kings

Dwayne's last tour of duty in Alaska would be a time of growth for the family—a seven-year bookshelf of familiar and new stories. This chapter would be set off by a pair of spectacular bookends: near the beginning, a long-awaited summer in the Lower 48; and toward the end, a history-making flight followed by an emotion-filled look into the past and the future.

9. GLENNALLEN: Committed

~

A ring by spring or your money back!
　　　—Dwayne King,
　　　　　advertising Alaska Bible College
　　　　　as prime mate-hunting territory

*In a comfortable world, the hard edges have been padded, rounded
and smoothed—it's the home of the foam-rubber lawn mower.
But where there is no risk, there is no achievement.*
　　　—Dwayne King,
　　　　　1991 missions conference

THE GLENNALLEN YEARS looked more like a slice of typical American suburban life than anything the Kings had experienced so far. But they still weren't the Brady Bunch—they didn't live in a typical state, and they weren't leading typical lives. Dwayne might be hunting musk ox above the Arctic Circle one week and, a few days later, running the time clock at a high school wrestling meet. For son Dave, spotting fish by plane for commercial fishing boats and attending Bible college was a perfectly reasonable combination of activities. It was the same for the rest of the family: a normal Alaskan mix of the conventional and the adventurous. "Becky working at Tastee Freez and learning to fly," Carolyn wrote.

It was a full, fast-moving seven years. "I'm tempted to just Xerox off a page of our calendar and see if you can keep track of everyone's comings and goings!" Carolyn told friends and supporters. And, in another letter: "Where has this year gone? As Job says, *My days go by faster than a weaver's shuttle.*"

The fall of 1984 was the longest and warmest in memory, a pleasant backdrop for settling into new roles: Dwayne as chief pilot for SEND and recruiter for Alaska Bible College, and Carolyn as college bookstore manager. Dave returned to the Bible college at Columbia International University. Becky and Jon started basketball at Glennallen High School. Joel played saxophone in the school band and joined Boys' Brigade, a Christian youth organization.

In 1985, Dwayne and Carolyn celebrated fifteen years in SEND with a summer in the Lower 48 and Canada. Carolyn summed it up: "eighteen thousand miles, twenty-eight states, five provinces, fourteen churches, thirty meetings and innumerable friends equal one joyous, interesting, successful, safe home service... It was an experience of a lifetime... We really grew closer to those of you who have been so faithful."

They arrived back in Alaska on August 17, their twenty-second wedding anniversary— "a great anniversary present!" Carolyn also gave thanks for generous financial support that left them only $263 short of their monthly expenses. Two more "praise" items were funds for a garage and the gift of a new aircraft navigation instrument—the latter a necessity for a flying missionary in the Far North.

Northern Smorgasbord

Carolyn's March 1986 letter was filled with the variety of mostly Alaskan life, including trips in which Dwayne was accompanied by Dave, who had transferred to Alaska Bible College.

> ... Dwayne is in Cheyenne, Wyoming, with a Gospel team from Alaska Bible College. They'll be in Wrangell [Alaska], Montana and Denver ... to recruit students and staff, and minister in many places. His last big trip, two weeks ago, was renamed a "Muskospel" trip. They went to Nunivak Island—the home of one of our students. Besides holding three Gospel meetings, they went on a musk ox hunt—a rare privilege for white men. Only a limited number of permits are issued over the whole state. So the trip involved spending the night in Bethel in the fish and game office to be sure to be one of the first to sign up ... and get one of the twelve permits. They had to go forty miles by snow machine to where the animals were. They came home with three musk ox and a big story. The meat is delicious and the hair is unbelievable—some of it as long as eighteen inches. A local gal is spinning the kiviut [soft under-fur] into yarn for mittens.

... we try to keep up with the sports events. Now that basketball is over, Jon is wrestling, Joel is goalie on the hockey team and Becky is waiting for track to start... Dwayne is learning to run the time clock while I learn to keep score for wrestling. At least once a month I help feed the visiting teams and bake dozens of cookies, etc.

... the winter has been too mild in Anchorage. For the first time in the forty-year history of the big Fur Rendezvous there is *no* snow, and the international dog sled races have all been cancelled and moved to Tok.

Our tenth annual men's and women's retreats are coming up soon. Dwayne will be song leader for the men's, and flying for both. I have a couple of seminars to do—one on "How do I keep up with Dwayne?" No, not really—it's on time management. Right after I agreed to that, I said "Yes, I'll teach the Pioneer girls—but only for ten weeks." That will be a good illustration for setting priorities, knowing your limits, not over-committing yourself, and being disciplined.

... It looks like the summer will be more than full. Dwayne has been asked to speak at two or three camps already, plus coordinate the new library project... He also wants to spend a week or so fishing with [son] Dave in Bristol Bay and go back up to some of the gold mines around Bettles. I'll have to keep the bookstore open, but with flexible hours.

Our biggest praise is that the pledges for our support requirement are all in! *Thank you!!!*

Dwayne spent much of the next few years in what Carolyn called his favorite places: "in the air and in the pulpit." One pulpit was KCAM Radio—he hosted the early-morning daily show, "As the Prop Turns," dispensing aviation tips and a devotional, "Thoughts to Fly By." A favorite was Isaiah 40:31: ... *those who hope in the Lord will renew their strength. They will soar on wings like eagles* ... Pilots throughout the Copper River Basin without phone service or two-way communication listened to KCAM for weather and flight conditions.

As a pilot, Dwayne airlifted Gospel teams to remote villages, flew hundreds of medical evacuations, and ferried missionaries, college staff and visitors, as well as conducting summer sightseers on a popular glacier tour. Ministry highlights included hosting a pastors' conference, presenting Gospel drama team skits, and recruiting students and faculty.

On one occasion, he promised potential students "a ring by spring or your money back"—resulting in what Alaska SEND Director "Steve" Stevenson claimed was a record attendance year, with several weddings at graduation.

He also made some new friends in this period, winning them with the personality that made him successful in his work. They included Don and Ann Lewis, members of Twin Orchards. Only Dwayne could have inspired a middle-aged, upstate New York couple to leave their comfort zone and eventually become team leaders for SEND construction volunteers in Russia. What's more, the Lewises recall, he did it without them being aware of it.

"Right away, he started working on us. He was a motivator," Don said. Ann added, "He's got a plan mapped out for your life. You don't even know you're being motivated."

Carolyn, meanwhile, chronicled the family's life as a whole, keeping friends and supporters abreast of details ranging from kids to college, from daily weather to the rhythm of the seasons. Her June 1986 letter was typical:

> With rain in December and three inches of snow on June 1, we began to wonder what happened to our seasons. Since then ... temperatures in the 70s, many forest fires and more mosquitos than are necessary to carry us away.
>
> May was full of graduation activities. Six graduated from the college ... Jon graduated from high school ... in April he took third place in the state wrestling tournament ... Becky went to Kodiak for student government meetings, then to Washington, D.C. for Project Close-Up—an in-depth look at the government. Joel is very busy doing odd jobs around the college here, and next week he will go to a wrestling clinic ...
>
> The library project is in full swing ... God has marvelously supplied the funds for Plan B—to get the building enclosed before winter. Four couples are here from Arizona and Florida to build it.
>
> Carolyn has had three jobs for the last six weeks ... receipting money in the administration office ... doing the inventory in the bookstore ... all the bookkeeping at the college since May 1... Today she stayed home and cleaned cupboards—a nice change.

The Glennallen years brought sadness as well as accomplishment. In 1988, Carolyn's stepfather, Dick Merritt, died unexpectedly, and a mission child, Tyler Kauffman, was killed in a parking lot accident.

Two vacations in Hawaii gave Dwayne and Carolyn a break from Alaskan weather, especially the notorious winter of 1988-89 with its wind chill of minus-126 in Glennallen. In 1990, Carolyn stood smiling with other capped and gowned Alaska Bible College graduates and was awarded her bachelor of arts in Christian Education. She received a computer from the boys, a gift suggested by Dwayne—who himself had become computer literate the year before. ("Joel is our real computer whiz, though," Carolyn noted.) In 1992, Dwayne would finally complete requirements for a master's in intercultural studies at Columbia International University.

Kings in Glennallen, 1989, from left:
Jon, Joel, Carolyn, Dwayne, Dave, Becky

The years also brought a combination of parental pride and nervousness as the kids continued to grow and take flight—usually literally. Jon got his private pilot's license and bought a Piper Pacer. Dave's newly rebuilt Super Cub was flipped over and damaged by wind in April 1988— he was unhurt, and the other kids were undeterred. "On July 27th Becky made her first solo flight, and mother lived through it," Carolyn wrote. "One more to go!" Joel got his private pilot's license in 1990 and his commercial license in 1992.

The kids filled their lives with other skills and activities. Dave guided hunters and, helped by Dwayne, set up an air taxi business. Jon worked on a crab boat in the Bering Sea. Joel worked at KCAM, helped make a Christian film in Brazil, won the state wrestling championship and was accepted at John Brown University in Arkansas. Becky went on a mission trip to Kenya, graduated from The Master's College—a Christian school in Los Angeles—and spent a semester in Israel.

Carolyn, as always, saw in nature the march of time. "The fireweed's gone, the leaves are turning. I was not ready for school to start, but it did anyway!" she wrote in 1989. Two years later, it was time to think of home service in the Lower 48 again, which meant finding replacements and deciding what to do on returning to Alaska when the furlough ended.

Dwayne and Carolyn pondered whether to resume work in Glennallen or minister in native villages. He picked the latter, deciding to focus on developing native churches in the Copper River Valley, which would involve more personal discipleship and evangelism.

God, however, had other plans. Russia changed everything.

Answering a New Call

Carolyn's Christmas 1991 letter was full of the repercussions of Dwayne's groundbreaking September flight to Providenya to check out ministry possibilities. She summed up the mission team's findings in one sentence: "They found people starving for the truth of the Gospel."

Two months after the trip, the Vestal missions conference of November 8-10 was the pivotal point where past, present and future met.

For three days filled with laughter and tears, Dwayne stood in the sanctuary of Twin Orchards in front of those who believed in his work, and gave an accounting of a life made possible by their gifts and prayers. He trumpeted the old call to service, but this time he threw out the challenge of a new mission field at the end of it. Alaska was in his bones and was the focus of the conference, but twenty-three years of continuous front-line service in missions had taught him to follow where he felt God leading. The Alaskan adventure was going on hold and the Russian journey was about to begin. But whether in Alaska, Russia or their own neighborhoods, he assured his hearers, the goal remained constant: "to accomplish the work that God has commissioned us all to do—to preach the Gospel to every tongue and every tribe and every nation."

He made it clear at the outset that this would be no dry-eyed report to some impersonal board of directors:

> There's just a flood of memories that come through me as I see some of you people who have been such a part of our lives ... I get tenderhearted ... so you'll forgive me for those times, but this is an emotional place, because this is where it all began with us in the work that God has called us to do. As Pastor Blasko said, we've been up there in Alaska. This is the place that God has called us to serve, and we're glad. We love it ... though I get awfully cold at times. Seems the older I get the colder I get, and sometimes I do wish the Lord would send us to Hawaii or some South Sea island or something. But He continues to give us warmth, warmth in the ministry as well.

He challenged his audience to hear and obey what he had heard and obeyed in Isaiah 6:8: *Then I heard the voice of the Lord saying, "Whom shall I send? And who will go for us?" And I said, "Here am I. Send me!"* Excuses, he quickly added, were not an option: "Forget the *I'm too old . . . I'm too poor ... I'm too weak ... I'm too quiet.* Forget all of that, and listen. Do you hear the voice of the Lord?"

Dwayne reviewed for supporters what their prayers and donations were accomplishing, not only for his work, but throughout SEND's North American territory. He distilled service on a distant frontier into something his suburban audience could feel, smell and taste:

> Many small towns in Alaska and the Yukon now have groups of believers fellowshipping regularly. Some meet in rented quarters, and others have bought land and erected their own building. Missionary counselors often care for a scattered flock... Visitation is sometimes done by plane or radio.
>
> A large number of people work behind the scenes to keep other SEND missionaries productive in a wide variety of ministries. The harshness of the climate and the vast distances demand skilled technical personnel. Planes, trucks, even cars, must run when they are needed, even if the temperature drops to 40 below zero. SEND takes advantage of the few short weeks of warm weather to hold Vacation Bible Schools and camps for kids of all ages, and to make evangelism contacts in villages. Summer is also prime time for work projects that can only be done when the snow is gone and the mud is dried up.
>
> The missionaries of SEND International have one purpose, with many ways to attain that goal. The nurse at Faith Hospital, the secretary using the computer, the teacher at Alaska Bible College, the radio announcer, the mechanic, the church planter—are basically the same kind of person. They are people who are personally committed to Jesus Christ, who enjoy reaching others. They want to see the church established in a vast, remote region of Alaska and northwestern Canada.

Many short-term volunteers, Dwayne added, had returned to work fulltime in Alaska, the Yukon and British Columbia, citing their summer experiences as part of God's plan to lead them into career ministries. Dwayne gave his invitation to missions a flavor of urgency, warning against the distractions of a world that, according to Biblical prophecy, might not have much time left.

God is preparing a world for a day of judgment ... for the return of Jesus Christ. Are we ready? Will we hear the words, *Well done, thou good and faithful servant!* Some of you have given your time and energy and money to the hilt ... but some of us are going on with our own plans. . . . We've heard the message so many times, it seems to go over our heads. We want to be faithful. We want to be effective. We want to be out there. We want to go. We want to give. But, Lord, somehow ... the things of the world just crowd out all of the most important things. Help us to zero in on giving our all, whatever the cost, to You, and for Your purpose.

Emphasizing that God gifts individuals differently to accomplish His purposes, Dwayne characteristically baited the stern hook of missions with the lure of his own gift. For the benefit of would-be pilots and NASCAR fans, he warned, in effect, that another excuse for avoiding God's call—missing out on fun—was not only unacceptable, but inaccurate. "I have gone fast. I love to do two hundred miles an hour at twenty thousand feet," he said. "Don't get the wrong idea, young people. If you want to go fast, do it in an airplane—not in a car."

Not surprisingly, the lure he dangled before the more daring attendees consisted of more than mere talk.

Tomorrow night we're gonna have a quiz on Alaska—and the people that get the best grades get a free airplane ride Sunday afternoon... Okay, some of you are saying, "You can have it!" But some of you are adventurous, and you'd love to see the Triple Cities and your very own house from the air ... and I'll keep it right side up, I promise you.

"Of course, you know," he added, "I don't have an airplane to do this with. I'm just trusting the Lord's gonna come up with something by Sunday." The Lord did, using Dwayne's networking connections. On a more serious note, he gave credit where it was due for the skills with which he wielded his primary mission tool.

After ten thousand hours in the air in some of the most difficult flying conditions, God has been with me... I think about the mountains you've seen in those slides ... the North Slope and the Brooks Range and the Alaska Range and the Wrangell Mountains, ascending up to sixteen thousand ... twenty thousand feet, how God has spared us and given us wisdom and care as we've flown safely through them. *You prayed.*

When the subject turned to Alaska Bible College, he turned the discussion from huge landscapes to little things: The school itself—"the smallest accredited Bible college in North America." Occasional encounters, at college and career fairs, with a few teens seeking God among thousands seeking advancement. A flash of spiritual understanding in the eyes of a child in a remote village. "The people of Alaska may be touched by a variety of tools and means, but the missionaries of SEND International realize that the final key is people touching people," he said.

The audience laughed at his description of the tiny Alaskan school daring to compete with prestigious icons of American higher education:

> Here I am in this little booth with the Alaska Bible College sign and poster behind me, and next to me is Yale, and down the way is West Point... Once in a while a kid will come up to my booth and say, "Hey, I want to go to Bible college!" Oh, man, a breath of fresh air! ... and I'll say, "Why do you want to go to Bible college?" He'll say, "I want to serve the Lord." Wow! . . . and I'm encouraged and I'm thrilled, and I just want to take that kid and hug him.

Dwayne spoke of the young people, including some who had approached his booth, who followed through and enrolled at the college. Some knew they wanted to be pastors or missionaries. Others could express nothing more articulate than a desire to know God more deeply and somehow serve Him. He spoke of his and Carolyn's work in helping them develop their gifts—preaching, singing, playing instruments, acting, puppetry—and throwing them into hands-on ministry:

> On the weekends, we'll load them into a plane and we'll head off to some distant village, and begin a ministry among people who don't have the opportunity of hearing good music [or] gathering together in a fine congregation in a beautiful church. They pour out their hearts—singing, and preaching, and teaching, and loving those people to the Lord... We want to be motivators. We want these young people to see how God can use them. As they begin to visit with the people and touch them with their lives, they see God using them in maybe just a little way—maybe just a sparkle in somebody's eye as they sing; maybe they look and they see the light come on. They give their testimony and somebody says, "Yeah, that was me ... that's me!"

A major part of Dwayne's message was gratitude for prayer, which he called a two-way blessing. Prayer, he said, makes the mission possible, and encourages those who pray to know that God answers.

Why do we give a missionary report? Is it because we want to show our worth, that all this support you've been giving us has been justified? Not really. Because when I look out over you, and I look at those slides, I think about all the prayers that have been answered.

I look at the people, the Native people, and I see Herbert Paul, one of the men you prayed for, for many years... Herbert Paul from Tanacross...

Years later, Herbert would reveal the result of the prayers, and Dwayne's part in the outcome. Dwayne continued:

I think about the prayers when I see the airplanes, that little red and white Pacer, how you put that into the air back in 1971 by [paying for] an engine and instruments. I think about how God used that little airplane to start that church in Dawson City ...

When I saw the picture of Faith Chapel, I thought of how many years you prayed for that little chapel. And you know, the Sunday just before I left [for Russia], we went to Tok ... and did the final step of turning that church property over to that body of believers ...

Many a time, Carolyn and I shared and were grateful, and praised the Lord together because of your prayers and your support. That's why it's important. We want you to be encouraged. We want you to continue to pray. We want you to know that God answers prayer, and that He'll do the same for you, beginning right here, in your ministry.

The Twin Orchards choir sang, prompting Dwayne to focus on the role of the churches from which many of the songs and voices of prayer had come:

If we don't get the message from that song about the crying, terrible need of souls around the world today, we're deaf to God's call. We can't hear. We can't see. We can't get in touch with what's going on out there in the world. That song is powerful.

... Carolyn and I have been traveling since I returned at the end of September from Alaska, and each church takes on a different character in terms of missions. This church [Twin Orchards] takes on the character of truly a sending church ... *Sweetheart, I need a Kleenex* ... There's about three pulpits I always cry in. One of them is Tok ... where we had our first pastoral ministry for nine years. I can't go back to that church but when

I look out over the congregation, and I see so many lives that God has worked in, so many changed lives, it affects me.

And this church.

And my church over at Cal Tab ... Ministry is our life—preaching, and teaching, and flying, and serving the Lord—so it was the ministry from these pulpits that really affected and motivated us to the calling ...

Dwayne had special reason to single out one object of gratitude at the conference, the person who had been with him the longest and whose presence was indispensable.

I want Carolyn to stand. I almost got through and forgot, but right there she is, that woman. If it wasn't for her, I wouldn't be standing here tonight. I would never have made it... Pastor [Blasko] is right. We are so different. I am so wild and so fast, and she is so calm and so slow.

Commitment: Risks and Rewards

"Commitment" was Dwayne's battle cry for the rest of the conference: commitment by others, and his own commitment, begun in childhood and already launching him beyond the western borders of Alaska. He urged Twin Orchards members to continue encouraging the resolve of would-be and fledgling missionaries "day by day, in the details of showing a kind word and a loving word to the young people, a kind act of slipping one of these missionaries a twenty, or a fifty, or a hundred." The audience laughed. "I shoot high!" Details of encouragement must be matched by details of obedience, he added. "You don't just become a missionary—*Boom! I'm gonna be a missionary tomorrow!* You begin by the little, faithful steps of obedience to God. And then it's a process."

It would be a commitment that not everyone would—or could—make.

I want to share with you something else tonight about being committed: *No turning back. No way out. No return.* These words often send a chill up the spine of so many whose lives thrive on non-commitment ... who are working, and striving, and looking forward to the time they can be comfortable and safe. If you're a pilot, your friends regard you with suspicion—boy, they do, too! They're always afraid I'm gonna go *loop-de-loop* with them. Any form of striving that once made people heroes—any quest that carries the acceptance of risk—now makes them crazies. To sustain comfort, we have to be safe—safe from confrontation with other people, objects or elements. In a comfortable world the hard edges have been padded, rounded and smoothed—it's the home of the foam-rubber lawn mower. But where there is no risk, there is no achievement.

He drew an image from Alaska, an image of flying a small plane without instruments from Anchorage to his home in mountain-ringed Glennallen.

When I head up into the pass, heading home, I've got to make a choice. Which will it be? The weather is low. The clouds are low. I'm flying down along the Matanuska River ... working my way on up to the Matanuska Glacier. I've got about fifteen miles to go when I reach the glacier—the pass begins to narrow and it gets really tight, and the clouds are pretty steady, with a ceiling of about 3,500 feet. The elevation of the pass is about 3,200 feet, and as I approach the pass and it's narrowing on both sides, I realize I've got to make a decision. I've got to make a commitment. Shall I continue flying through this narrow valley to the point at which there is no turning around? I've got precious cargo on board. I don't want to be foolish. But yet, if it's safe, we can make it through. Ah, I can see the sun shining up around the pass! It's clear up there. I'm gonna take this route to Tahneta Pass. *Committed.*

But it has to be the right commitment, he warned.

I told the kids tonight about Merrill Pass. Scattered with airplanes embedded in the rocks. Those who made the wrong choices. Those who committed themselves to the wrong way, at the wrong time, in the wrong weather. *Committed.*

Dwayne spoke of his first commitment, his decision at age 11 to give his life to Christ. "I walked an old sawdust trail at Lake Arrowhead Bible Camp ... in 1954, on a hot Sunday afternoon in the middle of the summer... That commitment will keep me safe through eternity." He retraced the path through his teen years and beyond, inspired by calls of faith from mission fields as diverse as India, Ecuador and Russia, overcoming poor eyesight and math skills to become an expert pilot.

"God had a plan, God had a purpose," he said of his own path, quoting Psalm 37:5 to show his listeners that their commitments, too, would unlock the power of God: *Commit your way to the Lord; trust in him and he will do this ...*

This is a two-way commitment. We commit to God, and God performs. His faithfulness is not dependent upon our acts of commitment, but we activate His response by our commitment. That's faith.

With commitment, Dwayne said, "the world opens up."

His next commitment was calling him to a world that wouldn't open up easily: the dying Soviet Union. But he had already taken the first step. Two months earlier, he had led one of the first missionary flights into post-Communist Russia, opening the ancient nation's Far Eastern door to an ongoing mission. It was a mission that would strengthen and expand the thinly scattered network of surviving Russian Evangelical and Baptist churches stretching from Ukraine to the Pacific.

The flight from Alaska across the Bering Sea to Providenya, he noted, crossed the International Date Line: "We flew into tomorrow."

Toward the end of the conference, he told of receiving a phone call "just minutes before I went to the youth group ... it was from Alaska, and as I answered the phone, a young girl spoke in very broken English, with a very Russian accent, and said, 'Hello Dwayne!'"

It was Maria, the believing daughter of the Providenya air traffic controller who had asked the mission team how he might pass from death into life.

Part 4

RUSSIA

Land of Sorrow, Fire of Hope

From the east I summon a bird of prey;
from a far-off land, a man to fulfill my purpose.
What I have said, that will I bring about;
what I have planned, that will I do.

—Isaiah 46: 11

10. LAUNCH: Eskimos, Courage, Cracked the Wall

I once made a note of the following statements at a missionary conference:

"The contradiction between Jesus and the world is always bloody."

"Suffering is necessary because the conflict between the world and the Christian community cannot be softened."

"Suffering is testimony to Jesus."

> —Winrich Scheffbuch, preface to *The Meek and The Mighty: The Emergence of the Evangelical Movement in Russia*, by Hans Brandenburg (1977)

You don't just hop in your little old missionary airplane and fly across that border.

> —Dwayne King

DWAYNE CALLED the September 1-2, 1991, flight the "Miracle of Providenya." It was no accidental miracle. The pieces, some going back decades, were already on the board and moving: the yearning of Eskimos to reunite with their trans-Siberian brothers and sisters; the courage of pro-democracy Russian demonstrators, which probably jarred loose a glacial bureaucracy; and Dwayne's own placement in Alaska, poised for a flight into tomorrow on the other side of the world.

Dwayne took this as evidence that God was in control. "He has a plan, and nothing will stand against His purpose and His plan," he said three months later at the Vestal missions conference. Dwayne's part in the plan brought him face to face with a church whose sufferings and hopes he had previously known only indirectly.

The plan included SEND's mission effort that had begun two years earlier in Eastern Europe and western Russia. The outreach got as far as central Siberia, but was too thinly spread to go further. That left Russia's Far East, the land beyond Siberia, almost barren of any evangelical witness.

Almost.

"God used the Eskimos," Dwayne said.

When the "Ice Curtain" froze shut in 1952, Eskimos, who considered themselves one people, were cut in two—those in Alaska and Canada on one side; those in Russia's Far East on the other. It wasn't until 1989, when the Soviet Union began to totter and SEND's campaign began far to the west, that the voices of a divided people began to be heard. Dwayne recalled in 1991:

> Three years ago, the Eskimos began to say, "Hey, look, we've got relatives over there, we've got people of our culture over there. We have people with the same names, the Eskimo Inuit people. . . . We haven't been able to see them or even communicate with them." And God began to work . . .

The Eskimos pressured their governments with pleas to visit their relatives, and permission was granted for limited visiting back and forth. An entrepreneur with an air taxi business was allowed to run a shuttle between Nome and Providenya every few days. "The only problem was that he charged the Russians rubles, and a ruble isn't worth two cents in America, so he doubly charged the Americans that wanted to go over there," Dwayne said. The audience chuckled as he added, "Yeah, it cost almost six hundred bucks to go on a one-hour flight over to the Soviet Union ... *Capitalist.*"

Exorbitant or not, the visits continued. Something else was working in the mix, something that got SEND's attention. "Some of these Eskimos were believers and Christians, and they began to see those people over there as people who need the Lord," Dwayne said. "And some began to win people to the Lord over there, other Eskimos, and white people."

Christian Eskimos who visited Russia brought back a bleak report of the results of more than seventy years of oppression: Organized religion was at best marginalized, and often totally rooted out. Except for one Orthodox church in Providenya and one in Anadyr, the entire Chukotka Peninsula, with an area the size of Pennsylvania and a population of about seventeen thousand, was spiritually empty, Dwayne said.

> ... we've been hearing about the underground church in Eastern Europe and the Bloc countries, and the western part of the Soviet Union, but in

the [Chukotka portion of the] Soviet Far East there is nothing. A total dearth of any spiritual or Christian influence. Nothing—in all those Eskimo villages and in the cities that line the east coast.

Countdown to History

SEND mission planners, Dwayne said, responded predictably: "Why don't we get in on the act?" In early 1991 they started thinking about how this could be done, and quickly saw that it wouldn't be easy. Other methods—radio broadcasts, tracts in bottles and balloons—hadn't made much of a dent. There was no substitute for live bodies. But if they didn't do it by the book, the result might be dead bodies.

"You don't just hop in your little old missionary airplane and fly across that border," Dwayne explained. Shuttle operators had permission to fly to Russia, "but if any other plane goes over there, woe be to it if you meet that Russian MIG, and you're not in the right place, at the right time, with the right code number!" Not only was a code number required, but also an identification number and a flight plan. The plan had to be followed exactly—the flight would have to arrive at the border within three minutes of its estimated time of arrival. And before all that, a letter of invitation was required from some organization approved by Soviet officials. Not to mention visas. "You have to be prepared in so many ways," he concluded.

Faith survives in Russia: baptism in Vladivostok, 1997

The obstacles generated a fervor that would eventually overcome them. For the planners, Dwayne said, "Planting a church has become a vision and a heart's burden." They had an important source of practical information: the Nome-based shuttle business. They also had expertise, patience, prayer, and what Dwayne suggested was God's intervention in history. They would need all of it.

Among the key planners was Dr. Robert "Bob" Provost, a former U.S. serviceman and communications expert. His specialty was breaking codes and interpreting transmissions, mostly military, coming out of Russia. When he left the Air Force, he went to work for The Master's College in Los Angeles. In 1989, which was turning out to be a pivotal year, Bob became a SEND International missionary dedicated to reaching the Soviet Union. He later became president of the Slavic Gospel Association.

The SEND team eventually secured an invitation from a national religious organization, the Moscow-based Union of Evangelical Christians-Baptists, or "Baptist Union." They applied for visas around June 1991, with plans to fly to Providenya on September 1. At the missions conference, Dwayne described the intervening weeks as a time of anxiety, an unexpected historical drama, and—for the team—an even more unexpected outcome.

> We waited. Waited. Waited. They don't give you any warning as to whether they're going to give you a visa. You apply and you wait. And that's all you do. You don't call them up and say, *Well, where is it? What's wrong with the mail? Let's get on the ball!* You don't do that in a Communist country. You wait. So we waited, and two months later came August 19th. What happened? The coup.

He was referring to the short-lived attempt by hard-line Communist officials to forcibly take back power and roll back democratic reforms sought by Soviet leader Mikhail Gorbachev. In Moscow, thousands of pro-democracy demonstrators formed a human shield to protect Gorbachev's government from military units mobilized by the hard-liners. The coup fizzled out.

> There was an uprising of the people against the military and the party and the KGB, and that country was a mess, and some of the people did as they did in China—they stood before the tanks and they were rolled over for the cause of freedom... Russians died last August for the cause of freedom for their people. And those Russian soldiers refused to open

102

fire on the crowds of people. Many of the Christians ran up on those tanks with Gospel tracts and jammed them down the holes—that actually happened—and said, "You can't fire on your brothers and sisters and mothers and fathers!" And they didn't. And God began to open up these doors of the Soviet Union.

The team didn't foresee one of the ways a door would open. Because of the turmoil, Dwayne recalls, "We thought, *This is it. No way will we ever get our visas.*" But he later came to believe that it was the turmoil itself, or at least the changes in Russia leading up to it, which sent out ripples that may have jarred loose the bureaucracy.

In any case, he believed, a higher power was ultimately involved. From time to time throughout the missions conference, he quoted God's cryptic revelation to Isaiah (46:11) to illustrate his conviction that God's will was at work in history: *My purpose will stand, and I will do all that I please. From the east I summon a bird of prey; from a far-off land, a man to fulfill my purpose. What I have said, that will I bring about; what I have planned, that will I do.*

"The coup lasted three days," Dwayne concluded. "Two days after the coup, our visas came in the mail."

They were about to enter a society that had never been run for the convenience of its people, who were as resigned to the inevitability of high-level oppression as they were to the cold and darkness that had gripped their land for winters beyond living memory. The mission team's charge was to be convincing bringers of Good News to people armored in the hard caution of those to whom all news had for centuries been bad. Looking back on it, the flight was the easy part.

Wounded Church, Wounded Land

The team flew to Providenya full of foreboding about the survival of Evangelical and Baptist congregations, known collectively as the evangelical church. The apparent spiritual emptiness they found in Far East Russia seemed to confirm their worst fears. A closer look revealed not corpses, but victors—victors who had been terribly battered and diminished, but who had survived against all odds.

Russia's dark side explains some of the challenges Dwayne faced. The sufferings of evangelicals and millions of other Russians, some continuing to this day, were sown centuries ago when Russia turned away from paths leading toward religious and political freedom.

In modern times, the evangelicals' hardships began under the policy of atheism imposed during the seventy-plus years of the Soviet regime, which ended on Christmas Day, 1991—not quite four months after the Providenya flight. It was not a policy of continuous persecution, but rather a freeze-and-thaw cycle of repression and limited freedom. Treatment of evangelicals and other religious believers ranged from public denunciation to execution, and included bureaucratic harassment, deprivation of organizational rights, internal exile, arrest, torture, and imprisonment in forced-labor camps.

The sporadic nature of the persecution, the infiltration of religious groups by police spies, and the pressuring of vulnerable believers into acting as informers—all crippled religious life by adding uncertainty, dissension and distrust. Anti-religious policies were not the only source of suffering for Christians. Religion historian Mark Sidwell writes:

> In the light of the millions who died, it is difficult to determine precisely how many Christians actually perished at the hands of the Communists for their faith. Many Christians likely died in the famines and other sufferings caused by Stalin's brutal industrialization program. [Author] Walter Kolarz cites statistics that indicate the effects of this persecution. In 1929 in the far east of the USSR the Baptists had 193 congregations and the Evangelical Christians had 118. In 1932 the two groups combined had only 85 congregations. (*The Russian Baptists,* research report, Bob Jones University, 2002)

Hardships endured by both Christians and Russians as a whole were graphically recounted in 2000 by a survivor from Russia's Far East, a church leader with whom Dwayne later worked.

> Vladimir Trossavitch Lebedev, a trim, square-jawed, gray-haired man, is a deacon at Central Baptist Church in Khabarovsk. He was born in 1931 into what he calls "the time of oppression" and grew up in the nearby village of Georgivka in the Amur region.
>
> Vladimir's parents and other villagers were living in a period of great scarcity and hunger when he was born. "All they had was taken away, including food. They had nothing to feed the kids," he said. The collective farm stopped operating for a time because the villagers had to raise food for their own families. Along the Amur River—about eight hundred miles—480 villages had been destroyed to make way for collectivization.

At one point, Vladimir recalls, his family and their neighbors lived on tiny rations of a husk ordinarily used for stock feed. They had no farm tools or horses, only shovels.

People lost not only their possessions, villages and food supplies, but also—starting in the 1920s—their money. Their savings were period-ically wiped out by financial "reforms" that made their money worthless. "That's why the Russian people are so poor. They were robbed every seven to ten years," he said. Under Communism, workers received only about three percent of what they earned, but some periods were better than others.

Many people lost not only their possessions, villages, food supplies and money, but also their churches and their lives. Between 1928 and 1938 in the Amur region, about thirty thousand Christians were shot, Vladimir said. During the seventy years of Communism, the brunt of repression fell sometimes on Baptists and sometimes on Orthodox believers. Those shot along the Amur included members of both groups.

In 1936 or 1937, Vladimir's father and three other Christians were lined up before a firing squad, but an officer ordered his father out of the line. Soldiers whipped him and forced him to sign a paper stating he would say nothing about his arrest. As he was leaving, he heard three shots. When he reached home, he pulled up his shirt and showed his family the marks of his beating.

Until the late 1930s, Georgivka and most other nearby villages had churches. In addition to killing or imprisoning Christians and their pas-tors, the Communists closed many churches, sometimes by destroying them. They destroyed the Georgivka church.

A baptism in 1932 was the last one near Georgivka for sixty-four years. In 1996, Vladimir and Dwayne baptized two women. Even then, several years after Communism ended, authorities still had problems with events they did not plan and could not predict or control, but which came from the people. Especially religious events.

Police came and said Dwayne was not allowed to be there. Vladimir told them the American missionary was his guest, and they permitted the baptism to proceed. Many people came to the riverbank and watched. (Excerpt from *Light: A "Jewish Cowboy's" Journey*, by Mark Winheld, 2004)

Vladimir Lebedev (right) shares memories of oppression

Despite tactical changes of direction, writes historian Hans Brandenburg, the goal of Soviet policy toward religious belief remained constant: "eradication."

The Soviet regime wasn't the first or only adversary of the evangelical church, and wouldn't be the last. In their nearly two centuries of existence in Russia, the evangelicals had also been persecuted at times by the Czars, often in cooperation with the Russian Orthodox Church, the nation's quasi-state church. Some social and legal discrimination continued after Communism ended, although—as Dwayne's friendly letter from Providenya officials suggests—attitudes varied widely from place to place.

More restrictions, starting in 1997, further limited the freedom of both Russian churches and foreign missionaries. The new laws, which began under President Boris Yeltsin and coincided with a resurgent nationalism led by his successor, Vladimir Putin, appeared to bolster the prediction made by some Russian evangelicals soon after the Soviet Union dissolved. They said the new window of relative freedom of religion would close again in about twenty years.

The challenge Dwayne and other missionaries faced would have been easier if their only task had been to help revive the evangelical community. But they also had to navigate a society that has never been user-friendly—for visitors, evangelical believers or the great mass of ordinary people. The end of the Soviet regime sparked hopes for progress, but the opposite occurred: Decay of the infrastructure. Economic chaos. Rampant organized crime. Massive corruption of business, government and law. Intimidation of the media and other potential sources of dissent. Public apathy. Declining population and health standards.

According to the Slavic Gospel Association's February 2007 *InSight* newsletter, "Russia is now the only major industrial nation whose population is steadily shrinking."

> The country is losing 700,000 people a year—the equivalent of a city the size of San Francisco—[because of] the fastest-growing AIDS epidemic in Europe, rampant heart disease and diabetes, pervasive alcohol and drug abuse, unrestrained smoking, a high suicide rate, and unabated industrial pollution... abortions surpassed births [in 2006] by more than 100,000. An estimated ten million Russians of reproductive age are sterile due to botched abortions or poor health.

Gorbachev, the last Soviet leader, moved toward democratic reforms. Conditions worsened, however, and Putin, a former KGB agent, chose a different route: strengthening the state. The result was the usual Russian trade-off: a little more economic security, but less freedom—for evangelicals and Russians as a whole.

The Light Endures

Dwayne came to Russia in 1991, when hope was strongest. I accompanied him nearly ten years later, visiting the Christians he was working among. Despite the wounds left by Communism, I found hope still strong because it was built, ultimately, on faith that transcended earthly victories and defeats. In an account of a brief visit to Siberia in *Light*, I tried to describe that hope, and the needs that SEND was helping to meet.

> **KRASNOYARSK REGION**—March is a time of dirt and promise in Siberia, just as it is near my home in upstate New York. Spring, like birth, isn't pretty at first. Melting snow releases the earth, uncovering the long winter's accumulation of trash littering muddy roads and naked fields still unsoftened by new growth. But more changes are coming, in the warm winds that blow across the land and in the hearts of the people.
>
> Where nature rules, the change is easier. Sparkling snow covering the taiga, the endless forest of birch and fir, silently gives way to green leaves and brown earth. It's noisier on Lake Baikal, where the crash of breaking, sun-weakened ice gives way to blue water. But only where men live is the change of seasons a metaphor for hope and despair. In

Ukraine, they say, many old people die when winter ends—not ground down by long months of cold, but in despair when the first thaws prove false, crushing hope that can somehow alone sustain life.

In the south-central Siberian village of Uzhur, a huge hammer and sickle the color of dried blood sits rusting in the mud. Nearby, on a pedestal, the standard statue of Lenin exhorts empty air. The grip of dead gods, like winter, dies hard here. In trickling meltwater and warm winds are the groans of creation laboring to be reborn. It's a good time to visit Russian Baptist churches, which are undergoing their own transformation, struggling to grow after a long winter of repression. Like the Son of Man who had nowhere to lay His head, evangelical believers in Uzhur and many other villages have no permanent houses of prayer to call their own. The church is in their hearts, and in whatever kitchens, community centers or rented warehouses they gather to worship.

Communist emblem rusts in Siberia.

Russia's spiritual light has not only endured, but some Russian evangelicals believe it will prevail. They have a vision of eventually becoming "sending" churches with mission outreach to the rest of the world, not merely continuing as recipients of aid from foreign missions. Russia has paid high dues to play such a role, judging from *Hope Against Hope* (1970) by the widow of Russia's great poet, Osip Mandelstam. Thirty million people or more, including the poet, died in the *Gulag Archipelago*, the name given by Aleksandr Solzhenitzyn to Lenin and Stalin's continent-wide network of prisons and slave labor camps. Nadezhda Mandelstam wrote:

> Russia once saved the Christian culture of Europe from the Tatars [the medieval Mongol invaders], and in the past fifty years, by taking the brunt on herself, she has saved Europe again—this time from rationalization and all the will to evil that goes with it. The sacrifice in human life was enormous. How can I believe it was all in vain?

The sacrifice was enormous because, perhaps, the evil was more focused than in other times and places. John 1:5 (RSV) says the darkness has not "overcome" the light. Other translations say the darkness has not "comprehended" or "understood" the light, but the first is a better description of what happened in Russia. There, the darkness understood exactly what it was attacking, but the sacrifice was not in vain because, despite all the efforts and expectations of the regime, the assault ultimately failed.

This was the land, with its history of agony, its future of uncertainty and its bulletproof hope, to which Dwayne was being called.

Contorted in agony: memorial at Babi Yar, Kiev, where Nazis slaughtered Ukrainian Jews in World War II.

11. STRETCHED: Russia Calls, Alaska Holds On

⟨⟩

Please pray about our future. More and more it looks like we could be heading for the Soviet Far East. The burden is growing. But also the burden for the Native [Alaskans] is there...
— Dwayne King,
February 1992 postcard to Paul Blasko

What God calls us to do is always impossible ... always too big... always too demanding... without His help.
— Carolyn King,
testimony

DWAYNE'S MOVE to Far East Russia may have been inevitable, but it would not be quick or painless. The dramatic flight to Providenya was one thing. Uprooting himself and Carolyn from Alaska and settling into a totally different culture was something else. The call to Russia seemed urgent, but so did the claims of Alaskans to whom Dwayne had been ministering for years.

From the Russian end, the note of hope and urgency was sounded by Bob Provost, then SEND's Eurasia director. In the crumbling Soviet Union of 1989, he described evangelism opportunities as "somewhere between unbelievable and unimaginable! Where doors have been closed for decades, I couldn't find a closed door! The harvest fields are ripe." Russian evangelicals were calling for help in strengthening doctrine, training pastors, countering cults, planting churches and reaching youth. But, Bob added, with Communist-era religion laws still on the books, the new freedom was fragile. Speed was vital.

... who [knows] how long this door of opportunity [will] remain open. We simply must figure out ways to begin seizing all these opportunities simultaneously.

On the other side of the world, Carolyn echoed Dwayne's search for guidance. "Pray about our future," she pleaded in her February 1992 newsletter. "We are burdened about the need and openness in Russia. Does God want us to serve there? We are open. We are also burdened about the need right in the Copper River Basin and Alaska Bible College."

Meanwhile, she and Dwayne were enjoying balmy South Carolina, where he was working on his master's degree. "In Alaska we wouldn't even be looking for signs of spring," she wrote. His thesis project would deal with church planting in Far East Russia, so he could look forward to more trips to Providenya. But research at Columbia International University was a long grind for Dwayne, always happier in the trenches than desk-bound behind the lines.

"This schooling is like eating an elephant," he wrote to friend Paul Blasko. "It's impossible—I can't see the end—I guess it's just one bite at a time." Characteristically, Dwayne didn't let his own frustrations stop him from encouraging others, including Pastor Paul and his annual outreach to hunters.

... I am praying for you on the venison dinners ... I am blessed by your commitment to those dinners. I pray God will work in the hearts of many men. I know many will receive Christ. I trust God gives you strength— do not become weary. II Cor. 12:15 reminds me of you. [The verse reads in part, *So I will very gladly spend for you everything I have and expend myself as well.*]

On most weekends, Carolyn said, she and Dwayne visited churches and friends. But they encountered attitudes that didn't bode well for a flood of recruits into their next major ministry.

Interest is high everywhere we go in missions in general, and especially about Russia. But very few seem to want to go—and fewer still want to go to the Far East of the CIS [Commonwealth of Independent States, which succeeded the USSR].

Dwayne, however, was an old hand at melting resistance to recruitment. True to form, he enthusiastically dragooned friends into Russian missions even before he was sure it would be his own fulltime field. Don and Ann Lewis, who later in 1992 helped him load a plane with Bibles and fuel for the second flight to Providenya, recall his words as they prayed just before takeoff.

"He said, 'Don, I want to see you in Russia,' and he told people we were going to do it. We said *yes* before we knew what we were doing," Don said. Ann added, "We probably never would've done it otherwise." She called Dwayne "kind of a prophet." The upstate New York couple had traveled overseas only once before in their lives, on a guided vacation trip to Germany. Starting in 1996, they made eleven trips to Far East Russia, leading church construction teams.

In the spring of 1992, Dwayne and Carolyn completed a grueling but fulfilling home service schedule—driving 36,000 miles, holding 136 meetings and visiting many friends and helpers—then headed back to Alaska. Dwayne worked with Native churches in Copper River Valley villages, coordinating evangelism and discipleship, and Carolyn filled in as Alaska Bible College librarian.

One highlight of the spring was son Jon's wedding on June 6. "It was a beautiful warm day," Carolyn wrote. "The mosquito army had not yet arrived." Another was the eruption of Mt. Spurr, which blanketed Anchorage with a quarter-inch of ash. Dwayne and Jon happened to be flying nearby during the second eruption, on August 18, and were the closest witnesses to the event. They got "fantastic" pictures, she added, quoting Yukon poet Robert Service: "There are strange things done in the midnight sun ..."

"I Can't Not Go"

Volcanic eruptions weren't the only new additions to Dwayne's Alaska routines. Trips to Russia were pulling him ever deeper into the new ministry, especially in Siberia, recalls "Steve" Stevenson, then SEND's Alaska director.

> Dwayne came into my office... We talked about the urgency and the need for personnel, and he told me he wanted to volunteer to transfer from Alaska to Far East Russia. I talked about the pros and cons and asked, "What's driving you?" Dwayne said, "Steve, I can't not go."

In less than two years, Dwayne would make fourteen more flights to Providenya. One of the earlier visits seemed guaranteed to activate his adventurous streak, judging by his summer 1992 letter.

"PREEVYET"—(roll the r). That means "hello, my friends," in Russian. It didn't take long, once we got to Alaska, to head for the Russian Far East... What an incredible blessing to minister to people so willing to listen to the Gospel. In the week there, I stayed again with Nicolai, the air traffic controller. He gave clear indication that he had indeed asked Christ to be his Savior. I also visited a TB hospital, giving gifts and pamphlets to the children there, distributed more Bibles and made new contacts.

While staying with a dentist, I was privileged to go by helicopter to visit several Chukchi reindeer brigades out on the tundra, where the herders received dental care and were checked for TB. Got lots of close-up video of teeth-pulling. After giving one of the men my Leatherman tool [multifunction pocket knife], he lassoed and killed a reindeer for our dinner. Carolyn is very glad this is not the video she had to watch two hundred times! This was the first American contact for many of them, as well as their first time to receive the Gospel and their first good Novocain. I will return in August to survey many new areas in the Magadan Region. We are still working on ways to use the airplane more easily over there.

Dwayne missed the third eruption of Mt. Spurr on September 16-17, the seventeenth also being his 50th birthday. He was in Providenya again, helping SEND's first missionary couple in Far East Russia, Robert and Robin Crane, get settled. If previous flights were exhilarating, the September trip was a more typical slog through bureaucracy. What wasn't typical, Carolyn wrote, is that most of the headaches were on the American side, and some unexpected helpfulness came from the Russian side.

Satan has done his best to prevent [the move] through a lost passport, which resulted in all the paperwork having to be redone. The date of the move had to be changed several times ... each time resulting in end-less paperwork. Just a week before the final date, U.S. Customs required [the] Cranes to itemize everything they were moving. Their boxes had been packed for weeks. But on the final day, everything went smoothly and they were moved in *with the help of the KGB border guards and the local militia!* [Emphasis added] They were very happy and excited to finally be there. However, Dwayne had some difficulty getting home again. On Friday (Saturday in Russia), there was no English-speaking person in the control tower. The next day, there was no customs agent. Today (Sunday here), both are on duty and he is on his way home. . . . The control tower told him it was O.K. to "open the store"—take off. He [the air traffic controller] had his phrases a little mixed up.

Hearts Beating Together

Two partnerships that began in the fall of 1992 were the first of several that would add to Dwayne's effectiveness in Russia. He and friend Dick Camp paired up to bring SEND's mission to the Far East, with Dwayne as point man and Dick coordinating from Alaska. The other partnership was with Gennady Abramov, the Baptist Union's chief pastor in the Far East. Gennady had traveled to Alaska in August at SEND's invitation, seeking help to increase the tiny number of evangelical churches serving his huge territory and to start theological education for pastors.

Gennady Abramov, a key partner

Like a good marriage, his and Dwayne's relationship wasn't always smooth, but—in Dick's words— "Their hearts were together. The working relationship between him and Gennady was really the key to that ministry." Dwayne and the Russian pastor agreed on the big issues, and the biggest, said Dick, was how to serve the Christian community that was asking for help: "We follow their agenda. [We ask them] How do you want us to serve? Our missionaries will come and work under you. We have no other work here except with the Baptist Union."

Late 1992 and early 1993 was a time of growth for Dwayne. "The Lord was higher on the totem pole," Dick said. Dwayne knew that flying would have to drop another notch in the scheme of his work, and both men realized that in their "youthful vigor," they had been depending too much on themselves.

From the early 1990s into the early 2000s, several Gospel expeditions committed Dwayne to the Russian mission, and brutally tested that commitment. They showed him just how much he would have to depend on God, and on the people he had come to help. In late November 1992, he plunged into the nation's Far East, including the far northeast Chukotka region—a remote corner of a remote part of the world.

> ... I departed Anchorage loaded to the gills with bags, Bibles and books, mail and supplies for the Cranes [in Providenya], and money for Russian pastoral support. In Magadan I met the team... I have never had so much fun, joy and tears in serving Jesus.
>
> Every day was filled with hauling boxes of Bibles and tracts to schools, airports, bus stations and meetings ... the routine was to go to the officials of the city, give the secretaries and leaders tracts and Bibles, and ask their permission to evangelize their city and schools. [At] each place, we were welcomed with open arms. We did much teaching ... the existence of God, the authority of the Scriptures, a bit of Old Testament history, life of Christ, redemption, repentance and salvation. Evening and Sunday meetings were much of the same, only longer—much longer, but they loved it. Everywhere, we were challenged with difficult questions ... atheists asked about our proof of the existence of God ... agnostics asked about all the religions and holy books—what makes us right? ... We sure were sharpening our apologetics ...
>
> In Anadyr we saw many come to repentance ... [it] would be quite dramatic. Leaving one's seat and coming to the front ... those repenting would confess before the group to God, usually with much emotion ... In Anadyr we also had opportunities in the local radio and TV stations for hour-long programs—all very well done.
>
> It is very cold here. We experienced minus-30, with thirty-mile-per-hour winds.

One night as he lay in bed, unable to sleep, he thought of the college students who had committed their lives to God. Many students wept because the team was leaving. *Who will follow up with these people?* he thought. "That was the tipping point of my ministry. I was committed to Russia." In February 1993, he returned to Anadyr for two weeks to encourage the new believers.

In Dwayne's priorities, flying may have been down, but it wasn't out—either for fun or missions. On one leg of the November-December trip, he flew to Providenya in a fifty-passenger Antonov-24 Russian air-liner—but not, he revealed, as a passenger. "The flight was a thrill, as I got to fly it myself. Aeroflot pilots love to have Alaska pilots up front with them. Most of the time I rode up front." Combining evangelism and aviation while revisiting Anadyr, he met with Russian pilots and their flight crews. In a session arranged by a helpful Aeroflot pilot, Dwayne demonstrated modern aviation tools, including a GPS, hand-held computers and hand-held radios. "The men had never seen such things even though they are commercial airline crews," Dick wrote.

Dwayne's ability to make friends in high places was another skill he turned to advantage for mission purposes. He established contacts in the Chukotka governor's office. Later, when some of the Chukotka officials visited Alaska, Dwayne and Dick were able to meet with both governors and briefly share SEND's purpose and work in Russia.

Despite successes, the months of transition from Alaska to Russia took a physical toll. Carolyn's spring 1993 letter started with a bedraggled cartoon figure plaintively announcing, *I try to take just one day at a time, but lately several days have attacked me at once.* Dwayne returned from the November-December trip "very excited," but with acute bronchitis. Another Russian trip, in March and April, triggered intestinal bacteria and a second bout of bronchitis. He spent three days rehydrating in SEND's medical center in Glennallen. Almost as an afterthought, Carolyn mentioned that in May—which included Alaska Bible College graduations, conferences and frequent house guests—she found out she was anemic, diabetic, and needed major surgery. "The surgery will be June 15," she wrote. "The anemia and diabetes are under control."

Her surgery was successful, and the mission went on. As they had in the past, she and Dwayne would soon take another giant step away from familiar routines. With support behind him, by his side, and waiting for him in Russia, and some firsthand experience already under his belt, he was ready to hit the ground running.

12. LEAPS OF FAITH

Loving God in a Hard Land

We are committed to helping this ministry. Working with the Russian pastors and Christians is the only way to go.

—Dwayne King

Russian people have so little and share so much.

—Carolyn King

THE DOOR WAS OPEN, as Bob Provost joyfully proclaimed in 1989, but when the Kings walked through it, they faced a hard road and a staggering challenge. In Far East Russia—about the size of Alaska and California combined—there were, according to Dick Camp, all of forty-three evangelical churches, only twenty-five of them with pastors, and no Bible colleges.

Living conditions were no worse than in remote Alaskan villages, but adjusting to an unfamiliar, impoverished society with a tortured history could be exhausting. And—despite a warm welcome from Russian evangelicals and surprising initial enthusiasm by local officials—some missionaries, foreign and native alike, would face harassment and life-threatening violence in the coming years.

Carolyn made her first visit to Russia in November 1992 and described her impressions in her Christmas letter.

> ... warm reception, showers of gifts "to give you good memories,"
> 1940s-vintage tiny, tiny bathrooms and kitchens, living rooms and bed-
> rooms with fold-out couches and chairs, too much walking in snow and

wind, *everyone* lives on the fifth floor! Wonderful people, more than willing to practice their English on us. Our Russian—*choot-choot*—very little.

A year later, she took the plunge into living there. She and Dwayne became resident missionaries in Khabarovsk, the region's second largest city, where they began learning Russian and helping to plan what became Far East Russia Bible College. An Alaska Bible College team arrived in 1993 to conduct short-term theological training for Russian church leaders. The Russian pastors' faithfulness was "an inspiration to the whole Christian world," Dick Camp wrote, but their previous training had been minimal by North American standards. Over the next few years, more SEND missionaries came to teach. The college would eventually become the evangelicals' center for ministry outreach in the region, housing Baptist Union offices and SEND's fulltime staff.

Welcome to Russia

Even someone as adaptable as Dwayne found living in Khabarovsk a challenge. Home was a sparsely furnished one-room apartment on Brestkaya Street, on the sixth floor, overlooking the Amur River. "Freshly painted, clean except for some creepy crawlers," Carolyn wrote in October 1993. "There is a *big* dog next door." In the unfamiliar environment, with winter setting in, accomplishing small tasks was a victory.

Friday—Some firsts today. Washed clothes in electric washer [with] manual wringer and siphon. Takes forever but does the job... Went out by *myself* to buy bread! Means getting in and out of apartment by self, getting to store, and home, and making myself understood. Not too hard when you only have to use one word. No hot water since noon. Has snowed a little every day—very icy on walks. Streets and drivers are unbelievable. Ice forming in river now ... Much cold air coming in windows.

Help and hospitality from Pastor Gennady Abramov's family and other church friends eased the settling-in process. But shopping for more than one item was a challenge, even with Russian friends along, Carolyn wrote.

We heard about an American company having a food show ... [Khabarovsk Deacon] Volodya [Lebedev] really thought that was great. This company will only sell wholesale, but we were able to buy some of the stuff they were demonstrating... So we have a case of toilet paper, paper towels and Kleenex, which you can't find here, plus some food. Shopping is a real treasure hunt. You never know where you'll find a store... Can usually only find two or three things you want in one place, and then have to look somewhere else. So it takes a lot of time... Golden rule of shopping: If you see it, and you think you might need it, buy it. You might not see it again or remember where it was.

Shopping can be a challenge: street vendors in Vladivostok, 1997

Local transportation was another challenge, Dwayne wrote. "Trams and buses are very crowded and don't always stop where you wish they would, so much walking is also involved. But we can do it, thanks to your prayers... God has taken very good care of us, met every need and kept us quite healthy."

At church, some details were unfamiliar, but the welcome in the small, rough-hewn log building was warm—in more ways than one. "It is full and very hot," Carolyn wrote.

Oct. 27—Go to prayer meeting. Uncomfortable experience having to sit on platform [up front]. Everyone is very glad to meet us ... Oct. 31— Again on the platform... Hard to know whether to stand or kneel for prayer. Decide to stand, since others are. Service does not seem too long. Nearly three hours. Couple sings, "Russia, O Russia—you have forgotten God" ... one lady repents in the middle of the song, then the song goes on again. Many people greet us.

Christmas 1993 in Khabarovsk was lonely for the Kings, but long-distance contacts with children, a flood of delayed mail, and visits with new Russian friends picked up their spirits, Carolyn wrote in January. They were saddened to hear that son Joel, working and studying in Arizona, had received no birthday or Christmas presents, but Carolyn said he "sounded good" and was pushing ahead with flight training.

"Christmas is really not for ourselves but what we can do for others," she added.

So we gave a few gifts to the kids of the people we work with, car parts to Volodya, tools to Gennady, and bought a washer for Vera [Gennady's wife] and one for me. This is a little more automatic than the one that was here. It drains the water out and spins, but I still have to fill it and partially wring the clothes by hand before I put them in the spin part. But then they come out almost dry, instead of having to hang all day and night all over the house. Vera had to wash clothes by hand for seven people, plus haul all her water! So she was really thrilled.

Trips into the countryside, including one with Gennady and other church friends in a Volkswagen bus, etched a Russian panorama into Carolyn's memory. Ten days of touring coastal Primorye shortly before Christmas featured visits to nine churches. She and Dwayne were warmly welcomed—and relentlessly fed—by hosts who remembered hunger and offered food as love. To Carolyn, the landscape was a trip back in time.

Roads are like the Alaska Highway twenty-thirty years ago. No restaurants, very few gas stations—if you are lucky there may be an outhouse. Little villages—cows, sheep, goats, chickens, ducks, geese roaming all over... Stayed in many homes. Some had running water, inside plumbing. As many did not. Services were packed. People very responsive even when you cannot communicate. They talk and talk, just as if you could understand. Must have "tea," which is a whole meal before each meeting, and dinner after! Mostly same food in every place. Always soup and bread. Then rice/potatoes with a little meat or meat gravy. Salads of pickled things—peppers, tomatoes, cabbage, beets, etc. Raw fish. Mushrooms in oil ... Russian tradition: eat out of the jam bowl with your own spoon. Breakfast is often the same as dinner. Sometimes *kasha* (buckwheat) with meat gravy.

A few weeks later, journeys into the Amur River hinterland offered more legendary hospitality—as well as a bout of stomach flu, memories of

massacre and seeds of renewal. Again, Carolyn faithfully saved the details of a different world: *Christmas trees don't go up until the more popular New Year's ... a pastor's wife with four small children serves a new group of guests at each meal, including breakfast— "had our first Russian moose meat there" ... in Tambovka, in the 1920s, Communists shot the church pastor, all the leaders and Sunday School teachers, imprisoned many others, and took the building: "There were eight hundred believers in 1927 ... last year there were fifteen in the church, and now there are fifty."*
... another evicted congregation, meeting in an old kindergarten building, will get its old church back under a new law of property restoration ... Dwayne visits believers in the Svobodny prison.

Dwayne described intercity train travel in the Far East as "always very hot, or very cold, or very slow." The ride back to Khabarovsk on the wilderness BAM (Baikal-Amur Main Line) Railroad was no exception. Carolyn wrote:

> The student workers forgot to fill the water tanks for heat, so there was very little warmth. Have to take your own food. You can buy sheets and a blanket for four hundred rubles [then about ninety cents] to sleep. I guess there is a dining car, too, but it is very expensive... These trips really tire me out because of all the jarring and jolting. So I'm glad to stay home for a while.

Back in their apartment the pace slowed down. "Seems like all I do is practice on [the computer], study Russian and sweep the floor," Carolyn wrote. "I can't believe how much dust there is here. Worse than Alaska in the summer."

The fulfillment of the work more than balanced the hardships, Dwayne wrote in March 1994.

> This is a rare privilege to be here and see what wonderful things God is doing, to work with such dear people and see their commitment to God's purpose to build His church. Everywhere you look ... almost every church has three or four brothers out in the surrounding cities or towns starting new works. It is church planting at its best. It is not because it's easy ... that it's been done, though. It is plain, old hard work, and faithfulness to see the vision God has for this country. I praise Him every day to have this peek into His mighty work in this corner of the world.
>
> So far, I've preached in twenty-five of our registered Baptist churches in the Far East. We have fifty-six churches and ministries, with

new ones starting almost every month. The people here are truly grateful to their brothers and sisters in America. There is one story after another of God's grace and blessing upon the work. But they need and want help. They have a great appreciation for SEND because we have adopted a servant role. Every gift and effort goes through the Baptist leadership.

Meanwhile, the Bible College was "going great," he added. Eager students started a church in a classroom and attracted about fifty neighbors to the first service. Elsewhere around Khabarovsk, he and Carolyn were welcomed into private homes and a civic center, where she taught children Bible stories and he led adults in Bible studies. Once a week, they opened their apartment to Bible College students, providing hospitality and practicing each others' languages. They spent the rest of the time in travel and more language study. "That is progressing very slowly," he noted. And, naturally, he wasn't neglecting aviation.

Twice a week I go to the Aeroflot Training Center. About three hundred student pilots and crew are constantly rotating through here from all over the Far East. I have an open door to teach Bible, as well as aviation. Both the *Jesus* film and Moody's *Signposts Aloft* have been shown. I also work with the international crews on their English.

Iron Sharpens Iron

Dwayne and Carolyn were learning more than a new language. With every passing day, they were learning that dependence on God was more than a proper Christian attitude—in Russia, it was a constant necessity for every step forward. So were the friends and partners who were placed in Dwayne's path.

"Piles of paperwork for each trip," Carolyn wrote in 1992. "Often the visas, clearance numbers, etc. come only at the last minute, with much prayer." Once inside Russia, Dwayne observed, the problems changed but the solution remained the same. "Shortages of seats on airplanes, shortages of flights, shortages of fuel ... caused a lot of delays and frustrations at airports. There were many dramatic, last-minute answers to prayer."

Air travel was only one example. Until the mid-'90s, said Dick, there was no e-mail, and it took more than an hour to make a long-distance phone or fax connection. They were learning what Russian Christians had known for years: Pray always, standing or kneeling, on all occasions—whether seeking God's grace to endure persecution or simply to jump-start a stalled meeting. "That's how they existed in the years under Communism," Dick said. It was a challenge Dwayne wholeheartedly absorbed.

Dwayne's other mainstay in Russia was a skill he already had in full measure: building and keeping relationships in which the participants learned and grew. Former SEND chief Frank Severn recalls how it worked between Dwayne, Pastor Gennady and God. Dwayne has never claimed to be a fire-summoning Elijah, but if that was the impression Gennady sometimes had to conjure up to keep the mission moving, Dwayne didn't object. Frank wrote:

> I remember story after story of high adventure during the first months and years in Russia. Dwayne would often be traveling with the head pastor of the region and would not have all the necessary papers to go from place to place. Very often, police stopped them. [Dwayne and Gennady] would say a quick prayer, then Gennady would say he had a man of God with him, and the police had better respect God. Most often they would be waved on their way without much delay. Dwayne would say, "Let's go! We will trust God to get us through!"

Gennady, now pastor of Central Baptist Church in Khabarovsk, called Dwayne his model, teacher and best American friend. "He loves people," Gennady said during a visit in 2005 to Davis College. He and other Russians, disarmed by Dwayne's humor and up-front emotions, returned the feeling and forgave his stumbles in learning their ways.

"He was a bad student—he had a hard time just sitting down and learning," Gennady said of his friend's early attempts to learn the language. "His teacher kept saying, 'Grammar! Grammar! Grammar!'" Gennady said Dwayne's first sermon in Russian "appeared funny, but many people understood it. He could cry in front of people—he could share his needs, even his deep needs, and his emotions."

Two more helpers—Lena Sidenko and Carl Kresge—added guidance and organization to Dwayne's spontaneous energy. If Gennady was Dwayne's gentle authority for the kind of mission assistance the region needed, Lena was the tough, street-smart guide who showed him how to give it without getting mugged, lost or arrested. Officially, her initial title was secretary and interpreter. What Dwayne called her was less formal: "Annie Oakley" or, occasionally, "sidekick."

"When he had a job for me, it was 'Annie get your gun!'" Lena recalled with a grin during a 2005 interview on a Trans-Siberian Railway coach carrying American church-building volunteers led by Don and Ann Lewis.

Interpreter Lena Sidenko, AKA "Annie Oakley," "Sidekick"

Dwayne and Lena met in 1993 at the Khabarovsk airport while Lena, then working for Interact Ministries, was meeting a flight from the U.S. The Russian woman said he approached her and "talked and talked and talked" about far northern Yakutia and reindeer. He made a good impression, but an odd one. "He told me so much information, and he's a stranger. Joking. Russian men don't *do* that." Lena became his secretary in 1994. "He said he stole me from Brand X." Her work also included helping him learn Russian, and interpreting for visiting summer missionaries and church construction volunteers.

They learned much from each other, but sometimes sparks flew.

He tried to make me jack-of-all-trades. He makes me do all these things I don't want to do, like go to driver's class, help him fix an old Mazda. It had no ignition switch, just wires. He gave me a screwdriver and pushed me, and said, "Do this!" I threw up my hands. "I don't want to do this!" I left, crying and crying... He says, "Use phones!" And I say, "You can't do it that way! I need to go there, see their face." I taught him importance of face-to-face dealings with Russians.

"We were a team," Lena concluded, although an onlooker, seeing two strong personalities butting heads, might have mistakenly assumed they were fighting. "Sometimes he didn't have to say anything. I knew what he was thinking."

They proved their worth to the mission over the next few years, whether coordinating communication between Russian congregations and foreign helpers or, during an economic crisis in 1998, extricating a home-bound construction team from frustrating delays and expenses. At the Khabarovsk airport, an American volunteer praised Don and Ann Lewis—the team leaders—and Dwayne and Lena, who had just foiled an attempt to jack up the exit fee levied on departing visitors. "We'd follow Don and Ann through hell! And if we ever got stuck there, Dwayne and Lena could use their connections to get the heat turned down."

Things never got quite that bad, thanks in part to Carl Kresge. Carl arrived early in 1995, just in time to stave off an organizational meltdown. He was on a one-year assignment from SEND to teach at the new Far East Russia Bible College and help oversee a new team of missionaries. The assignment changed when Carolyn had to return to America to care for her ailing mother. "If you know anything about Dwayne's administrative prowess, you could guess that Dwayne without Carolyn is a disaster waiting to happen!" Carl said. Dwayne agreed, and asked him to be his administrative assistant, helping with scheduling, travel plans, e-mails and other tasks. According to Alaska colleague Leander Rempel,

> What made Dwayne such a success as the Far East Russia area director and [later] the [Eurasia] regional director was the people he teamed with. Gennady and Carl both chose to focus on his strengths rather than ... his weaknesses. When I told one party in Alaska that Dwayne was being considered as a regional director, his loud exclamation was, "You've got to be kidding!"

Carl has fond memories of getting to know the colleague who would become partner, mentor and friend.

> My wife Lori and I, and our three daughters, flew from Anchorage to Khabarovsk, arriving after dark one February evening with forty-one boxes [containing household items, food, a computer and printer, and educational supplies]. Our first memory of Dwayne is "The Marshmallow." Lori and I still remember his huge fur *shapka* [Russian winter hat] that reminded us of a perfectly browned marshmallow, and his big smile and loud laugh after we struggled through customs with all those boxes.
>
> My first impression of Dwayne was a friendly, outgoing, down-to-earth visionary with a "can-do" approach to life and ministry. He has had

a very significant impact on my life and work. I've never worked with anyone whose gifts and abilities were such a good fit. When he asked me to be his administrative assistant, the comment of one of our missionaries was, "Either that's going to be the best thing that ever happened to Dwayne, or it's going to be the worst thing that ever happened to you!" As it turned out, it was a great blessing for me to work so closely with a man of such vision and faith.

Carl kept Dwayne coordinated with SEND International and Lena continued helping with Far East Russia details, an arrangement that lasted until December 1995, when the Kresges returned to Michigan. In April 1996, Lena officially became Dwayne's administrative assistant.

Close Encounters of the Scary Kind
Merely being guests of the Kings in Khabarovsk could be an adventure, several old friends discovered.

Day-to-day errands were usually tedious, sometimes frightening. On one occasion, buying gas for the SEND van was both. One Sunday in the mid-1990s, while Leander and Louise Rempel were visiting, they and the Kings went looking for motor fuel, which was in "extremely short supply," Leander recalls. "We drove through the downtown, dodging open manholes—the people stole the covers and sold them for the metal content. Dwayne watched the gas stations—all four of them. They were closed because they didn't have any gas."

Using his still rudimentary Russian, Dwayne finally learned that one of the stations might be getting gas at 7:30 p.m.—more than two hours away. The men sent their wives home by bus, then settled into line with fifty or sixty vehicles ahead of them. Leander described a typical Russian shopping scenario that quickly turned threatening.

The whole retail business was designed to frustrate the potential buyer and drive him out of his gourd ... you had to wait in line for hours, sometimes, just to get to the pumps, then you waited in line to pay. Then you got out the gas cans you were carrying in your trunk—everybody who drove a car had five or six cans in his trunk. These were duly filled, as well as the tank. Then you waited in line to get your change, and your transaction is completed.

While we were waiting patiently in line, I observed a hiccup in this "efficient" system. Every five minutes or so, a car would wheel up past the car that had just pulled up to the pumps, [then] back into position close enough for the filler hose to reach his gas cap. He then went to the front of the line of people who were waiting to pay, and to the front of the line to receive his change. It sort of irked my North American sense of fairness ... I asked Dwayne what was going on here. He just said they are *Krutoy*.

Dwayne explained: "Three or four *Krutoy*—young gangster wannabees in Land Cruisers and other pricey cars—had busted into the line while the 'peasants' waited." One of them pushed ahead of the SEND van and started backing up to the pump. Leander resumed the narrative. The former hockey player and tractor-trailer driver went into action, or rather, inaction:

> ... I just stood there with my arms folded across my chest. I really wished for a lead pipe or a good hockey stick, but there were none to be found. He got out of his car and came to where I stood blocking his way and lectured me on the finer points of Russian civilization. At least I thought that's what he said, because I didn't understand a word of it. He then got in his car and started to back up. I gave a foot or two when he reached my legs, and received another lecture. I gave a little every time his bumper touched my legs. Finally, he was close enough to pump gas, but he wasn't properly positioned. So he pulled forward and then backed up, but he was so frustrated that he backed right into the concrete island [protecting] the pumps. He got out and inspected his bumper, all the while lecturing me in Russian. He got his gas, we got our gas, and we all lived happily ever after.

Despite being a pretty tough dude, Leander was probably relieved that Dwayne waited until they were driving home before answering his question, "What does *Krutoy* mean?" He replied that the term—literally, "one who stands like a pillar of stone"—is the Russian equivalent of "Mafia." Meanwhile, as Louise tells it, she and Carolyn were having their own problems on the bus.

> *One*—it was getting dark, with very few outdoor lights, either on the streets or the various apartment grounds. *Two*—various and sundry men who had first filled up on alcohol somewhere were also headed home. *Three*—non-Russian people stand out whether they try to blend in or not, especially in those early days of Western contact.
> We did not find a seat, so we stood in the very crowded bus, trying to "blend" in. Not successful! One "exuberant" man noticed us and wanted immediately to "learn English, help us find our address," and numerous other "helpful" and forceful things. The closer we got to our stop, the less funny the situation seemed. We decided that if he got off at our stop, we would get back on.

About the time the doors of the bus opened, a woman—an angel!—
appeared from out of nowhere, roundly "admonished" the exuberant and
told him where to go, etc., grabbed us both by our arms and escorted us
off the bus, across the street and dark apartment grounds, and almost to
our apartment door. Then, just like she had appeared, she was gone—we
have no idea where she went and we never had a chance to thank her.

Louise described Far East Russia as "definitely" a place of missionary
pioneering in the early days of SEND's ministry. "It was *not* an easy place
to live, but one thing Dwayne and Carolyn made sure of was to have a
broad circle of prayer warriors surrounding them with their prayers."
Contemplating whether those prayers rescued her and Carolyn from the
bus situation, she stated, "In my mind, the answer is a resounding *yes!"*

Cups and Bowls of Love

Another scary incident in Khabarovsk, involving another visiting
friend, was responsible, in a roundabout way, for hundreds of beautiful
butternut wood communion sets used in Russian churches.

Dwayne's driving skills kept him and Durland "Dur" Vining mostly
intact in 1996, when their van was smashed between two heavy trucks. "We
were sort of an Oreo cookie between the trucks," Dur recalls. "Dwayne
kept apologizing, but it wasn't his fault. His foot was on the brake—if
not, I wouldn't be here!" Dur credited his friend with the same lifesaving
reflexes that had kept him from wrecking Dur's beloved roadster decades
earlier on Vestal's winding roads.

Dwayne passed a police breathalyzer test, "more than can be said of
the other two drivers," Dur added. Dur sustained cuts and possibly a mild
concussion, and Dwayne suffered a whiplash injury. The van was totaled.
Dur was taken to a hospital and later transferred to another hospital. He
was afraid the language barrier would keep him from being found, but
Gennady and Lena eventually rescued him.

Dur and his wife Jan, members of Dwayne's home church in Vestal—
Cal Tab—were in Russia visiting the churches their friend was starting.
"The people and their needs became very real to us as we labored side
by side with our missionary," Dur said. Shortly after the Vinings returned
home, Dwayne e-mailed Dur—a skilled woodworker—asking him to
make a communion set for a church planned in Amursk. Dur finished it in
time for the new church's dedication service.

Ten years later, thanks to donated trees and labor, Dur's craftsman-
ship on a borrowed lathe, and sewing by the women of Cal Tab, that first

offering of golden wood, gleaming with many coats of polyurethane varnish, had multiplied three hundred-fold. Russian churches from the Far East to Siberia to Central Asia were receiving his unique gift of love: boxes each containing two chalices and two bread bowls, wrapped in about six baby quilts.

Dur Vining and communion sets: a labor of love

"Now, new parents and the newborn receive a gift, as well as the church itself," Dur said. "And my joy is complete, knowing that all this, in a very small way, is helping those who have suffered for so long in the name of Jesus Christ."

Dwayne, as usual, injected some humor and practical encouragement in his message to the churches: "Double your congregation and we'll double your communion sets!"

Short-term Missions, Lifelong Transformations

In recruiting workers for the harvest, Dwayne knew his best tools weren't his own words—eloquent as they were—but what his listeners could see for themselves. "Take them to the uttermost ends of the earth," he recommended. "Let them experience pioneer ministry, and they won't ever be the same." Just as in Alaska, where he had packed routine flights with passengers so they could learn firsthand the needs of remote villagers, he depended on short-term projects in Russia to open the eyes and touch the hearts of potential career missionaries.

"You don't have to be special. The Lord can use all of us in a different way if we're willing to go," veteran volunteer Virginia Russell told visitors at a Russian missions rally in upstate New York. "It's amazing how many hunks of your heart you can leave in different places!"

*Vladivostok, 1997: Author (right) leaves heart in Russia—
and hat with a young Russian friend.*

Throughout much of the 1990s and early 2000s, Dwayne's arrangements pushed hundreds of new volunteers beyond their comfort zones into a bleak world where seeds of faith struggled to grow in the ashes of a destroyed society. These are some of my memories of a 1997 mission to Vladivostok:

Vladivostok, 1997: Good News Baptist Church choir sings at baptism.

I think I'll always have in my ears the singing of the Russian women and the laughter of the men as they raise a living church, brick by brick, while across the bay, under a dark sky, the steel tower that once choked the voices of faith and freedom stands silent.

... Aleksandr Solzhenitsyn has written that the prison camps of the Soviet Union can never be fully comprehended because those who knew them best are dead. But, he added in *The Gulag Archipelago*, "To taste the sea all one needs is one gulp." Similarly, our team needed only two weeks in one Russian city to see a light spreading through the vast land that only a few years ago still lay under a great darkness—a darkness that swallowed uncounted lives and, like some moral black hole, seemed to swallow light itself. In the receding shadow of that darkness, we helped build a small evangelical church in Russia's eastern outpost.

... We had crossed fifteen time zones to reach Vladivostok, [including] hours on planes and an overnight ride on the Trans-Siberian Railroad... We cleaned bricks, mixed cement, dug ditches, shoveled stone, hammered reinforcement bars straight [and] climbed narrow ramps to rickety scaffolding with heavy loads of cement. We used a medieval outhouse at a work site that was fifty years behind American standards of construction safety.

[We were told that] anti-religious harassment survives, aggravated by a shaky economy. The weak economy, rife with bureaucracy and corruption, results in periodic cutoffs of salaries, building supplies and electricity. Pastor Alexander Drozdovo said opponents of Good News Baptist Church ranged from the mayor of Vladivostok— "he said he wouldn't let us build this church"—to a squatter who threatened to meet church builders with gunfire.

Our irritation at our comparatively minor inconveniences vanished under the love that grew between us and our Russian hosts. Together we worked, prayed and sang on the dusty hilltop. Together we ate under a log lean-to while chasing wasps away from huge meals prepared without running water in an old donated trailer, a former Russian Army field kitchen.

... "Your coming to us was like a love-gift in action," Pastor Alexander said at the team's farewell dinner. "We hope God gives another opportunity to see you—if not here, then near His throne." (From *Light: A "Jewish Cowboy's" Journey*)

Dwayne (left) at Good News site with
Pastor "Sasha" Drozdovo (right)

Another church-building mission, in 1998, found us on the road from Khabarovsk to the mountain town of Obluchye, a rural servicing stop on the Trans-Siberian line.

> The sparsely traveled road had no side stripes, and often no center line. The blacktop later gave way to gravel as we headed west into the high country toward China through birch-covered hills flanked by distant mountains. It was dark when we rolled in. We got a warm welcome, supper, and finally, after we were parceled out among the host families in the small congregation, beds.
>
> ... we struggled to process a mass of new, often conflicting impressions. Green mountain pastures and a clear, cold river were a backdrop for weather-beaten but picturesque wooden houses surrounded by fenced vegetable gardens. Chickens pecked busily for scraps in uncovered trash and garbage dumps. Cows, goats and preschool children wandered along potholed, curbless, frequently unpaved streets next to railroad tracks crowded with tank cars and flanked by repair sheds and stacks of rusty pipes.
>
> Homes, at least those of our host families, were simple, well-kept havens where privacy and comfort depended on mutual consideration rather than space or furnishings.
>
> ... "They survive with such joy," team leader Don Lewis said of the Russians. (From *Light*)

Above: Dwayne's "Car-Hood Café" on road to Obluchye.
Below: Dwayne works on church construction.

Another mission site was Blagoveshchensk, on the Amur River separating Russia and China. American volunteers wrote names, dates and home churches on the ceiling beams of the church they were helping to build. It was a thrill to think of the scrawled messages enduring for a lifetime or more, hidden under paint and drywall like spiritual time capsules.

Dwayne and Lena were frequent visitors to those and other sites throughout the Far East. He planned and she translated, but both of them got their hands dirty with every imaginable construction task. Lena's jobsite savvy enhanced her effectiveness as an interpreter immeasurably—sometimes amusingly. When a sound system donated by an American sister church proved difficult to install, she convulsed some Obluchye Christians and their American helpers with a graphic hand gesture illustrating a male-female electrical connection. She called it a "mama-papa plug."

As an American volunteer in Obluchye, frustrated by my lack of skills and the poverty I saw, I wondered if I was really doing anything worthwhile. The local evangelical pastor's faith, and Dwayne's ever-present vision and humor, put things into perspective.

> ... Akif Askerov said God lets nothing happen by accident, including mission team journeys. "All our separate lives have been preparing for this time in Russia, to build His church."
>
> The other reassurance came from Dwayne, trying to dispel a Russian contractor's suspicions about the American team's motives. First one of us, then another, quietly walked over to hear the conversation during a work break. It became one of those defining, dramatic moments in which one person sums up and articulates the unspoken convictions of others.
>
> Team members have no hidden agenda, Dwayne told the contractor. Most are not rich, but have scraped together enough money, their own or donations from supporters, to come and help their Russian brothers and sisters in Christ. "We worship the same God," he said.
>
> Building a church creates work—including work for contractors, he added pointedly—and stirs up interest in the community. The volunteers don't do all the work, but their presence encourages Russian believers who have been persecuted harshly for many years. American volunteers, he concluded, know the importance of religious freedom, especially those with Russian ancestors or relatives still living in Russia.
>
> For Dwayne, humor is indispensable in a society where nothing is routine or predictable. He was unflappable, whether delightedly greeting a near-sighted *babushka* [grandmother] who mistook the worksite-bound mission van for the dilapidated village bus and climbed aboard, or scrambling high in the none-too-secure rafters of the future church to attach a pulley.

*Whatever Dwayne was saying, it was cracking up Lena
and Obluchye Pastor Akif Askerov.*

"He is monkey!" said Lena. "Give him a banana."

Triumphing over hardships ranging from hostile bureaucrats to endless journeys on terrible roads, nurturing the seeds of faith among steadfast believers emerging uneasily from a century of murderous darkness, he would probably agree with [author Conrad Hyer's] comment: "Humor is not the opposite of seriousness. Humor is the opposite of despair." (From *Light*)

SEND would soon give Dwayne something more than a banana: responsibility for a much larger territory. But there was some unfinished business and another long journey to tackle first.

*an example of what Russians and foreign mission volunteers
accomplished: Central Baptist Church, Khabarovsk, Far East Russia*

13. SHARING THE ADVENTURE
New Home, Big Territory, Long Flight

⌒

When in Russia, drive like the Russians. Otherwise it's dangerous—they don't know what to expect.
— Dwayne, in fast traffic
near Krasnoyarsk

IN 1999, DWAYNE was promoted to head SEND's mission in all of the former Soviet Union—a region stretching from the Polish border to the Pacific Ocean. Carl Kresge rejoined him, and, like Lena a few years earlier, acquired an unofficial title in the process. Frank Severn, introducing Dwayne as the new Eurasia regional director and Carl as his deputy, said something about sweeping up the dust behind Dwayne's whirlwind. Someone shouted, "Oh, that makes Carl the Deputy Dustbuster!"

Before starting the new assignment, Dwayne and Carolyn worked on their new home about eighty miles northeast of Anchorage. A team from Twin Orchards in Vestal—Don and Ann Lewis, Richard and Dawn Davey, and me—spent two weeks that spring helping with the project. The next year, I accompanied Dwayne on a tour of his new mission territory and shared a memorable flight home.

As a bush pilot and missionary, Dwayne had originally appeared on my radar screen as a visitor to my church who might be interesting to write about. He soon became something more: a friend who let me into his world, which offered not only high (literally!) adventure, but also a front-row seat at a drama in which faith and history were being played out. Whether crossing paths with him on mission trips, working in Alaska or traveling across Russia, it was endlessly fascinating to watch this enthusiastic player in that drama in action.

*Above: Daveys (left), Lewises (right) and author
worked on the Kings' new home (below).*

Many details found their way into *Light*, a mostly autobiographical book I wrote in 2004, edited portions of which follow. These excerpts are neither comprehensive, nor—as the author is a fellow believer—objective, but are simply firsthand glimpses by one observer among many whose faith has been strengthened by Dwayne's modeling.

Close quarters revealed many sides of Dwayne.

Alaska: Work and Play in Paradise

Dwayne and our group of helpers would stand on his hillside before breakfast, chilly hands cradling warm coffee mugs, looking out past beetle-killed spruce trees into the Matanuska Valley. The early June sun burned the mist off the snow-covered flanks of the Chugach and Talkeetna ranges. Dwayne usually started the day by squirting water from a hose onto a dusty patch of slope loaded with grass seed, which, he insisted, would spring up any moment into a lush lawn. We moved slowly while our aging bones warmed up, jealous of young Daniil Marchenko, the Russian pastor's son, who ran—literally—from task to task.

Dwayne was the only middle-aged member of our group who needed no warm-up. Even in those hopefully far-off last moments before he hears his *Well done, good and faithful servant*, I doubt that his body, mind or spirit will be holding still.

Things didn't always go smoothly—especially on June 12, the day from hell. It started well enough. With his usual ingenuity, Dwayne used an arc welding outfit and some plastic piping to rig up a truck-mounted sprinkler to settle the dust on the dirt roads. Things went downhill from there. The hired plumber didn't show up. The laundry room flooded. The sprinkler truck got stuck in a ditch. The bulldozer ran out of fuel, so it couldn't rescue the truck. My daily post-lunch energy collapse, usually gone in ten or fifteen minutes, lasted two or three hours.

Daniil was one of many young Russians whom Dwayne helped launch into ministry. After spending the summer with the Kings and learning to fly, his next stop would be Alaska Bible College. "He's a good boy," said Dwayne. The few times Daniil was late for anything, he could generally be found in our trailer, glued to a training video or a tape of one of Dwayne's adventures.

*Daniil was the first of Dwayne's mission
aviation trainees from Russia.*

Dwayne made sure that recreation breaks were times of inspiration, not just relaxation. His gift was vision, which he shared where it's most contagious: high above the earth. One clear, windless day, he gave us the afternoon off and took us flying. His own airstrip wasn't finished, so we used the dirt runway at the homestead of his friend, Hal Farrar, an aging but energetic country singer, poet, tomahawk-thrower, bullwhip-snapper and all-round wilderness character.

Ann, Dawn and Don went up in Hal's four-seater. I was in Dwayne's Cessna 150, a single-engine two-seater with a cockpit no wider than a two-hole outhouse. Never having flown in anything that small, I assumed I was supposed to be folded up like a jacknife, with my knees jammed against the instrument panel. I was delighted when Dwayne showed me I could move the seat back.

Dwayne buzzed a running mountain sheep on one of the Talkeetna mountains, then frowned at a set of snowmobile tracks visible high on the tan, rocky slopes. "They oughta ban those things . . . guns and sex too," he added with a straight face, glancing sideways to see if I was paying attention. He banked and turned south, flying over the edge of a high meadow that suddenly dropped a few thousand feet down to the Glenn Highway and Matanuska River, briefly taking my stomach with it. Minutes later, we were across the valley and into the Chugach Range.

Circling for altitude to clear one snowy pass, Dwayne responded to the grandeur with song: "Oh Lord, my Lord, how majestic is Thy name in all the earth!" Snatches of Job ran through my head, competing with the whine of the engine—*storehouse of snow ... frost of heaven ... newborn mountain goats.*

He let me take the dual controls for five or ten minutes over the Matanuska Glacier as we headed back toward Hal's. I wish I could say I swooped and dove and mounted up with wings like an eagle, but I flew more like a little old lady trying out a new Crown Victoria—white knuckles coaxing the stick into slow turns, feet timidly nudging the rudders.

Gateways: The Engines of Heaven
... do you love me?... Feed my sheep... Follow me!
—John 21: 17, 19

A few days later we drove to Glennallen in Dwayne's 1980-something Ford Club Van. The van has sentimental value for Don and Ann, who logged many miles on it in 1992 while training to become mission team leaders.

... Daniil and I spent a sweaty hour with a vacuum cleaner, Windex and rags, making the maroon workhorse presentable for the trip. We took turns riding in a lawn chair we had put into the back to expand seating space, a homey touch that reminded me of Tom Joad's California-bound jalopy in *The Grapes of Wrath*. The Chugaches and Talkeetnas fell behind as we headed east though flat pine forest, but soon, straight ahead, loomed Glennallen's signature backdrop: a huge, misty mountain in the Wrangell Range.

Glennallen, like the van, is something ordinary that becomes locked in memory by being bound up with where the direction of a life changes. It was from the Glennallen airfield that Dwayne embarked on the September 1991 flight to Providenya. It's at the Bible college at Glennallen that Daniil will learn to follow in the footsteps of his father and Dwayne. And it's at Glennallen that an Alaskan cliché—small planes and big mountains— became, for me, something more. It's where I finally saw what it looks like, and sensed what it must feel like, to fly for God.

At the airfield, dwarfed by the snow-capped Wrangells just beyond, rows of little planes were lined up, noses pointed at the sky. In my mind's eye I could see Daniil and other missionaries in frail craft like these, trusting tiny engines to float them like gossamer-winged seeds through clouds and darkness, over mountain ramparts that would break and freeze armies, to land on waiting soil and take root.

Glennallen airfield: "... what it must feel like to fly for God."

Millennia ago, nomadic Siberian hunters who called themselves the People of the Raven trudged east on foot across a frozen sea in search of food. How appropriate, I thought, that the place they found and called the Great Land—*Alyeska,* in their tongue—should become a jumping-off point for returning an imperishable food, the bread of life, back over the western ice, this time on wings. How natural that this land, where life is an adventure, should be a breeding ground for missionary enterprises— which are, after all, leaps into the unknown sustained by faith in things unseen. How fitting that Alaska, which still lures gamblers, should mold other kinds of seekers as well—those who count on a sure thing for the greatest adventure of all.

I asked Don, who had very much wanted me to see Glennallen, why I was increasingly finding myself in such far-off places relatively late in life.

"You're in deep," he said, grinning.

As different parts of what we believe is the body of Christ, we each have different roles, but we depend on each other. Don and Richard build, run and fix things, and I help. Ann, Dawn and Carolyn bring order and comfort to our little frontier society. The ladies also boss me around occasionally; they have the living credentials to do it, so I bite my tongue and obey. We all support Dwayne and Daniil, whose part it is to spread the Word and give others the vision to do the same, until the body is complete and the Kingdom comes.

Meanwhile, I trust my friends, on whom my safety depends. They take good care of their equipment, which reassures me. But more than that, seeing in them He who lives through them, I can join in Dwayne's cockpit song. Fear of falling yields bit by bit to a growing faith that I will rise in God's time, not before, to those mountains of which these Alaskan peaks are but emblems, and wake in that eternal light of which these nightless northern days are but shadows.

So you're right, Don. I'm in deep. And even if I never learn anything more about engines, I'll know, when I hear you and Dwayne and Richard talking about them, why they remind me of heaven.

A Journey through Darkness and Light

Dwayne planned to survey his vast new SEND territory in 2000. While we worked on his home, he dropped a bomb as casually as if he had merely told me to fetch some more roofing nails. Would I, he asked, like to accompany him as a writer and photographer? Being reasonably sane,

I responded appropriately: "Do bears commit indiscretions in the woods? I'll need some time to think about it, like five seconds. One, two, YES!"

The three-week journey in March and April would span five thousand miles across eleven time zones, not counting travel to and from Eurasia. Dwayne would be delivering the SEND payroll and other supplies, reviewing plans for new churches, distributing gifts from American and Canadian sister churches, and listening to the concerns of missionaries and Russian evangelicals.

On Sunday, March 12, 2000, the day before departure, he demonstrated his usual ability to multitask. In his home at SEND headquarters near Detroit, he paced around the living room in socks, slacks and T-shirt, fine-tuning a sermon he would give in an hour at a Russian evangelical church in Detroit and simultaneously watching NASCAR tape from Atlanta's Cracker Barrel.

"Go, Bobby!" he yelled, rooting for Bobby LaBonte in the pack of cars screaming around the track at nearly two hundred miles per hour—coincidentally, the same speed he and a stiff tailwind would coax out of a pumped-up Cessna 172 a month later between Anchorage and Detroit, the last leg of our globe-circling journey. Dwayne headed for the closet to get a tie, shouting over his shoulder, "Hey, Mark! Is the caution flag up?"

"How would I know?" I yelled back, trying to overcome the TV noise and penetrate his hearing aids with more volume than the uninsulated engines of the bush planes he has piloted for thirty years in the Alaskan wilderness. "What is there in the background of this sheltered, Northeast, urban, leftwing, Jewish intellectual that makes you think I'd know squat about NASCAR races?"

"Well bless your *heart*," Dwayne boomed back. "That's just the kind of writing we *need* to reach a non-church audience!"

His refusal to sit quietly in the missionary box is typical of a life of leaping over walls that others have erected to box in or shut out God's love. The biggest leap, the flight to Providenya in 1991, combined a heart for the Gospel and a passion for Russia. In Dwayne's view, spreading the news about spreading the Gospel was another box-breaker. That's why he invited me along.

Strictly speaking, it was a business trip, but that's all it had in common with the redeye to Kennedy for the monthly marketing meeting of boring-bigbiz.com.

The hallway next to his office was cluttered with books, clothing, snacks, medications, letters and software, all bound for missionary families scattered across Russia. A money belt, lovingly sewn by secretary

Lisa Mollencamp, was packed with more crispy hundreds than you'll ever see outside a gangsta movie. The luggage didn't all fit into SEND's Saint Bernard-sized green duffle bag, so I sullenly made space in my own carry-on. I thinned out my already small supply of clothing, thereby adding smelly-socks anxiety to half-excited, half-scared expectations. We even had a few birthday presents for "MKs"—missionary kids—stuffed into our bags.

After a quick trip from Farmington to Detroit Metro Airport—Dwayne drives like his NASCAR heroes—we boarded a big 747-400 for Amsterdam, with connections to Kiev.

Before we could take off, a U.S. Customs agent came aboard, checked our seat numbers and asked Dwayne, "Are you Dwayne King?" He asked to see the $86,000 Dwayne had declared he was taking abroad. "Not here," Dwayne replied, quietly explaining the dangers of displaying a large sum of money in public. He and the agent walked to an exit row and repeated the dialogue. Then they left the plane and walked to the terminal concourse, where the agent again demanded to see the money. "Not here," Dwayne said, again pointing out the risks. The next stop was the men's restroom, where—between the sinks and urinals—the scenario was repeated a fourth time.

They ended up in the handicapped toilet stall and spread the stacks of crisp bills on the floor. The determined agent counted it while Dwayne prayed that nobody would open the door and draw the wrong conclusions.

In answer to more questions, Dwayne said the money was earmarked for missionary salaries, church construction, Bible schools and to help Russian pastors. He also told the agent some facts of life about post-Soviet Russia: No, there was no way to transfer the money to Russian banks, which could not be trusted anyway. No, he did not intend to declare the money to Russian customs officials—the declaration would immediately become "street knowledge," with predictable results.

Meanwhile, I sat in the plane, wondering if I would make the trip alone. Dwayne eventually reboarded. Minutes later we were airborne for the Atlantic and Ukraine—some forty-five minutes late.

We later switched to Russian carriers. Despite Aeroflot's scary safety record—some smart-alecs call it "Aeroflop"—we had no complaints about the Russian planes. Like any flier who has to be a passenger, Dwayne kept up a running critique of our pilots. He gave their performances good grades, except for one landing in Siberia. It seemed OK to me, but he said the pilot hadn't left enough extra runway in reserve if something had gone wrong.

A Million Meetings

The days blurred together in a panorama of changing scenes, from elegantly restored turn-of-the-century buildings in Kiev to the broad boulevards of Moscow, past ramshackle wooden villages strewn like *Fiddler on the Roof* movie sets across the snow-covered fields and forests of Siberia, to the bustling downtowns and dingy apartment buildings of Vladivostok and Khabarovsk. We lived on the run, serenaded by droning jet engines, clicking rails, and bouncing vans slamming along potholed roads. We wrestled our extra suitcases and grabbed meals, beds and showers when we could.

Dwayne visits with SEND missionary John Wicker in Siberia.

I lost count of all the meetings with SEND staffers, church workers and Bible college teachers. Dwayne summed it up as "getting to know the missionaries' needs, and the heartbeat and vision of the Russian Baptist leadership."

In addition to listening, that meant sharing tips ranging from nutrition to cross-cultural sensitivity. He advised Siberian Baptists seeking to buy a church site from Russian businessmen, "Don't take us along. They'll smell American money and raise the price." To Bible college officials worried that students' attention spans were succumbing to hunger and fatigue, he recommended vitamins and protein to supplement the usual bread and potatoes. He listened sympathetically to volunteer work teams enamored of "fast-build" wooden churches and frustrated by the Russians' preference for time-consuming masonry construction. But he reminded them that efficiency is less important than helping the Russian church lead its own revival in its own way.

Above all, Dwayne told Russians and their foreign helpers, God uses people and their varied gifts to do His work. That means teaming up, networking and personal contacts. Is a congregation bored by an introspective, study-oriented pastor? Well, pair him with an evangelist-type helper who's good at relationships. Is the pool of short-term volunteers drying up? "Reach those old friends. Try your home church."

The Russians you want to reach—do they skydive or play soccer? "Go out and do it with them." Are the usual donors in Peoria tapped out just when you want to equip a summer Bible camp in Ukraine? Reach beyond the usual newsletter: *"Tell* donors about your projects. It makes more impact that way."

Hard, Happy Charger

Hearing Dwayne bark marching orders on a busy day could make you wince. "Make it happen! I gotta teach you to be a *secretary,*" he snaps at interpreter Lena Sidenko, bullying her to find some elusive telephone number in a search for a cheaper air fare. She starts to reply but he cuts her off, chanting, "La-la-la!" She scowls, eyes narrowing in a strong, high-cheekboned face. "Wear a tie," he tells me one Sunday morning in Khabarovsk. "We'll be sitting at the front of the church, and you'll be giving a testimony." In church, enforcing some detail of Russian propriety, he leans over and whispers to me, "Don't cross your legs!"

A funny thing happens on your way to feeling indignant about this obviously abusive Type A boss.

Lena breaks into a grin and replies: "Dvayne, dat's so *stupid!* How come *you* don't know zose numbers?" In church, I reply to his legs directive: "Aw, c'mon! You never let me have any fun!"

He laughs when his targets give back as good as they get. That's because he and they know something a casual observer might not. They know that the work they're doing isn't about anyone's rank or ego, but about focusing on what they've been called to do for God's glory.

That means humility and humor go along with the hard-charging style. Preparing for a difficult encounter—a meeting with a Russian church member smarting over criticism of a translation of an American theological work—Dwayne asked Lena to do something an ego-bound boss wouldn't normally request: "Be there. I want your take. Maybe you'll think he's right." And he's not above practical jokes. On a Russian airliner, as I uncertainly examined something on my lunch tray that appeared to be a foil-wrapped candy, he hastened to be helpful.

"White chocolate," he declared. Reassured, I popped it into my mouth and nearly gagged. It was butter.

Some of Dwayne's energy goes into drama, unnervingly. At least twice, he thought he'd lost his wallet, a thick leather organizer stuffed with cash and just about every important number and contact in the former Soviet empire. What appeared to be an imminent coronary subsided when he remembered it was in the jacket he wasn't wearing that day.

During one bout of in-flight bumpiness, he announced dramatically, "We're in the grip of the CAT!" My anxiety spiked off the chart. "...Clear Air Turbulence," he explained. I felt much better.

Travel Tidbits

Russians sitting next to us on planes and trains seem thoughtful and interested, not uneasy, when the conversation turns to religion. This is a response partly to Dwayne's friendly, non-confrontational manner and partly to history. Russians have endured so much unimaginable horror and bureaucratic harassment that they're inclined to be curious about alternatives.

....

Many sales clerks and government officials take the attitude that customers are an inconvenience or a threat unless proved otherwise. So it's surprising how quickly the ice melts when a foreigner or stranger proves to be a fellow human being in need. The ice melts even faster if one can personalize the encounter, as Dwayne often does, by flashing a few wallet shots of grandchildren.

....

Overall, police "like to lord it over the citizens," Dwayne says. However, some cops are capable of joking. One excuses an alleged traffic infraction after seeing the smiling face on Dwayne's license: "We can't throw such a happy man in prison!" Russians assume that only Americans, missionaries and idiots smile for official photos. Near Krasnoyarsk, another officer stops another SEND missionary for some minor or nonexistent infraction: "*Harasho* [good]! We finally caught the Canadian [missionary]. Someday we're going to catch the German."

....

In a land where apartment foyers are dark because light bulbs are stolen as quickly as they're screwed in, the level of trust is similar to that in the South Bronx. But in large and small gestures, many ordinary Russians perform acts of solidarity, practicality and kindness that defy or ignore a dehumanizing system.

As in America, blinking headlights in the oncoming lane are a helpful tip-off to a police speed trap up the road. Pedestrians seeking rides routinely flag down private cars and negotiate a fee on the spot for specific destinations. At the Vladivostok airport, while Dwayne and I are in a no-win argument with customs officials, several men within earshot urge them to let us go.

In Bryansk, in western Russia, a choir director brushes snow from our coats. In Irkutsk, Siberia, the Bible Institute vice president serves us the soup himself in the school's tiny, brick-walled kitchen/dining room. Both times, I see Jesus washing the feet of the disciples.

In Uzhur, Siberia, I promise to tell the church's story. An old woman, a transplanted Ukrainian, squeezes my hand in an iron grip and whispers, "*Spasiba! Spasiba!* [thank you! thank you!]"

Dwayne talks with Ukrainian woman in Siberia.
She wanted the church's story told.

....

On the train from Ukraine to Russia, two men we don't know share our four-bunk compartment. We wait until they leave—for a drink or a trip to the bathroom—so Dwayne can take off his money belt, which has become unbearably hot and irritating. He stashes it in the luggage storage space beneath his lower bunk.

Several things happen at once: Our fellow passengers return. The train stops at the Russian border. Border guards will enter our compartment any second to check papers and search baggage. There's no time for Dwayne to put the money belt back on. Transporting money is technically legal, but if the guards find it and tip off criminals—highly likely in corrupt, post-Soviet Russia—our possessions and lives, and those of the church people with whom we've arranged to stay that night, won't be worth the proverbial plugged nickel.

The cops look everywhere except in the crucial storage space. "Why?" I ask later. "God blinds their eyes," Dwayne replies.

....

We're delivering a gift from an American congregation to an unregistered church in the run-down, unpaved outskirts of a large Russian city. The church risks being fined and closed for operating without official permission. It stands in plain sight, displaying a cross and a sign stating its purpose.

"Why can't the police find it?" I ask.

"God blinds their eyes," Dwayne replies.

....

In Siberian airline terminals at 3 a.m. or on dark, cold railroad station platforms, we hope God is blinding the eyes of whoever might be thinking of mugging two lonely Americans loaded down with bags. Aware that even minor feelings turn my face into a flashing neon sign, I practice Manhattan body language and close my face up so tight I'm afraid it might disappear into my head. Even Dwayne seems nervous.

We feel exposed and vulnerable, but still more secure than Major Joe Makatozi.

Makatozi, a fictional American test pilot of Sioux and Cheyenne blood, is the hero of Louis L'Amour's *Last of the Breed*. Imprisoned near Lake Baikal during the Cold War, Makatozi has only one escape route: the one used by his mammoth-hunting ancestors millennia ago. He must make his way east on foot across a few thousand miles of subarctic wilderness, elude capture and somehow cross the Bering Strait undetected.

We quickly join the ranks of SEND missionaries for whom the adventure novel has become a cult classic. From Siberia, where we borrowed it, all the way to Far East Russia, we fight over the dog-eared paperback ("C'mon, Dwayne, it's my turn! Why don't you do some Bible study?").

Our challenges in leaving Russia are trivial next to Makatozi's. All we have to do is put together an itinerary made slightly more complicated by Alaska Airline's dropping the Khabarovsk-Anchorage shuttle.

Source of Strength

Days are filled with long meetings, short food breaks, arguments with Russian customs bureaucrats, and endless rides on bad roads to inspect new church sites. At the end of each day, Dwayne falls exhausted into bed — or a plane seat — and rises refreshed the next morning. That's how it was on this trip, and many before it.

From what deep well, besides the coffee pot, does he draw his strength? What balances the cost of weeks away from home and family?

"I gain a reward in heaven," he says in the straightforward manner of one stating a fact, not reaching for a pleasant symbol or metaphor.

It was God, he said, who made sure he was living in Alaska when the Soviet Union imploded across the Bering Strait, giving him the challenge of a new ministry that opened up when the old order closed down ... God, who gave him the spiritual gifts and physical drive to take up the challenge ... God, who broke his heart with the sufferings of the Russian church and showed him that "this is the hour for helping that church be re-established and rebuilt."

He said his life was also directed by the people God put in his path. He initially wanted to fly missionaries, not be one. His mind was changed by the late Gordon C. Davis, former president of his alma mater, Practical Bible [now Davis] College. Dwayne encouraged leaders of the Irkutsk Bible Institute to encourage in their students any signs of tenderness of heart and avoidance of pride, "like the president of Practical saw in me."

"I think all your words are right," said Constantin Galeiko, chairman of the Siberian school.

Anyone can say the right words about God. The long journey from Ukraine to the Far East showed that Dwayne lives them: in his willingness to preach to Russian congregations in their own language, plunging happily ahead in the complex tongue he has largely taught himself, improving with each visit. In his acceptance of a thousand tasks and some dangers involved in coordinating missionary activity across the vastness of a difficult, unpredictable land.

He lives them in the eyes of missionary children as "Uncle Dwayne," and in the hugs of longtime Russian friends, who see in him the solidarity of Christians caring for brothers and sisters. In his enjoyment of sharing testimonies of faith with fellow travelers on whatever level they invite the conversation.

Khabarovsk, 2000: taking time to play (above) with missionary kids; making time (below) to witness

He lives them in something I rarely paid attention to on the trip, but which I think about more and more now—his undivided attention to everyone he speaks with; his unwillingness to sacrifice anyone to a deadline or a timetable. It's like the unwillingness of a good shepherd to be content with the safety of ninety and nine while one remains beyond the fold.

Life Flight: In Good Hands

Once back in Alaska, the next stop was SEND headquarters in Michigan. We planned to board a jet, but Dwayne spotted an opportunity that would make the journey more interesting. A flight school in Tyler, Texas, co-owned by J.C. Harder, was buying a single-engine four-seater from a Civil Air Patrol squadron in Alaska. The school needed someone to deliver it, and that seemed like a fine idea to Dwayne and me. We'd had enough of crowded jetliners, trains and bad roads. We'd save airfare, too, and the little Cessna 172 promised a relaxing, scenic ride back to suburban Detroit.

The flight school sent up Andrew De La Torre, a trainee who needed some supervised mountain flying time. Dwayne and I would get off at Detroit, and Andrew would fly the Cessna the rest of the way to Texas. A soon-to-be commercial pilot, Andrew was a friendly, open-faced young man with a Southwestern drawl. He said "Yessir, Nosir," and was respectful toward his elders. We liked him. The sight of snow-capped mountains and a few moose outside his motel window immediately won his heart to the north, an ardor that cooled considerably a few days later.

Andrew fell in love with the north ... for awhile.

We planned to stay on the ground in bad weather, or fly around it. This was to minimize exposure to conditions that can quickly freeze condensation into a fatally heavy shroud on a small plane lacking de-icing capability. At least in the mountains, we would fly only in daylight and usually by Visual Flight Rules, relying not on instruments, but on observation of ground landmarks. Andrew would ride "left seat" as the designated ferry pilot. Dwayne, co-piloting with dual controls, could immediately take over in situations requiring more experience, such as threading narrow mountain passes under low cloud cover. The trip to Detroit would take about three days—four, tops.

That was the plan. We were able to follow most of it.

The usual Russia-induced deficits—steak, sleep and reliable showers—were quickly remedied. We were ready to go, but nothing else was. For nearly four days we cooled our heels at the King Ranch, waiting for the weather to break and the plane paperwork to clear. Late Tuesday morning, April 4, south-central Alaska was still socked in and it was snowing in Anchorage. Dwayne's son, Dave, picked at his guitar while I looked across the Matanuska River and saw only the lower slopes of the cloud-shrouded Chugach Range.

The night before, I had prayed for my anxiety about small planes to lift, along with the clouds that were holding us down. It was the second time in five years I had prayed for help against an enveloping darkness. The first time, the enemy was pain. Both times, the answer was immediate and in an unexpected form: The assaults did not subside, but assurances rose to meet them.

We had to move fast when the ceiling lifted Tuesday afternoon. Dwayne jumped into his two-seat Super Cub, bounced along the dirt runway and took off for Anchorage, where Andrew and the Cessna waited. Dave followed along on the Glenn Highway in his pickup with me and the other pieces of luggage.

We took off in the red-striped white Cessna, but less than an hour out of Anchorage we had to make an unscheduled landing because I'd forgotten something. I'd forgotten why, in better-equipped craft, those of us older than 50 prefer aisle seats. I thought my approach to the airstrip office was no faster than a brisk stride, but the manager, resplendent in a World War I-vintage leather aviator's helmet and goggles, smirked and said something about knowing who was hell-bent for the restroom.

Dwayne topped off the fuel tank and, sensitive to my needs, requested a "range extender": no high-tech astronaut diaper, just a couple of empty soda cans in a resealable plastic bag.

Comfortable once more, especially after learning how to attach the Cessna's safety harness correctly, I settled into the right rear seat, behind Dwayne. The seat next to me was stacked with luggage, and a five-gallon plastic container of extra gasoline sat snugly on the floor in front of it, behind Andrew's seat. More bags in the small cargo hold made up a full load.

Underway at last: The calendar said "April,"
but the mountains said "winter."

Climate control settings seemed limited to "steambath" or "meat-locker," but the temperature evened out after I stuck some tape on a small hole in the ceiling. We wore headsets to hear each other and the radio over the whine of the engine in the uninsulated cockpit. I was delighted with my new toy and wanted to sound just as professional as Dwayne and Andrew, with their crisp babble about "niners" and "vectors." I keyed the mike, triggering an attention-getting blast of static, and issued my first jargon transmission:

"Passenger to cockpit crew, passenger to cockpit crew, do you copy? You are advised to maintain level flight and refrain from aerobatics and evasive maneuvers while range extender is being deployed. Estimated time to deployment three minutes, or as soon as I can get out of this . . . [*inaudible, static*] ... safety harness. Please acknowledge. Passenger out."

As the passenger, I was the lavatory attendant, food service specialist and chart librarian. That meant I emptied the range extenders, made sand-wiches, and—generally after I was all strapped in—was asked to rummage around in somebody's bag for airport approach charts. I was also the ground crew intern, helping to push the plane to its parking space, tie it down for the night and brush snow off the next morning.

Dwayne and Andrew kept busy flying the plane and, at fueling stops, checking weather reports and filing flight plans. Dwayne usually had to start the latter tasks by himself. As soon as Andrew's feet hit the taxiway, his cell phone swung to his head for the daily reports to his girlfriend and Texas flight instructor. Dwayne was starting to mutter about this, then recollected that Andrew was, after all, 21.

Fifteen Minutes, "Fifteen Thousand Years"

This river has been a terror to many ...
to the palate bitter and to the stomach cold ...
—John Bunyan, *The Pilgrim's Progress*

The routine was interrupted on the second day in the air. What followed was considerably tamer than some of Dwayne's previous aviation adventures, but it was exciting enough for a novice—and a good illustration of life lessons learned in his company.

Just over an hour out of Whitehorse, Yukon Territory, we were flying by instruments in thick cloud cover at eleven thousand feet, nearly as high as we could go without a pressurized cabin and auxiliary oxygen. Despite zero visibility—a sock's-eye-view in an over-soaped washing machine— we were at a safe altitude, high above some six-thousand foot peaks in the Canadian Rockies. I assumed everything else was safe, too, although I didn't enjoy the feeling of racing along blind.

Then the engine started coughing.

When you don't know enough about planes to know what's normal, any change in sound or motion tells your stomach: *Something's Wrong.* The warning bypasses your brain and goes straight to your gut. It's probably your guilt gland Just Serving You Right for going out of your way to trust your life to something other than a boring, airborne office building like a 747.

But in this case, there really was something wrong. So when Dwayne and Andrew started talking in low tones about engine trouble, my freefloating anxiety congealed as quickly as ice on a wing.

High above the Canadian Rockies, the engine was starting to quit.

We had to get out of the clouds quickly and find an airstrip, a road, a frozen lake or even a treeless piece of ground. We needed someplace to land before or immediately after the engine died—which it was going to do in minutes, as soon as the ice clogging the air intake got thick enough to shut off the air supply to the engine.

Andrew raised the Teslin airstrip and was speaking with the soft urgency of controlled, focused fear. The conversation went pretty much like this:

> *... Teslin radio, this is Cessna 1357 Uniform. Do you copy?*
>
> *... Cessna 1357 Uniform. This is Teslin Radio. We read you loud and clear. Go ahead your request.*
>
> *... We've experienced a partial loss of power at eleven thousand en route to Watson Lake. We're gonna try to land at Teslin Lake.*
>
> *... Roger. Teslin Lake weather two miles [visibility] in snow, temp minus three degrees Centigrade, altimeter two-niner-o-five [barometric pressure at airstrip so plane crew can set altimeter].*
>
> *... We're descending out of eleven thousand and we have the highway on our GPS [Global Positioning System].*

Meanwhile, I was tightening my harness and having my own conversation, a silent one, consisting of all I could remember of certain parts of Romans and Psalms. Dwayne, already wearing a lap belt, told me to hand him his shoulder harness. I was very happy when we got out of the clouds and saw the ground. I was even happier about ten minutes later when I saw, in the distance far below, the gray ribbon of the Alaska Highway winding through the forest.

We weren't out of trouble yet.

Up the highway and behind a hill, just above Teslin's location, the sky was black. The airstrip dispatcher confirmed our suspicions: "... now our visibility is one-half mile in heavy snow. What are your intentions?"

We couldn't land in a snow squall. Dwayne made a decision.

"We're approximately five miles south of the field, with good visibility. We're over a straight section of the highway and very little traffic. We're going to land on the highway."

"Roger... The RCMP [Royal Canadian Mounted Police] is on their way south along the highway to assist you."

We circled over the two-lane highway a few times to lose altitude and wait for the Mounties. My spirits sank with each swing away from the road. With each swing back, I thought, *Why can't we just LAND? NOW?!* The engine was missing more frequently. A pair of white sport-utility vehicles finally appeared, racing south, lights flashing. The Mounties were setting up roadblocks at each end of our "runway."

"We're lined up," Dwayne radioed. "Landing to the north, on the highway at this time." And he did, smoothly.

When our hearts stopped pounding, we pushed the plane onto the shoulder. Dwayne removed the culprit: the air cleaner, a book-sized filter, slushy with now-melting ice. He said that in thirty years of medical and mission flying in all weather conditions, he had never run into the kind of wet, sticky snow that would clog an air cleaner so quickly. He kept the filter out until we were much farther south, where icing would be less likely. The next decision, which Dwayne and I announced to each other more or less simultaneously, was to spare our wives the exciting details until we got home.

I was glad to be on the ground when I learned a few more of those details. Dwayne and Andrew had initially thought the engine was starving for fuel, so they adjusted the mixture to enrich the fuel-air ratio with more gasoline—which nearly shut down the engine completely. Quickly realizing they had the opposite problem, they "leaned" the mixture to match the reduced air intake, a balancing act that nursed the dying engine just long enough to keep the prop spinning until we landed.

"You goin' up in that again?" a smiling onlooker asked.

"One decision at a time," I replied. For some reason, he thought that was a very funny answer.

Dwayne flew the plane the few miles to the Teslin airstrip, where the squall had subsided, while Andrew and I rode in one of the RCMP vehicles. Andrew made the understatement of the day: "Sorry for the trouble. This wasn't on the agenda."

We babbled our thanks to Corporal Tim Ashmore and Constable Ben Dyson, and to dispatcher Sue Swereda, who had started putting together an emergency response at the first hint of trouble. She had fed us answers almost before we asked questions, such as reporting ground temperatures just when we were wondering if ice conditions would permit a lake landing.

Friendly villagers drove us to and from the nearby Yukon Motel & Restaurant. We spent much of Thursday at the airstrip, napping, snacking, and waiting for the weather to break. Reading material included, appropriately, a woodcut-illustrated volume of Robert Service's poetry ("The Shooting of Dan McGrew," "The Cremation of Sam McGee," etc.). We went to the general store and replenished Sue's kitchen supplies. Comments from other shoppers indicated that most of Teslin's approximately five hundred residents—about half of them Tlingit people—knew why we were in town. We didn't know whether to feel honored or embarrassed.

Sue's comment— "It worked out well"—carried more personal weight than the words suggested. In her four years at Teslin, there had been one other serious incident involving a small plane. Four people had been killed. She and the Mounties had not been optimistic about our chances.

"It didn't look good. We didn't think you'd make it," one of the officers said.

We had gotten into trouble around 5 p.m. Teslin time. In Vestal, that would have been 8 p.m., when the Wednesday prayer meeting at Twin Orchards breaks up. Two days earlier I had called Pastor Paul Blasko, asking him to put our safety on his list of prayer requests. Between realizing we had a problem and landing on the highway, fifteen minutes had elapsed, Dwayne estimated. "It felt like fifteen thousand years," Andrew said.

Ups and, Mostly, Downs

... You got to know when to hold 'em, know when to fold 'em ...
—Don Schlitz, "The Gambler"

"Should be clear sailing the rest of the way in," said Andrew, looking beyond the last few high ridges and snow-filled clouds toward the easier skies over the prairie provinces.

"Not necessarily," Dwayne replied.

I could overlook the reason Dwayne had asked me to pass him a rubber band the previous day: to hold a couple of non-critical controls in place. I was even willing to overlook what happened Thursday, right after we took off from our next stop, Watson Lake: The directional gyro, a compass that aids navigation, had decided to stop working. But we still had the magnetic compass.

However, I started to do some hard thinking Friday evening when electrical problems forced us to turn back from our Winnipeg heading and return to Saskatoon. That would take about forty-five minutes, and I wasn't happy about fighting fear for a period three times longer than those fifteen minutes over Teslin.

I was relieved when Dwayne explained that the latest problem wasn't dangerous, just inconvenient. Our alternator had quit, throwing the electrical load onto the battery—which could last only about ninety minutes. Without electricity, the plane would be flyable, but would have no lights, radio or transponder, effectively making it invisible to air traffic control. Ninety minutes gave us plenty of time to make Saskatoon, but if we continued toward Winnipeg and lost the battery, we'd be landing at night at a big city airport without landing lights or communications—akin to dropping a refrigerator into a day care center and hoping no one would get hurt.

"And we'd be in the refrigerator," Andrew offered helpfully.

Clearing us to land at Saskatoon, a controller—sounding almost hopeful—asked, "Are you declaring an emergency?"

"No! We just want to fix our problem," Andrew replied. The airport would have to wait for another opportunity to stage a fire-and-rescue drill.

I was ninety-nine percent ready to take a short walk to the terminal and buy a seat on the next jet to Detroit. I had no sentimental attachment to our cranky little craft, and, more to the point, no more confidence in it, either. I told Dwayne that I had gotten back on after Teslin and Watson Lake by trusting God, but reboarding after the latest problem might amount to testing Him with the equivalent of a swan dive off the Temple.

158

Dwayne was very understanding. He assured me there would be no hurt feelings if I chose a different route home. After all, we agreed, he and Andrew were more comfortable with small planes and their quirks than I was.

But, Dwayne added, I would have to make a decision by about 11 a.m. Saturday.

"... Think of the life ..."

... There'll be time enough for countin,' when the dealin's done.
                                                    —"The Gambler"

Did you ever make a decision by not making a decision? By just waiting until it was no longer possible to make any choice but one?

I had plenty of time to think and pray Friday night and Saturday morning. I didn't have anything else to do. I certainly wasn't going to be of any use to Dwayne and Andrew, who were checking out the Cessna's circuits with the kind help of West Wind Aviation, which provided hangar space, tools and consultation.

I couldn't find any holes in my decision to bail out. By getting back on after Teslin, I felt I had already pushed the boundaries of what I could handle. I was too ignorant about aviation to sort out minor problems from real dangers. I didn't enjoy being afraid, and it was exhausting to be constantly summoning up the spiritual energy to keep fear at bay. Dwayne even admitted there was some danger inherent in flying small planes.

And yet ...

I had started this flight with Dwayne and Andrew, and it would be much more fun to finish it with them in Detroit than to arrive by myself, no longer part of the story. I was starting to know what they liked for breakfast. I was starting to share the rhythm of grabbing catnaps on airport couches, then scrambling aboard armed with a decent weather report and kicking the Cessna's 180 whining horses skyward into blue sanctuaries between passing storm fronts.

Sure, I could buy an airliner seat. But did that mean it was okay to start a journey on faith and trust, then buy my way out when faith and trust wore thin? Sure, safety is important. But even with the best piloting, maintenance and judgment, something can go wrong. A tiny piece of technology can fail, in a 747 as well as a Cessna. A weather system can move unpredictably. A safe situation can slide into a dangerous one, then out again. Should I step aside from living whenever the path is in shadow?

All this was swirling around in my head as we were driving around looking for parts. Dwayne called Winnipeg and located an alternator and voltage regulator we could pick up there.

Meanwhile, it occurred to me that time was getting short, and I still hadn't checked airline schedules. God, as usual, didn't answer my questions with Charlton Heston's voice in an echo chamber. He just made me think about something else Dwayne had said after acknowledging the risks of private aviation: "But think of the life you have!"

I was thinking about it when the three of us took off from Saskatoon about 11:30 a.m. under broken cloud cover, running nearly two hundred miles per hour before a stiff tailwind. Dwayne had hand-cranked the prop to start the engine. After takeoff chatter with the tower, we turned off the electricity to save the battery, then switched it back on for the final approach to Winnipeg.

I was still thinking about it when we left Winnipeg, fully operational at last. The Cessna banked like an amusement park ride that had slipped its moorings, and I thought of landscapes seen and still to come from a vantage point I'd never had before. I thought of unseen things known in a way I'd never known them before.

There were snow-covered mountains and silver rivers snaking through pine forests, all tilting and turning far below, the forest a rumpled white sheet dotted with tiny, dark-green spikes. There were endless cotton fields of clouds beneath our wings, touched with gold where the sun was sinking. There were flurries whipping past in the darkness, the snowflakes frozen into a million motionless sparks with each strobe-like blink of the wing lights. There was the approach to Midway Airport in Chicago, transformed by night into a black velvet field strewn with glowing jewels from horizon to horizon.

In the six days of our journey, from Alaska through the Yukon, from the prairies to the customs office at Grand Forks, from Minneapolis-St. Paul to Chicago and finally to a little airport outside Detroit, the unseen things that are the objects of faith remained invisible. But faith itself took more shape as it was used, a ghost-shield becoming half-visible in the hand, energized by trust, in constant exercise against fear. Emotionally, in my human skin, I couldn't fully possess the peace of Paul's win-win promise in Philippians: ... *to live is Christ and to die is gain.* But fifty-one percent is legal ownership.

Life is sweeter after you come close to losing it. I used to call that a cliché, but I'll call it something more respectful now, like a truth, because this time it happened to me. The sweetness remains even when the time

160

before the end is short, knowing that the end is a new beginning when time shall be no more.

So can you blame me if tears and laughter are a little closer to the surface now? Can you blame me if I waited a few minutes before helping unpack Cessna N1357U, which Andrew has since named "Lucky"? Soon after we landed, another little plane took off. And because I didn't know who was in it or where it was going, I was free to imagine any destiny for it. The one I imagined was, of course, the one I would wish for myself: to hold life firmly enough to keep it for awhile, but lightly enough for it to fly where my heart would go. I stood still until the little plane disappeared from sight and the drone of its engine passed beyond my hearing.

....

My adventure with Dwayne was over, for the time being. His was beginning a new dimension.

14. THE MISSION GROWS
Dispatches from Eurasia

Proclamation of the Gospel in Eurasia is the adrenaline that flows through the missionary's heart to bring people to Christ.
— Dwayne King,
Harvest Heartbeat, 2002

AS THE NEW HEAD of the biggest SEND territory on earth, Dwayne still gloried in riding the adventurous edge of the Great Commission. But he could be a practical realist in other ways, adjusting to changes ranging from post-Soviet shifts in Russian society to encouraging a new generation of missionaries.

Harvest Heartbeat, SEND's Eurasia newsletter, gives a blow-by-blow account of his new ministry. The May-June 2002 issue featured a trek that demonstrated one of Dwayne's permanent traits: unhesitating willingness to risk his hide and health on the front lines—in this case, a mission with a six-man Russian Baptist Gospel team in Siberia in the dead of winter. For three weeks in March, they traveled in the Buryatia region northeast of Lake Baikal, witnessing to Russians, Buryats, and Evenki reindeer herders. The only other Christian outreach, serving about 270,000 people in thirteen towns and villages, was a lone missionary from Moldova.

"This trip was the most challenging and dangerous of his life," states the newsletter—edited, thanks to Dwayne's persuasion, by Ann Lewis.

The team moved in a ground convoy, braving blizzards, snowdrifts, sketchy or nonexistent roads, broken-down bridges, frozen lakes, river crossings and mountain passes to reach tiny settlements and a few larger communities. They endured meager meals, little sleep and constant travel.

Dwayne, who became very sick, was the only American and SEND member on the team, and he had never been colder—even in Alaska.

A few days after that trip, while he and Canadian missionary John Wicker were visiting other villages in the area, they rescued a man who had fallen through river ice. John held on to Dwayne's legs while Dwayne pulled the man from the freezing water. While he warmed up in one of the convoy vehicles, he was asked if he believed in God.

"*Nyet* [no]," he replied.

Was he afraid?

"*Da* [yes]."

Why?

"When we die, there is God," the villager said.

"I will never be the same person," Dwayne wrote after the trip, calling it a "total immersion" in Russian language, culture and faith. "God has burdened me all the more for the importance of reaching Russia with the Gospel, and to see churches planted where there are none."

"The trip was worth every hardship," the newsletter concluded. Remote villagers met a man who had traveled around the world to tell them of God's love. Dwayne's own inspiration was revived, as it had been many times before, by working with national missionaries. Plans were made to organize a SEND team for the area.

Dwayne did not take part in an even more ambitious journey two years later, an effort to crisscross Russia in a caravan of four- to six-wheel-drive, off-road vehicles. "Miles were covered on winter trails and roads in order to reach the hidden people groups of Russia," he wrote, adding from his own experience that breakdowns were not necessarily a hindrance: "Sometimes, the best evangelism happens when you get stuck."

Freedom Flight Gets Bumpy

On short-term mission trips, SEND team leaders Don and Ann Lewis always got a laugh by reminding checklist-focused volunteers they had to be "flexible"—illustrating the reminder by flopping their arms and heads in a rubbery, boneless motion. On a bigger stage, flexibility was becoming increasingly vital for all mission efforts. The dramatic collapse of the Soviet Union was receding into the past, and the honeymoon of spiritual openness and official tolerance was cooling. "Since 1991," Dwayne wrote in the September-October 2002 *Harvest Heartbeat*,

> ... I've seen the methods of evangelism change. We began by drawing people to meetings by holding an American missionary out on a string

like bait. Good-looking Russian guys played guitar and sang to attract crowds. We saw Russians coming to Christ by the dozens. It was amazing to watch someone receive a Gospel tract, stop in his tracks and read every word. But in the mid-90s, I saw people take a tract, wad it up, and throw it down. Times were changing. Mass evangelism became more difficult.

The response, Dwayne wrote, included determined outreaches into remote areas, such as the 2002 and 2003-2004 expeditions, and "friendship evangelism," in which missionaries offered English classes and musical events to build personal bonds for presentation of the Gospel. "Clowning around," a circus-inspired Western technique, was catching on with many young Russian and Ukrainian evangelists. "It catches the attention of young and old, and shows that Christianity doesn't really fit the common stereotype."

Foreign and national missionaries worked together, using old as well as new evangelism tools. "We learned how to give and take with our Eurasian brothers and sisters," Dwayne wrote in 2002.

We have learned from them how to use the "old-fashioned ways" that still work there. Tent evangelism, putting up posters, traveling around town with loudspeakers, announcing meetings, and inviting folks out are proven methods ... in Eurasia. People walking the "sawdust" trail, repenting, and calling out to God for forgiveness are still witnessed there today ... and it happens every week somewhere across the former Soviet Union. We've been helping by buying tents and setting them up—or holding them down in the windstorms ...

Pastor Paul Blasko and many others have gone to teach in some of the twenty-four Bible colleges and seminaries. Street evangelism, surveys, and prayer walks have produced fruit that will last. The Gideons have been faithful to provide Bibles for millions of people.

On our trip across his new territory in 2000, Dwayne visited with SEND missionaries, absorbing their concerns and insights and commending their achievements. During a stop in Krasnoyarsk, Siberia,

... Chad Wiebe praised the "innocent, childlike faith" of many new believers, but worried about their vulnerability to cults and watered-down theology. He prayed for leaders with "pastor hearts" to strengthen their faith and knowledge during a period of spiritual ferment he likened to the Reformation in Europe centuries earlier.

Repeating a common SEND theme, John Wicker said foreign missionaries can best help as partners of Russian Baptists, under their church's leadership: "We want people who want to serve the Russian church. We don't want Great White Hunters coming to 'save' the Russians."

For missionaries, the high point of serving, the payoff, comes when God cycles through channels made smooth by love, faith, study and language training. At those times, there's no ambiguity at all. "This is the crowning moment of ministry," Dwayne said proudly while [missionary-teachers] James Leschied and Chad lectured in Russian at Krasnoyarsk Bible Institute. (From *Light*)

Dwayne and SEND missionary Dick Camp traveled to Moscow a few months later to help arrange the publication in Russia of *Practical Christian Theology* by the late Dr. Floyd Barackman, then a retired Practical Bible College professor. In the mid-1990s, Dwayne had successfully urged that the massive 930-page work, already in limited use at Far East Russia Bible College, be translated into Russian. Publication made it available throughout Russia and Ukraine, giving a valuable teaching tool to national and foreign mission workers alike.

In his travels, Dwayne also warned Russian church leaders to avoid a dependence mentality, urging them to trust God for help from many sources, not just one. He counseled them not to pray for American money, "just that God will provide for our needs from people around the world."

Ultimately, he stressed, it wasn't evangelism techniques, books or donations that changed hearts: "It is the power of the Gospel and the work of the Holy Spirit that produces the Harvest."

Ironically, as the climate of religious tolerance in Russia started to cool down, the vision of the Russian Baptist Union was warming up—thanks in part to its president, Yuri Sipko.

"It's one of the greatest privileges I've ever had in ministry to serve with such brothers as Yuri," wrote Dwayne. It's easy to see why he was excited about the Baptist Union's new leader, elected in 2003 to a four-year term. With a risk-taking personality similar to Dwayne's, Yuri staked out an ambitious vision for a society in which even the growing chill permitted more freedom than in Soviet times. A profile in *Harvest Heartbeat* states:

He realizes that now is the time for change and openness in order to reach all Russian and ethnic groups for Christ... "In one word, I want to see churches not closed in on themselves, but part of society, where church members are preaching the word of God everywhere," Sipko said [during a visit to New York State in February 2003].

In his early 50s, his rugged aspect accentuated by new Levis and a gray work shirt acquired on the obligatory American shopping pilgrimage, the former laborer shared a vision of outreach that has not only survived, but prevailed over, a century darkened by mass murder playing out into a continuing twilight of state-imposed harassment and limitation.

... Sipko envisioned "all kinds of ministries," including top-to-bottom education and outreaches to children, teens and the elderly. He spoke of developing prayer groups and leaders "who can reach hunters, intellectuals... We are doing this now with help from Americans. My great desire is to make our churches be missionary churches."

His vision for the next several years embraces evangelization, home visits, church construction teams and foreign missions.

Investments in Eternity

... my word ... will not return to me empty.

—Isaiah 55:11

In 2004, Dwayne compared training Eurasian church leaders to building a Boeing 747: "taking millions of pieces, small and large, to make it fly. But man oh man, when that baby lifts off with all those passengers and cargo and flies so far away, it is so amazing!"

Since SEND began working in Eurasia, twenty-four SEND-supported seminaries, colleges and Bible institutes had graduated well over a thousand students. They scattered across the former Soviet Union, and a few went beyond. Dwayne called SEND's outlays for construction, operating expenses and volunteer teachers "very minimal" in light of the number and quality of Christian leaders produced.

Combining faith and caution, he added, "The total impact of this effort ... may not be felt for many years." SEND's leadership training was only one part of its program, which *Harvest Heartbeat* reported as including about seventy long-term missionaries, twenty-one short-term teams in 2002, and plans for nearly thirty such teams in 2005.

None of the work of foreign missions could have been done without a living body of believers to work with, testimony to the endurance and dreams represented by the Baptist Union's approximately seventeen hundred churches in 2005. If Yuri Sipko's vision "seems ambitious," *Harvest Heartbeat* commented in the May-June 2003 issue,

> ... consider how far the evangelicals have already come. Soviet authorities once turned [Sipko's church in Omsk] into a stable. When Communism ended, the Baptist Union numbered fewer than three hundred churches serving fewer than twenty-four thousand believers in all of Russia. Inspired by SEND and other international helpers, and their own dynamic of spiritual survival, Russian evangelicals have quadrupled those numbers into a light that promises to someday shine beyond the borders of their vast land.

Dwayne's brother Dave, called by God (with Dwayne's help) to Russia, was impressed with the quality of the SEND missionaries he ministered to in Siberia. "These servants of God are not wimpy, sad, discouraged, or wounded warriors of the cross." But, he added, they were not supermen or women, either:

> Do missionaries experience loneliness, frustration, and the need to rediscover God's *joy*? Missionaries are people just like the rest of us. They have bad hair days, get tired, and experience situations that we will never experience in our entire lifetime. Missionaries live behind triple doors with triple locks, live in a culture where crime, muggings, and theft are a normal way of life... Sometimes they just want to see green grass for a change and not the dirt and dust outside their apartments. (*Harvest Heartbeat*, July-August 2003)

"Been there. Done that," Dwayne wrote of his own experience. "God has given me terrific opportunities and thrilling experiences." But, he added, it was time to find others who would "go there and do that, too."

Even under ideal conditions, he recognized, missionaries don't live forever or multiply miraculously. And, there were growing signs in Russia that those from other countries would not always be welcomed by the government. There would have to be more missionaries, and more of them would eventually have to come from their own native land.

"We need to mobilize many, many more effective missionaries to do their part in the great spiritual harvest God is sustaining across Eurasia," Dwayne said. He urged anyone who would listen to use the tools of prayer, persuasion and offers of monetary support to bring in friends and relatives. "Maybe," he concluded in the newsletter, "God is calling *you* to go."

But it would be those born in Russia and other lands of the former Soviet Union who would make the difference. Eurasian evangelicals told Dwayne the future of the church depended on equipping children. Not so many years before, they told him, children in an earlier generation had played a part in helping the church survive into the present.

> During the years of Communist control in Eurasia, children were not allowed to be in any church programs. Gennady [then chief Baptist Union pastor in the Far East] and Vera Abramov tell stories of how they taught their children anyway. When the authorities found out, they often raided the homes where such activity was going on. Young people would sometimes stand in the way of the authorities' vehicles so those responsible for teaching ... could not be hauled off to jail. One courageous young believer and her friends all crammed into the police car so there was no room for the youth leader to be hauled off. (*Harvest Heartbeat*, May-June 2004)

"Today, children's ministries are flourishing all across the Eurasia field," Dwayne said in the May-June issue, praising those involved in instructing Sunday School teachers and other children's workers: Vonnie Howard, Eileen Starr, Lena Sidenko, Chris Richie, Steve Hostetter, and Steve and Nancy Wooden. "I have listened to the stories of children whose lives have been changed because a Bible camp was provided for them to hear the Gospel."

Kazakhstan: "Four Miracles in 48 Hours"

I told the airline pilots I couldn't get a ticket. They said,
"No problem! You fly with us in cockpit."
—Dwayne King

A major target of SEND's Eurasia outreach was Kazakhstan, the second biggest country in the former Soviet Union. It's one of the places that enhanced Dwayne's reputation for chutzpah and improvisation, especially in the art of finagling transportation.

Missionary Garry McDowall called the Central Asian country a land of "tremendous opportunity" for the Christian community, having the world's ninth largest national land mass and about seventeen million people representing more than 130 ethnicities. Islam is predominant, with evangelicals comprising only .15 percent of the population, but increasing, he said in the September 2005 *Harvest Heartbeat*.

SEND decided in 2002 to open a ministry there, and Dwayne and Carolyn visited in 2004 to start planning a team to work under the leadership of the Kazakhstan Baptist Union. But first there had to be a feasibility study, and that's where Dwayne's talents came in handy.

He did some scouting alone in 2001 and sent back glowing reports. SEND then sent along the rest of the feasibility committee: Eurasia Co-Director Carl Kresge, Ukraine Director Everett Henderson, U.S. Director Dave Wood and missionary Chris Richie.

They met in Atyrau, in western Kazakhstan, with Baptist Union President Franz Tiessen and Pavel Hagalgund, the director of a German mission. The group then went to the airport to fly to Uralsk, in the northwest, for more meetings. Franz and Pavel already had tickets, and that's when things got complicated.

Here's how Dwayne tells it:

Franz goes to the counter and tries to get five more tickets. The clerk says, "No more tickets. The plane is full." The group decides that if she can find one more ticket, Dwayne will be the one to go with Franz and Pavel. They all pray.

Franz returns to the counter for another try, this time with Dwayne, but the woman repeats, "There are no more spaces! NO! NEIN! NYET!" Franz and Pavel tell the group, "Let's just pray that God will take the two tickets and make them into three"—you know, like Loaves and Tickets—"Miracles happen, and we ARE apostles ..."

"I prayed like an American," Dwayne recalls. "Lord, give the plane a flat tire so passengers will leave. Let the plane break so they'll send a bigger plane." They hear the boarding announcement and the three of them go to the gate. Pavel hands the lady the two tickets.

"All three together?"

"Yes."

"But you only have two tickets!" (Pavel and Franz must be thinking that they'll bud like Aaron's Rod into three tickets) "... only two of you can go!"

It becomes evident that Dwayne isn't the only creative spirit in the group. Franz—or maybe it was Pavel—says, "This American has to go with us... He's a famous Alaska bush pilot—another . . . CHUCK YEAGER! ... He knows—YURI GAGARIN!" [Russia's first cosmonaut]

The ticket-taker replies, "Ohh! Our pilots would like to meet him!" She takes them to the ramp of the Antonov 24, a forty-eight passenger turboprop, and they talk to the four pilots. Dwayne shows them pictures of planes and flying in Alaska. The airport is about the size of the Tri-Cities Airport, a small field in Endicott, New York, but there are four big corporate jets lined up at the ramp—from the OPEC nations, British Petroleum, and Chevron. Dwayne tells the Antonov pilots he's flown one of them.

By now, almost everyone has boarded, including Pavel and Franz. The pilots tell Dwayne, "We must go now. Are you on flight?" He tells them he can't get a ticket. They say, "No problem! You fly with us in cockpit."

"We had a great time," Dwayne says, talking aviation and trading autographs. That night in Uralsk, he adds, "We told the people in the church how God provided a miracle."

MIRACLE NUMBER ONE!

The next leg will be a twelve-hour train trip to Aktyubinsk, but for five hours the train will cut through a piece of Russia—for which Pavel and Dwayne do not have visas. Pavel asks the station lady what will happen if they get on the train without them. She says that at the Russian border, they'll be kicked off in the middle of nowhere, and if they make it into Russia and get caught, they'll be thrown in jail—"Big risk!"

They pray. The brothers are afraid, but Dwayne tells them he's willing to go because God sometimes blinds the eyes of the police. They buy tickets and board.

The train stops at the Russian border at night, and they hear the guards coming down the aisle to check documents. The guards go into the compartment next to theirs. "We were quietly praying in the dark," Dwayne recalls. Then there's a loud ruckus next door, and they're still arguing when the train whistle blows. The guards run off the train without checking the missionaries' compartment, or the remaining ones.

... MIRACLE NUMBER TWO!

Early next morning the train stops again before re-entering Kazakhstan, but before the next set of guards can reach their compartment, an elderly Kazakh vendor beats them to it. She's selling kumis (fermented mare's milk), camel-hair belts—which supposedly have curing properties—and camel-hair socks. Dwayne buys a belt for Carolyn's back problems.

A pair of guards tries to push the vendor away from the doorway. "I was scared," Dwayne says. "I figured this is where we go to jail—but this little old babushka stood her ground!" By this time, she's trying to sell him socks and kumis. The guards say "ladna! [Okay!]"—and go on to the next compartment. "I was ready to buy anything she had!" Dwayne says.

The whistle blows and the guards jump off, and the train continues into Kazakhstan.

... MIRACLE NUMBER THREE!

Another leg of the trip, another name-dropping story. But this one is true, Dwayne insists. They take a cab to the Aktyubinsk airport to get tickets to Almaty, the country's biggest city, but all flights are full. Dwayne tells the airport people that Don Bell, a big mission supporter and CEO of Bell Aviation, wants him to buy planes from the Kazakhstan airline for Kingdom Air Corps, Dwayne's missionary pilot training center in Alaska.

The employees tell the group to go see the president of the airline. They do, and Dwayne is impressed. "Wowee! He had this big office with mahogany paneling, five phones on his desk," Dwayne says. "We were joking and looking at pictures of pilots in Alaska. He was calling everywhere to get us a ride on a plane or helicopter. But no luck."

They go back to the counter, hoping and praying for three tickets. The clerk gets mad and shuts the curtain. The boarding announcement sounds from the loudspeaker and everyone leaves for the plane. The mission group overhears the clerk answer her phone: "Da! Da! [Yes! Yes!] ... THE AMERICAN IS STILL HERE." The president comes striding into the terminal and grabs them. He escorts them past security to the plane, puts Franz in a jumpseat, Pavel in the cargo hold behind the passenger cabin, and Dwayne, of course, in the cockpit.

... MIRACLE NUMBER FOUR!

That night they tell the church at Almaty about four miracles in forty-eight hours. There is much rejoicing.

By September 2005, SEND missionaries were either in place or soon would be: Garry and Kim McDowall, Michelle Gillespie, Chris Richie, Don and Esther Parsons, and Julia Potter. Dwayne and Carolyn went to Kazakhstan next month for a three-month stay, to help the team get started in church planting and evangelism in partnership with Kazakh Christian leaders.

The McDowalls began ministry where an earlier generation of Kazakh Christians had blazed a trail years earlier. Alpha & Omega Baptist Church in Almaty, founded in 1931, had about six hundred members in 2005 and had planted nearly thirty other churches since its inception. Garry said SEND's goal was to help the Baptist Union develop Kazakh ministry "today and years into the future." However, he warned in the September 2005 *Harvest Heartbeat*, changes in the country's ironically named "Freedom of Religion Act" signaled that the road ahead would not be easy.

Christianity today in Kazakhstan is under high scrutiny, especially since the passing of several new amendments... The new amendments have and will put many restrictions on the Christian community in the areas of evangelism, especially among the Kazakhs. One of the primary restrictions limits drastically the distribution of Christian literature.

In the April 2006 newsletter, Dwayne stressed the urgency of the mission task in a context that went beyond earthly politics: "As we see the day of Jesus Christ approaching, we should all increase our commitment to reach the nations with the message of redemption before it's too late."

His commitment to that cause would increasingly focus him back into the sky.

Part 5

"OPEN THE SKY"

Advancing Mission Aviation

Dwayne and Kostya, the young Russian professor and pilot trainee, were pleading the case for general and mission aviation to the stony-faced vice president of the Transportation University.

"We prayed that as God had broken down the wall, He will open up the sky," Kostya said. As he and Dwayne prayed, Kostya watched the official's face intently: "All his life he was a Communist and he's hearing all this Christian stuff!"

The vice president's expression softened. "He was okay. His face was good," Kostya recalls. "He said, 'Let's do this!'"

—Khabarovsk, Russia
March 2006

Russia has restructured its airspace in a move that's bound to foster more GA [general aviation] activity, pledging to reduce the amount of closed and restricted airspace ....

—Av*web* aviation news service,
November 2, 2010

15. KINGDOM AIR CORPS
Passing the Torch

They took off from the King Ranch and headed north beyond the Arctic Circle for the Brooks Range Bible Camp with no extra aviation fuel, no extra money, and no guarantee that any children would show up.

— Kingdom Air Corps Bible
Camp mission, 2006

... as they fly so far from home,
you can hear their loved ones pray,
"God give them strength and wisdom
keep them through another day."

—Hal Farrar poem,
"Missionary Pilot"

A TURNING POINT that Dwayne saw on the horizon at the 1991 missions conference became a reality nine years later. It was time to prepare the next generation. Starting in 2000, he made his first love—aviation—his latest gift: training young men and women to carry the Word on wings to souls beyond the reach of roads. The result was Kingdom Air Corps (KAC).

KAC trainees at Brooks Range Bible Camp: summer 2010

Before there was an air corps, there had to be an airfield. A few years earlier, his son Dave began carving one out of 160 acres of forest he had acquired in 1996 on the Matanuska River in the Chugach range northeast of Anchorage. Dwayne, who shares part of what became known as the King Ranch, later came to help. "Bud" Austin, former president of LeTourneau University, recalls trying to keep up with him.

> We started cutting trees... Of course, in the Alaskan summer, the sun sets only for a short time. We would start early in the morning and cut all day, stopping only for some nourishment. We would cut, step back and look, and Dwayne would say, "Oh, look at the tops of those trees! We should get those out of the way for a safe departing plane," so we would cut another twenty or thirty. I thought it time to stop, as it was 10 p.m., but he would say, "Let's take another look ... got to get those so we can take off out of here tomorrow." So down came more—and it went on and on. Over the years, we have lengthened and widened the flight path by removing trees, grading, making it a safer environment from which to operate and train. But this reflects Dwayne's spirit: "just a few more."

KAC trainees learn to fly in mountains (above),
fog (below) and everything in between.

Another of Dwayne's qualities prompted an insight from another old friend. "Dwayne is not locked into one little experience or responsibility," said Paul Blasko. That flexibility makes for some odd juxtapositions, one of which I encountered on the first day of a visit to KAC in August 2006.

Dwayne was out bear hunting with one of his two guests, an Iranian Jewish man, Soheil Najibi, an orthopedic surgeon. The other guest was Soheil's fiancée, Jerilyn Latini, Dwayne's urologist who had treated him after his prostate surgery. *Where but in Alaska with Dwayne King,* I thought, *would it seem perfectly natural for a Baptist missionary to go bear hunting with the fiancé of his prostate doctor?*

And where else, in who else's narrative, would it seem perfectly natural for a long-serving missionary in his 60s to reject the notion of a well-earned

177

retirement, and pour his energy and expertise into a wilderness flight school for students ranging from their 20s down to well under voting age? In 2008, 15-year-old intern Lydia Fairchild, boarding an airliner in New York State for her first trip to KAC, was chagrined that her parents had decided she was too young to travel without a flight attendant assigned to watch over her.

Not the Air Force Academy

In 2006, KAC, despite its name, wasn't operating out of some spit-and-polish complex of barracks, offices, paved runways, and hangars full of late-model planes. As often as not, 27-year-old Angela Parrish, a third-year trainee, had to chase her dogs, Blaze and Riley, off the grass airstrip before taking off in one of school's donated vintage Cessnas.

The nerve center, then Dwayne's garage, looked more like a trapper's cabin than an Air Force Academy classroom. Perched against a backdrop of snowcapped mountains and warmed by a wood stove on chilly, late-summer mornings, the work space was littered with wilderness tools and communications gear. A shiny section of airplane wing dominated one wall. Dusty binoculars and a welder's helmet hung from caribou and deer antlers. On the workbench were boxes of .308 and .30-30 rifle shells aimed at keeping the freezer full. Dwayne's young air cadets, dressed in the uniform of the day—jeans, flannel shirts, hiking boots or sneakers—tossed firewood into the stove and huddled over laptops and steaming coffee. "Our garage has gone from Internet Café to Situation Room," Carolyn quipped.

The Kings' garage (left) was KAC's first center of operations.

"We're planning sixteen things to do tomorrow," said Dwayne. Paul Blasko's account of a typical day suggested that wasn't much of an overstatement.

I'd see him bringing devotions to [trainees], giving them specific work assignments, counseling a young man who'd failed in a responsibility (holding him accountable, but still believing in him), salvaging from a wrecked plane one tiny screw that would be just right for a plane he and the students were rebuilding (teaching them you can't make equipment compromises), and explaining to me the workings and purposes of KAC—as he no doubt does for any visitor—to share the vision.

Another typical day found Dwayne assigning students to mow the runway, pressure-wash Carolyn's truck and finish drywalling a room in the new hangar. Between fielding phone calls about the Kazakhstan ministry and KAC business, he gave welding lessons, showed trainees how to salvage a damaged propeller and checked out one young man's flying skills.

He credits the Russian pastor's son, Daniil Marchenko, and his own son, Dave, with inspiring him to transform two long-held visions into the reality of the new ministry.

"It's always been a strong vision to see mission aviation in the former Soviet Union—and I was passionate about preparing missionaries to live and fly in the Alaskan wilderness," Dwayne explained. "I want to leave people who'll carry on the work I gave my life to. I want to spend more time in Alaska, training and mentoring missionary pilots. When I began training Daniil at the King Ranch in 1999, I realized this could be the training base."

KAC's grass runway with Matanuska River in background

179

In addition to the site, Dave and Katrina—then his wife—contributed enthusiastic support. Their daughter Briana, then 15, contributed the name. The working relationship between father and son is a good fit, practically and spiritually. Dave's business, Last Frontier Air Ventures, has offered a variety of back-country helicopter services, and he and Katrina felt strongly that the property ought to be dedicated to the Lord. They wanted to reach people for Christ in whatever venture they undertook—preferably humanitarian missions using large transports and helicopters. Dave and Dwayne share equipment and expertise in their respective missions.

A few KAC newcomers learn aviation from scratch, but most already have some experience and all are committed to missionary flying. The majority are in their early 20s, licensed in various aviation specialties, and are graduates of schools ranging from small Bible colleges to major evangelical centers like Moody Bible Institute, Columbia International University and LeTourneau. A few are from Russia, and the current roster includes two Alaskan Eskimo trainees. Typically, twenty-five interns spend two months at the school between early May and late September, for two or three years. The operation is funded by their donations, the Kings and other supporters.

Trainees learn real-world mission aviation skills: mountain flying, bush operations, and judging the limits of their equipment and themselves. That means catching ascending winds over mountains to save fuel, avoiding dangerous downdrafts, and making repairs when no mechanics or hangars are available. They learn to land and take off on short airstrips or no airstrips, using mountain tops or gravel bars. They learn navigation, which a LeTourneau student defined in very practical terms: "How to tell if you're going to clear the ridge!"

Trainee Mike Palmiter services plane.

On breaks, recreation is what might be expected in Alaska: hiking, camping, mountain climbing, hunting and fishing. The atmosphere is intimate, not institutional. Tired students sprawl like family over the furniture in the Kings' living room, inhaling a late supper of pizza, soda and leftover dessert. Dwayne sits next to them, inscribing "Solo/King Ranch/2005" T-shirts for those who, in the previous year, have taken the giant step of flying alone for the first time.

KAC's mission, as described in its brochure, is a distillation of his experience and beliefs.

> We teach our interns that their love of airplanes and flying is not the end result, but that airplanes are tools to use in winning souls for the Lord. Each intern will participate in village ministries, including witnessing, church planting, and organizing Bible camps for Alaska Native children, displaying a willing servant attitude.

Heartbeat of the Mission

The new nerve center of KAC is the hangar office, but the heart is the dining hall, next to the runway. The big, log-walled hall and kitchen is where students grab coffee, study, nap, and play songs on the keyboard, and where everyone gathers for the after-breakfast devotional hour. Dwayne sets the tone, hears reports and issues marching orders for the day. They're not the types of lessons and announcements that could be expected at a typical church in the Lower 48.

As antlered trophies of the hunt look down from the walls, Dwayne occasionally has to remind his students of the message in the brochure. He tells them to stay focused on God's purpose and not get sidetracked by the sheer excitement of learning an adventurous craft in a spectacular setting.

Dwayne (left) and trainees share a prayer.

For the newcomer or occasional visitor, however, the pizzazz offers powerful images and experiences that engage the emotions and lead quickly to a deeper appreciation of KAC's spiritual mission. I tried to express that appreciation—first, to the trainees at a morning devotional during a visit in July 2010, then, a few weeks later, at Twin Orchards:

> Going to Alaska in July is a dirty job, but somebody's got to do it. To say that Kingdom Air Corps has beautiful mountains, old planes, nice kids and Dwayne's dynamic personality—that doesn't quite do it justice. Think of Moses and Peter on their mountains, overwhelmed by the glory they saw. And for those of you who love pilot movies, the title of a KAC movie could be *Dawn Patrol and Top Gun Meet the Book of Acts*. It's like being initiated into some clean-mouthed college fraternity where the wind from the Matanuska Glacier blows all the nastiness right out of your head.
>
> By now, you're probably thinking like the snotty Major Winchester in *M*A*S*H*: "Should there by any chance be a point to all this, I wish you'd get to it!" Well, this is the point: KAC is having a powerful spiritual impact on me ...
>
> When I started my research on this book five years ago, I didn't think anything interesting would happen inside me. I had reached a good, proper level of Christian spirituality, and I didn't need any more, thank you! And I was going to write a book about a great Christian, and that was nice, and that was all there was to it. Well, you can imagine how that tickled God's funny bone . . .
>
> And just in case God needed to draw me a picture, He brought me up here to KAC. When you're next to these gigantic, cloud-covered, snow-capped mountains, watching a bunch of really good kids learning to serve God under the shepherding of some kind of spirit-filled NASCAR ace bush pilot—if you can remain unmoved by this, you've got a flat EKG. And if you predicted ten years ago that I would actually enjoy riding in a very small plane with a student at the controls, doing touch-and-go landings and takeoffs, and getting close enough to the cliffs to spit in a mountain goat's eye—I would've said you were a couple of tacos short of a combination plate.
>
> And for those of us who are old enough to have parents in the generation that flew P-40 Warhawks with Claire Chennault's Flying Tigers in China, or Spitfires and Hurricanes in the Battle of Britain, and you see Dwayne's young pilots taxiing down grass runways and roaring into the sky toward a different kind of battle—if you can watch that without getting goose bumps, there's something wrong with your heart.
>
> Fifty years from now, our descendants can say of these kids what English poet Stephen Spender said of an earlier generation—words

that can apply to anyone who dares greatly for God or country. Spender wrote:

> *I think continually of those who were truly great ...*
> *[Who] never ... allow gradually the traffic*
> *To smother with noise and fog the flowering of the spirit.*
>
> *... Near the snow, near the sun, in the highest fields*
> *See how these names are feted by the waving grass*
> *And by the streamers of white cloud*
> *And whispers of wind in the listening sky;*
> *The names of those who in their lives fought for life*
> *Who wore at their hearts the fire's center.*
> *Born of the sun they traveled a short while toward the sun*
> *And left the vivid air signed with their honor.*

So thanks, God ... and Dwayne, for the good words that are shrinking my doubts into a size that's too small to wear. And thanks to you young pilots for being doers of the Word, pushing out the perimeter of the Kingdom toward a horizon that's big enough to fit everyone.

"... roaring into the sky toward a different kind of battle..."

During another devotional, Dwayne spoke of some distinctive witnessing techniques and occasions for prayer. He described an encounter at an Anchorage pizza shop, where he stopped to buy a snack for himself and two visitors he had picked up at the airport. The visitors waited outside in Dwayne's truck while he went in to order a pizza. The counterman, whom Dwayne described as a rough-looking "skinhead" type, had a tattoo of a cross entwined in barbed wire.

Dwayne told him, "Somebody proud enough to wear a tattoo should be proud enough to explain what it means."

The counterman replied, "I believe in the cross!"

"So do I," Dwayne said. "But a lot of people just *wear* a cross ..."

"All people are children of God," the counterman shot back, to which Dwayne replied, "Without repentance, there is no forgiveness."

Dwayne recalled that he began to wonder if it was wise to continue a conversation that seemed to be growing confrontational.

"Who are you?" the counterman demanded.

That opened up the dialogue. The counterman stepped outside for a cigarette. Dwayne explained his mission, introduced him to the visitors and invited him to visit KAC.

In another example of using an apparently negative situation as an opportunity to witness, Dwayne talked with a pair of trainees who were planning a one-day flight to Anaktuvuk Pass. There was some discussion about a foul-weather prediction for the far northern village. Dwayne advised them to tie down the plane securely, then offered some startling advice.

"Get stuck," he told them. "Stay overnight. It's really good to get stuck in the village. Drink tea and talk with the kids." He called the process "Letting God work."

During the same devotional, he stressed the importance of prayer in what he acknowledged was a sometimes risky enterprise. He spoke of Carolyn's prayers for him, whether he was flying on a routine errand or training a student in emergency maneuvers.

"How many times has Carolyn breathed a prayer when that [Cessna] 206 roars overhead? You know how many times my wife's prayed me back home? Do you think she knows what's going on when I go out with one of you guys and I pull the power?" he asked, referring to idling the engine to simulate an engine failure. "Her heart jumps—*Is that engine failure for real?*"

Hal and Sherron Farrar

Hal Farrar, to whom Dwayne had flown coffee and warm cinnamon rolls on the Glenn Highway years before, invoked the purpose that made the risks acceptable. The rugged 84-year-old sang "Missionary Pilot," Christian songwriter Ruben Hillborn's tribute to all who fly for God in the Far North:

> *LORD, grant him a safe journey, as he flies for you today,*
> *Give him strength and wisdom, I heard his dear wife pray.*
> *O'er the great land of Alaska, in his own humble way*
> *As a Missionary Pilot, he serves the LORD today.*
>
> *Out across the frozen tundra, in the distance I can see,*
> *Wings glisten in the sunshine, as he climbs over the mountain peaks.*
> *But it isn't always sunny, for some days the clouds are low,*
> *And the passes fill with snow squalls, as on the deck you go.*

185

I've watched them follow rivers; every turn, yes, every bend.
You can reach and touch the willows, as he puts that plane
on in.
For a hundred miles an hour, the ground zooms by below;
And you wonder just how anyone could see through all that
snow.

As you approach the village, you're blessed by a cross wind.
Wings shudder in the turbulence, he holds her steady then.
One last look out the window, as he puts that plane on in,
What a glorious sound as you touch down; you're back on
earth again.

Yes, winter, summer, spring or fall, you'll find him in the air.
Preaching, praying, working hard, as God's love he shares.
O'er the great land of Alaska, in his own humble way,
As a Missionary Pilot, he serves the LORD today...

Isaiah (40:31) had the last word. Dwayne and the students ended the devotional with a prayer for the success of an upcoming Bible Camp, a high point in the training program: ... *those who hope in the Lord will renew their strength. They will soar on wings like eagles ...*

Downtime: Lydia Fairchild (above) bandages trainee
Pete Spear's arm; Dwayne and trainees (next page) enjoy a story.

186

On Wings and Prayers

Throughout his career, Dwayne has used the in-your-face reality of mission assignments to transform lives—not only the lives of those he serves, but those he trains, and an occasional awed bystander as well. The annual Bible camp for Native Alaskan children in the Brooks Range, north of Bettles, is no exception.

The July 2006 session was more challenging than usual. Dwayne and eight young pilots set out in seven planes to organize the two-week session. They took off from the KAC airstrip with no extra aviation fuel, no extra money, and no guarantee that any kids would show up. An overprotective soccer mom in the Lower 48 probably would have been horrified by the *make-it-up-as-you-go-along* unpredictability, both for the trainees and the kids. But the trainees had a different perspective. For them, the assignment was a typical exercise in faith and hands-on experience.

However, this trip threatened to be exceptionally unpredictable. While camping out during a stopover in Fairbanks, the team quickly learned that the session at Brooks Range Bible Camp might have to be scrubbed. They had planned to earn gas money for the rest of the trip by inspecting and repairing planes for some local pilots. Unfortunately, an old friend of Dwayne's who was supposed to have lined up the jobs—Dave Chaussé—had been unable to do so.

Dave could have shrugged his shoulders and walked away. But when he saw his own faith being lived out by the young pilots, he did something else. He told them, "Here's my credit card. I'll buy the gas." Dwayne replied in amazement, "Gas for seven planes, two weeks flying in the Arctic? That's two thousand—three thousand—dollars!"

Dave simply repeated, "I'll buy the gas."

Trainee fuels one of KAC's planes.

The challenges weren't over yet. The children were supposed to be assembled at Bettles, but none showed up. So the team flew three planes sixty miles downriver to two other villages, and another old friend, an Athabaskan man, came to the rescue. He offered to collect willing children in his pickup truck. Unfortunately, the pickup was out of gas, so the KAC team siphoned five gallons from one of the planes—enough for him to shuttle five loads of kids to the local airstrip, where Dwayne flew them in small groups to the Bible campsite. (The hypothetical soccer mom would have been relieved to know that the kids were flown in only by Dwayne, not his trainees.)

The campers seemed to be multiplying like loaves and fishes. After each truckload and plane ride, more would appear, asking, "Can we come too?" Some were brought to the airstrip by their parents, who themselves had been led to the Lord by Dwayne and Carolyn more than twenty years earlier.

"God gave us twenty-one kids," Dwayne said. As for the camp, "We threw it together Dwayne-style." A chuckle emerged from his audience, twenty-five or so worshippers in the log-walled sanctuary of Mendeltna Community Chapel, up the road from the King Ranch. They knew their man. The young pilots and mechanics "sang a lot of songs, witnessed to the kids, played in the tundra and climbed mountains," Dwayne recalls. Some of the kids were undisciplined, especially two teenage boys. But the night before the campers were to be flown back to their villages, one of the "bad actors" tugged on his sleeve and said, "Dwayne—*we accepted Jesus last night.*"

"About eight kids gave their hearts to Christ," he said. "One of them told me, 'This is what I want to do with my life.'"

For Lydia Fairchild and other trainees, KAC is not a one-time experience that they or those they serve can walk away from. Lydia—then from Vestal, Dwayne's home town—returned in the summer of 2009. But this time, she reported happily, there was no babysitter in the jetliner—and no instructor sitting next to her in the flight school's Cessna 152. At age 16, she accomplished a milestone of aviation training: her first solo flight.

Before Lydia left for Alaska, her pastor—Rev. Kyle Kaurin, who succeeded Paul Blasko at Twin Orchards—asked, "Didn't you get enough adventure last time?"

She answered by repeating what a neglected girl had told her on her previous trip: "I really wish you could come back and be my mom." Lydia spoke of other children raised in loveless families scarred by alcohol, drugs and near-poverty. She spoke of old superstitions and their paralyzing effect on children. "They're very scared of everything," she said. "We show them that God is bigger than the bogeyman."

Discipleship must be continually reinforced or the momentum and the lessons will be lost, eroded by peer pressure and the absence of role models at home, Lydia explained. She, like Dwayne, told of occasional dramatic victories—the acceptance of Christ by another troubled teen on the last day of the camp.

That's why she keeps coming back.

Slices of Alaska: moose calf (upper left) outside Dwayne's house; Tom Cobb (upper right), KAC missionary and maintenance worker, alert for bear near kitchen; Dwayne (lower left) welcoming youngster visiting KAC; takeoff practice (lower right)

16. "OPERATION OPEN DOOR"
Another Historic Flight

He can open doors where nobody else could.
He's opening a big one now.
> —Ann Lewis,
> missions colleague

We got work to do, kid!
> —Dwayne to Russian assistant
> before Khabarovsk flight

R EWIND TO 1991: Dwayne was poised in Alaska for a short flight
to a land struggling to wake up from a long, dark winter. He took no
credit for being in the right place at the right time, giving God the glory
for the strategic positioning of His servants. He would continue moving
out beyond the Providenya bridgehead, walking point for hundreds of mission workers who gave up their time, treasure and comfort to help Russian
brothers and sisters heal and enlarge the evangelical church.

Fast-forward to 2006: Dwayne was poised in Alaska for another flight,
this time with a different purpose. The night was coming down again.
SEND's work was being increasingly crippled by government restrictions
throughout the former Soviet Union. In a few more years, the mission
organization would shut down its operations in Far East Russia. However,
Dwayne didn't see this as a defeat. Thanks in part to what the missionaries
had already accomplished, he reasoned, the Russian church had become
strong enough to keep alive the spark beneath the snow until, in God's
good time, spring would come again.

But spiritual birth, like physical birth, couldn't be frozen in mid-labor, waiting for another political contraction. A harvest still remained to be gathered in, even though it wouldn't be foreign missionaries doing the gathering. In vast areas of Siberia and the Far East, tens of thousands of souls, representing nearly 140 nationalities, had no access to the Gospel. The road network was nearly nonexistent. Travelers depended on rivers in the summer and, in the winter, drove old tracked vehicles on ice roads through taiga and tundra.

"These are real people, but you can't get there," Dwayne said. "It's only by flying."

It was time to look to the sky.

Dwayne's mission, as he understood God's leading, was to fill the sky with hope in the form of pilots leapfrogging the Gospel over remote stretches of wilderness and supporting church workers on the ground. It was the same work he had done in Alaska years before, only now it would be carried on by others—Kingdom Air Corps-trained fliers (Russian politics permitting), and in any case, by increasing numbers of Russians themselves.

But before mission aviation could take off, there had to be a network of general, or private, aviation—which, like a good road system, was also nearly nonexistent. Marlin Beachy, pastor of Glacier View Church and an Alaskan mission volunteer, recalls working on the roof of a church in the Far East in the early 2000s. A small plane passed overhead and the Russians ran outside to stare at the strange sight. "No one sees small planes," Marlin said.

"We are the sowers," Dwayne told his KAC trainees in 2006. "A spearhead that will open the way."

Winning Hearts and Opening Wallets

The spearhead, he had decided, would be a 2,400-mile flight from Alaska to Khabarovsk, demonstrating to Russians the feasibility of general aviation. The flight, a first for Dwayne on that route, would be technically difficult. So would the preparation. He had to drum up support in two countries, find a plane and crew, absorb a mass of Russian aviation protocols, and—by far the biggest hurdle—secure approvals from the Russian bureaucracy.

Dwayne shared his vision in forums ranging from small Alaskan churches to a major university in Far East Russia. In the Mendeltna chapel, eight days before the planned September 4, 2006, takeoff, he summed up the years of prayer and months of preparation. He opened with a rousing chorus of "Victory in Jesus" and greeted his and Carolyn's old friends from the bush pilot years. Then he unleashed his not-so-secret weapon,

KAC trainee Konstantin A. "Kostya" Rudoy. At 31, Kostya held a doctorate in physics and taught at Khabarovsk's Transportation University— where, ironically, interest in private, peaceful aviation was centered in the Military Sports Club.

Their first meeting, in a hallway at Kostya's church in Khabarovsk, had been memorable. Kostya, wearing an expensive flier's jacket, strode up to Dwayne and announced, "Dvayne Keeng! I vant to be meessionair peelot!" Already a strong Christian witness at the university, he visited Alaska several times and, under Dwayne's instruction, became an excellent pilot. Dwayne's work and Kostya's position opened up numerous aviation contacts, and their eloquence softened Russian and American hearts.

At the Mendeltna chapel, Kostya drilled through the statistics with an image of one man and one church, telling the Alaskans of an encounter in his homeland. The man was a homeless beggar and the church was Kostya's church, Transformation Baptist, founded in 1992 by American missionaries. He bought the man a meal and witnessed to him, but the man was perplexed, saying he smelled bad and nobody cared about him, and there was no government record of him. "I don't exist," the man told him.

"You're in God's database," Kostya replied. "God loves him," he told a curious onlooker, explaining why he was taking time to care for a vodka-soaked beggar. Kostya said the people of his church would seek out others like him, with planes if necessary. "Our best love-share is time," he told the Mendeltna congregation. "Jesus shared His love by giving eternity."

Kostya: professor, pilot, and Dwayne's key contact in Khabarovsk

Kostya, like Dwayne, won hearts with humor as well as eloquence, especially when plunging into a new language despite lack of total mastery. On his first flying lesson with Dwayne in Alaska, his attempt to say he was amazed by the scenery came out as, "I am amazing!" His usual superlative—"such-much!"—originated in his good-natured ribbing of two Russian friends, reputedly good translators. One of the young interpreters was either admiring Dwayne's watch or trying to ask what time it was.

"Dvayne, how much dat vatch?"

"Forty bucks."

"Zat is pretty late! Zat is such-much vatch!"

Those whose hearts were softened included Transportation University leaders, whom Kostya and Dwayne had visited in March 2006. The visitors not only made the case for general aviation, but revealed a deeper agenda. "We prayed that as God had broken down the wall, He will open up the sky," Kostya said. He recalled anxiously watching the school's stony-faced vice president while they prayed. "All his life he was a Communist, and he was hearing all this Christian stuff," Kostya said. "But he was okay. His face was good. He said, *'Let's do this!'*" Later, visiting Alaska, the university officials were thrilled by the sight of hundreds of small craft at the Lake Hood Seaplane Base near Anchorage. "They have no examples of this in Russia," Dwayne said.

He and Kostya left no doubt about who was ultimately overseeing events. After visiting the university, they were in line at the Khabarovsk airport, bound for Alaska. An official demanded to see Kostya's return ticket, but he didn't have one because he planned to return on Dwayne's demonstration flight. At that moment, another official, processing an adjacent line, told Kostya, "I want you!" He checked Kostya's fingerprints, asked the purpose of his trip, and said, "Have a good time!"

"God was working," Kostya said.

A Mission Comes Together...

While God was working, Dwayne was networking. The search for a plane, crew and funding put two businessmen on his radar screen who were ready, willing and wealthy: Winnipeg construction contractor Harold Barg and his business partner, Dylan Fast. Harold already knew Dwayne as both a pilot and the mentor of his son Jonathan, who had started a missionary career in the 1990s as a SEND summer volunteer in Khabarovsk. Dylan owned an air charter service. With those positive associations, and both partners being adventurous types, Dwayne's request for help was no shot in the dark.

They told Dwayne they wanted to fly with him to Khabarovsk, and they would supply the plane: a seven-seat, twin-engine Piper Cheyenne turboprop owned by Dylan's company, Fast Air Ltd. Dylan would be the pilot and Dwayne would be the copilot.

"That was an answer to prayer—a major piece of the puzzle," Dwayne said.

The third piece of the puzzle was navigating the Russian bureaucracy. Dwayne already had considerable expertise here, but more was needed. Another Alaska-based aviation group—SOAR International Ministries—was happy to supply it. SOAR—the acronym stands for Service and Outreach, Alaska to Russia—specializes in humanitarian and evangelistic missions, mostly to the Chukotka region of Far East Russia.

Dwayne, Kostya, J.C. Harder—Dwayne's old friend and flight instructor from LeTourneau—and I flew to Soldotna on a sunny day in late August 2006. The planners hit it off famously with SOAR Director Dick Page, who provided a wealth of information that included a twelve-inch stack of Aeronautical Information Publications (AIPs) in Russian and English, and checklists of fees, application forms and other requirements. "This is a gold mine! God love ya," Dwayne exclaimed—and, turning to Kostya, added, "We got work to do, kid!"

J.C. Harder and trainee Lydia

Drawing on SOAR's experience, Dick reminded Dwayne that dealing with Russian officials depends primarily on personal relationships. Thousands of regulations—none of them ever repealed—have little to do with the process. "If you get people who want to help you do it, it'll happen. If not, it'll never happen," he said. A favorable decision, he added, can move the fearsome Russian bureaucracy faster than any American agency steeped in a culture of standard procedures and brisk efficiency. Conversely, an unsympathetic customs agent can pick any law he wants to bury an application forever. Getting the bureaucrats on your side, he concluded, includes practical things, like paying fees in rubles and filling out forms beforehand; and little things, like putting official-looking stamps on the paperwork—"Russians love them!"

"Pray that they'll think it's their idea," Kostya added.

Dwayne cautioned Kostya to forward every conceivable detail to Russian agencies in advance. "Grease the skids," he told Kostya. "We can't wait 'til we're there, because they'll be surprised and say, 'Maybe next time.' But there may not be a next time."

We took off for the King Ranch after nightfall, elated with the trove of information. But my friends were a little nervous about a temporarily repaired cylinder as Dwayne nursed the Cessna 175 through the darkness over the black expanse of Cook Inlet. When I saw how relieved they were after we landed, I decided I should be grateful for my blissful ignorance.

Dwayne, as usual, was alert for networking and teaching opportunities. At Soldotna, he had transformed what should have been a quick information pickup into a three-hour bonding session, complete with a proposal to enlist SOAR in training KAC students. Back at the King Ranch, he explained to the trainees the importance of monitoring potential problems: "It was a night flight over the inlet. We were watching oil pressure ... oil temperature ... RPMs ... *Everything!*"

At least once before the flight to Khabarovsk, Dwayne prayed with his trainees: *"We are out on the limb by faith ... we pray that you will open up the way before us ... we pray for those who support us ... that it will not be an adventure for us, but a mission—to spread seed across the great land of Russia and Kazakhstan ... let us demonstrate Your love by our lives."* To their prayers were added those of the Russian Baptist Union, which, as in 1991, issued the government-required invitation, and the Mission Aviation Fellowship, which serves hundreds of faith-based groups in bringing humanitarian aid and the Gospel to unreached parts of the world.

... And Almost Crashes

Dwayne predicted that powers of darkness would try to stop the flight.

"Everyone has received their visas, but the clearance to make the flight has not yet come," Carolyn wrote.

Prayers were being answered, but Dwayne's prediction also came close to being fulfilled. As sometimes happened in the past, not all the help came from America—and not all the obstacles came from Russia. One Alaska-based travel agency tried to charge the mission planners $500 for information that should have been routinely available. But in Moscow, the official who had the last word about the planned flight—Gennady Feodorovich, in charge of international air traffic inside Russia—was very encouraging. On Tuesday, August 27, "He wished us good luck," Kostya told worshipers at Chickaloon Bible Church.

On Friday, September 1, the mission team received permission to fly. God was working, but not without opposition, Carolyn wrote in e-mails to SEND, describing the final countdown.

To you faithful ones who are praying: Satan did his best to discourage the guys enough to cancel the flight ...

Sat. a.m. [Sept. 2] the plane was due to leave Winnipeg to fly to Anchorage. A critical part was broken and needed to be repaired. Of course, this was a holiday weekend [Labor Day]. The part arrived on Sunday a.m., was fixed, and the plane finally took off for Anchorage on Monday. Since the window to fly into Russian airspace was now gone, Kostya had to start the paperwork all over again. This took many phone calls to Russia, and his staying up until 3 a.m. printing out paperwork, etc.

Sun. a.m. Kostya was due to speak in Anchorage. Dwayne flew him as far as Palmer and had to leave him there for someone else to take [him] the rest of the way, as Anchorage was fogged in. Dwayne flew back to our church, landed on the road, parked, hit his head on the strut and managed to knock his hearing aid out on the gravel. Two, then three, then four of us searched for an hour trying to find it... Then all of a sudden there it was—quite a ways further from where we thought it would hit. We heard ten minutes of the sermon. Now that seems like a minor thing. But if you wear hearing aids, you will understand that it is *not* minor. Satan must have been snickering. But you were praying.

Mon. afternoon the Cheyenne arrives in Anchorage. The Canadians are picked up and brought out to the ranch. More paperwork... All the charts, etc. they need are not there. You can't get them until you get into Russia. Too many things could happen—like not having gas available, not the right paperwork, etc. Finally, they agreed they should go.

Tues. a.m. everyone is up at 5. Breakfast is at 6. [Dwayne and Carolyn's son] David is ready with the helicopter to fly them into Anchorage, and they take off around 7 a.m. Our favorite Russian interpreter [Kostya] is not going to get his peanut butter and "pine" syrup—

he means maple syrup. Plus a few other things get left with me. Too heavy. I came back to the house and found Dwayne had left his travel kit—including hearing aid batteries. Called and told him, and they were going to figure something out.

Her announcement that the plane was finally in the air, and wouldn't land until it reached Russia, was almost an understatement.

After unloading more weight, they are on their way. The last call I got was from Nome, about noon (Alaska time), and they were heading for their first stop—Anadyr—and if the winds were favorable, hoped to go on to Magadan by tonight.
Bless you all for praying.
In His Hands,
Carolyn.

[**Thursday, Sept. 7**] Dwayne called last night at 11:30 p.m. Alaska time. After spending the night in Magadan with one of our former Bible College students, they landed in Khabarovsk around 4 p.m. Thursday Khabarovsk time—(9 p.m. Wednesday Alaska time) and were very happy to be there. Had a good flight except for strong winds from Japan's Super Typhoon that is now headed for western Alaska. It was a bit frustrating to work around airport closing times on the way. For example: Khabarovsk airport is closed to all traffic from 1 p.m. until 3 p.m. for lunch. Some things never change. Fuel stops took three-four hours in both Anadyr and Magadan, to pay all the taxes/fees, etc. Fueling the plane alone takes an hour and a half. I'm sure Kostya is still exclaiming how "amazing" this flight is.
Thank you for all your prayers.
Carolyn.

The prayers were welcome. Carolyn's letters did not reveal everything that could have gone wrong, but didn't. The Piper Cheyenne had a fuel range of five hours—not much longer than the nonstop legs of the flight—and there were no authorized landing strips between Anadyr, Magadan and Khabarovsk. Unauthorized landings would have resulted in confiscation of the plane.

Headwinds were forecast when they took off from Magadan, which would have slowed them down and cut even further into an already small margin of safety. But the winds shifted favorably as they climbed, giving them a slight tailwind when they reached their operational ceiling of twenty-eight thousand feet.

"There can be a huge difference between forecast and actual winds aloft," Dwayne said. "All the way to altitude, we're calculating ... calculating ... calculating."

Not quite halfway from Magadan to Khabarovsk, approaching the point of no return, they made the *go-no-go* decision.

The decision, of course, was *"Go for it."*

17. "MIRACLES Are Worth Believing"

*I like the theory that the Creator puts a dream in our hearts
and gives us the means to fulfill it.*

—Anatoly Danilov,
self-taught plane builder

THE KHABAROVSK FLIGHT and Kostya's connections gave new
life to the unique aviation saga of one Russian dreamer who was
unwilling to wait for official approval. Anatoly Danilov's story testifies
that Dwayne's aviation outreach, like SEND's spiritual outreach, was re-
energizing powerful currents that already existed.

In the best biblical tradition of God's unlikely instruments, Anatoly—a
hard-partying, admitted atheist—became one of Dwayne's most fervent
supporters and students. But he was more than a dreamer. Among Russia's
many flying enthusiasts, he had gone further than most. Between 2005 and
2008, he built a plane remarkably like a Piper Super Cub at his home near
Khabarovsk, using the Internet to study aeronautics and locate blueprints.

"I am an ordinary engineer, nothing to do with aviation, but I think that
if you like something very much and you have a desire to learn, you can
achieve success in any matter." Anatoly wrote those words in "Miracles
Are Worth Believing," an article in the January 2009 edition of *Grand!*—a
Russian magazine featuring extreme outdoor sports.

Kostya, a friend of Anatoly, introduced him to Dwayne. Kostya called
his friend a "mechanical genius." Anatoly had not only built his "Super
Cab" from scratch, by hand, with no specialized tools or training, but was
ready to fly it, illegally, without lessons. (The Super Cub model is a venerable but punchy little performer, nothing like a taxi, but a translation error
in the article rendered it "Super Cab.")

Dwayne tried to persuade Anatoly to come to Alaska for training, but some close associates were leery. Like many other Russians, they were suspicious of what they regarded as sects. Their fears were expressed in a friend's warning not to become involved with an evangelical Christian organization: "They put you in a white robe and make you sell posies!" So Anatoly flew his "Super Cab" in Russia, without lessons, and crashed. The doubters quickly adjusted their attitudes. They and his wife Victoria told him: "Go to Alaska! Take lessons!"

He did, and Dwayne trained him at Kingdom Air Corps in the summer of 2008. Anatoly bought a two-seat Cessna 150 and had it shipped home— "It's the first Cessna in Far East Russia," Dwayne said. They intended to assemble and fly it in November 2009, as well as "christening" what Dwayne said would be the first private runway in Far East Russia.

It looked like the gathering of a perfect storm. A pilot's ambition, a missionary's vision and God's plan seemed to be converging.

To celebrate their plans, Anatoly rented a restaurant and band, bought plenty of vodka and threw a huge party. His friends—all flying enthusiasts, but only one of them a pilot—drank many toasts. As the designated driver, Anatoly abstained. Several toasts were offered in honor of Victoria, whose kitchen garden he had confiscated for space to build a hangar.

In a dramatic flourish, Anatoly named his makeshift aviation setup the "Baikonur Cosmodrome" after the giant Russian space launch facility in Kazakhstan.

Reviving an Old Dream

In the *Grand!* magazine article he co-authored with editors Mickhail Nepogodin and Yelena Kochegarova, Anatoly told of a long period early in the last century when the Soviet government encouraged and supported flying clubs and pilot training. He voiced the sadness many flying enthusiasts felt when that era ended.

> That was the time of dreamers and heroes. And we know that heroes don't live long. They were followed by cowards and [the] fearful who wrote hundreds of laws and regulations. They say it's for our own good or, even better, for the good of the country. They have employed thousands of supervisors who are too keen to see the laws enforced and don't care about real people. They don't see the sky. They don't need it. Therefore no one needs it.

The article, not surprisingly, expressed Anatoly's love of flying in Alaska:

We are flying over glaciers and mountain rivers. Underneath ... all is turning. The task is to fly over the river bed, altitude 10 metres. I am going down and the instructor gives a command: "Lower!" But it already feels as if the wheels are about to touch something! And he says: "Altitude 20 metres! You are not low enough yet! Pull it down, down ..." Then he goes: "My plane. Look, it's going to be 1 metre now." I let the handle [control stick] go and we fly right between the trees and the river banks! Our small red plane blends into the curves of the river easily like a bird. Dwayne is at the front, I am behind him. He is the pilot and I am a trainee. "My plane" means that Dwayne took over and I can relax. There is only one feeling—complete excitement!

He was also full of praise for American general aviation and the infra-structure that supports it:

... light aviation in America is as important as car industry. In Anchorage, for instance, there are more parking lots for planes than for cars. It's part of their culture. People go to visit each other by planes, not cars... There are hundreds of airports across Alaska and every small plane can land there absolutely free. You are allowed to land at closed military airports with automated equipment. When you are landing at night time you just have to send a radio signal and the field will light up. There is no one around but all is clean and tidy.

His statement about landing at closed military airports was inaccurate and his comment about parking lots was an exaggeration, both attributable to his enthusiasm and unfamiliarity with new surroundings. But there was nothing exaggerated in his enthusiastic description of KAC and Dwayne's hospitality:

I was amazed at what I saw at Dwayne's: there were students from Texas pilot's college, 17-18-year-old boys and girls and the kids from the neighborhood—all learning to fly. They all work. They mow the lawns, cook and do repairs just for an hour of flight. And all are cheerful! All are happy! Every time you land they come to the plane with congratulations.

From the very beginning it was wonderful: I got out of the plane in Anchorage early, it was 6 a.m. There were Dwayne and three girls meeting me. They got up at 3 in the morning and drove 80 miles to meet a Russian who they didn't know! That was a shock!

Less expected was what this man, who called himself an unbeliever, sensed behind his and Dwayne's joy in flight and the events that brought them together. As the magazine article relates, it began with Anatoly's question to his new friend:

> "How is it that you, an intelligent man, technically minded and a pilot to the core, believe in God? How does it all match?" Everybody went quiet, waiting for the answer. Dwayne smiled ... and said: "I believe in miracles. We both live thousands of kilometres apart. Yesterday we didn't know anything about each other! But our passion for aviation and love of planes brought us together at this table as close friends. It's a miracle!"

Dwayne's answer struck a chord in Anatoly and helped the Russian seek his own answers. "I can believe in such miracles, too," Anatoly replied. Continuing in the article to sum up his thoughts and conversations, he came tantalizingly close to understanding the source of the miracle:

> Dwayne is 67. He probably flew all kinds of planes. But he is not tired, because he and his friends have a purpose in life—they are missionaries. For them it's a celebration. "We have been chosen," they say. "God gave us joy to experience being pilots."
>
> We are tougher, our dreams and wishes are more earthly. Not all Americans are probably like them, but those who I had an opportunity to meet first get approval [for their plans] from the guy who sits somewhere up high and you just need to believe in him. Although I am an atheist, I envy them a little, because not everyone in this life is lucky to have such a true friend and a teacher (and the teachings are plentiful in the Bible) ...
>
> I like the theory that the Creator puts a dream in our hearts and gives us the means to fulfill it ... Once in the evening [Dwayne] was treating us, his trainees, to some ice cream. Suddenly he said: "There are several billion people on this Earth, but only thousands are pilots. I'm happy that God gave me a chance to become one of them."

Nuts, Bolts, and Connections

The 1991 flight to Providenya opened Far East Russia to SEND, and the 2006 flight to Khabarovsk showed the feasibility of general aviation. But both were accomplished by outsiders. One thing more was needed to inspire Russian aviation enthusiasts to take ownership of the movement themselves: a demonstration flight by a Russian, in Russia. The catch-22: it would be highly illegal—but such flights would never become legal without the enthusiasm triggered by the event itself.

That was enough to motivate Dwayne and his unlikely ally, Anatoly, to forge ahead. They were delayed by a false start and threatened by bureaucracy. But they were helped by Anatoly's connections and Dwayne's networking skills—not to mention spare parts that included a famous carburetor.

The countdown began in Vladivostok, where Anatoly took delivery of the Cessna 150 he had bought in Alaska. He loaded it onto a flatbed truck for the trip to his makeshift airstrip in Vinogradovka, a village near Khabarovsk. Police stopped him at every highway checkpoint and threatened him with fines for transporting an unlicensed, unregistered plane. At each stop, he phoned a higher-ranking officer he knew and was waved through, but not before he further sweetened relations with the checkpoint squads.

"I'm sure this cost him about six bottles of vodka or so," Dwayne observed.

In November 2009, Dwayne and aircraft mechanic Tom Reiger traveled to Vinogradovka, where, Dwayne said, they immediately faced a good-news-bad-news situation. The good news: Anatoly had already assembled the plane by himself. The bad news: He had done it with "various and sundry nuts and bolts" from old motorcycles, derelict washing machines and other junk. The hardware was a haphazard mix of thread sizes, tolerances and head designs, and many parts were missing.

"The airplane looked good from fifty feet away," but was obviously not airworthy, Dwayne added. He and Tom decided to go home and return in April with proper parts. Tom, of Reedley, California, was a former FAA inspector with worldwide experience repairing Missionary Aviation Fellowship planes. He had been introduced to Dwayne by Dave Ketscher, the Kings' friend from the Bettles ministry.

Tom, said Dwayne, brought more to the team than mechanical expertise alone. "God was really working in his heart. He spent thousands of dollars of his own money to get the right parts into Anatoly's plane." The parts included a carburetor from the *Voyager*, an experimental lightweight craft that, in 1986, was the first to circle the globe without stopping or refueling. It was given to Tom by a friend, the manager of a California repair facility used by Dick Rutan, one of the *Voyager* pilots.

Dwayne and Tom returned in April as planned to work on the plane, accompanied by Kostya, Dwayne's key contact in Khabarovsk. Several of Anatoly's aviation-minded friends—young men in their 30s and early 40s—gathered in his hangar to watch, and help when they could. Dwayne saw them as "a cadre of future Russian pilots—the general aviation pioneers of Khabarovsk—all unsaved." Every lunchtime and evening they told flying stories and offered numerous toasts. They eventually gave up trying to persuade the Americans and Kostya to drink anything stronger than fruit juice.

"It was a riot," Dwayne said of the ten-day visit.

It took a week to put the finishing touches on Anatoly's plane—"it ran beautifully," Dwayne said. That left a three-day window for the test flight. But it rained the first two days, turning much of the nine-hundred foot runway into mud, and on the afternoon of the third day—Monday, April 26—Dwayne had to be in Khabarovsk for his flight back to Seattle.

Launching Hope from a Muddy Runway

Monday dawned bright and clear. To reach the runway, the plane had to be towed over a deep gully on two military surplus steel bridges somehow acquired by the ever-resourceful Anatoly. He and Dwayne made six high-speed taxi runs to find dry spots between the mud puddles left by rain and melting frost. On the last two practice runs, they lifted off about three feet, testing the Cessna's ability to become airborne and, presumably, clear the trees at the end of the runway.

"This was a very anxious time," Dwayne said. "We had no authority to do this."

A high-ranking Russian aviation official who shared their dream had privately encouraged them to go ahead, but warned them not to get caught or crash. Dwayne understood that if the authorities learned he was the pilot, they would arrest him, expel him, and possibly bar him from returning to Russia. Anatoly would face lesser penalties.

(If the escapade were discovered after Dwayne was back in America, he was asked later, wouldn't he be concerned about never being granted a visa again? Dwayne smiled and shrugged, invoking the *it's-easier-to-get-forgiveness-than-permission* rule. He pointed out that if the flight had made a splash big enough to alert the authorities, it would have done its intended work: spreading ripples of inspiration.)

It was April 26. The moment had come.

Dwayne, Anatoly and their friends huddled Super Bowl-style on the field. Dwayne said, "Boys, this is a momentous occasion. Let's pray and ask God to bless this flight right now." The two boarded, with Dwayne flying "left seat" (command position). "Everything was so marginal, I had to be where I had the best feel for the airplane," he explained. But he again reminded Anatoly, "If there's a problem, *you're* the pilot!"

They took off around noon and flew for about three minutes, crossing the Amur River. As soon as they were airborne, Anatoly yelled, "Oorah! Chudah! Chudah! Eestoria!" (*Yea! Miracle! Miracle! History!*)

Dwayne remembered the aviation official's warning to stay under one hundred meters to avoid detection, but was momentarily confused because the Cessna's altimeter numbers represented feet. Anatoly's urgent question snapped him back: "Why you fly so low? We're right on treetops!"

People ran out of their homes and stared upward. "They'd never seen a little plane fly over their villages before," Dwayne said. As they landed, a mob of villagers ran onto the field to greet them. In the crowd was Dwayne's former interpreter, Lena Sidenko, whose home was on the approach path to Anatoly's airstrip. "The mud was flying!" Dwayne recalls.

Anatoly's friends begged for a ride, so Dwayne and Kostya made five more quick flights, each carrying one passenger. They got a chance to handle the Cessna's dual controls. "They'd practiced on computer games and thought they were pilots," Dwayne said. "In ten seconds, they found out they weren't."

*Dwayne (in KAC jacket) and Anatoly embrace
after demonstration flight.*

After a big celebration, there was just time to drive Dwayne to the airport, still in his dirty pilot/mechanic clothes.

If his and Anatoly's dreams were to become more widely shared, inspiring Russian officials to again make them real — as they were made real a lifetime earlier — then, Dwayne reasoned, the sky would be opened to far more than general aviation.

The sky began to open up sooner than many expected.

On November 1, 2010 — one hundred and eighty-eight days after the flight from Anatoly's muddy airstrip in the Far East — new freedoms for general aviation went into effect. The Russian government streamlined time-consuming requirements for filing flight plans and "pledged to reduce the amount of closed and restricted airspace," AV*web* aviation news service reported on November 2.

"We're overjoyed," said Dwayne. "These rules have moved us 75 percent toward what's in the United States."

Overjoyed, but not surprised: "I believe it's an answer to prayer." He also credited Aleksandr Pavlov, Aeroflot safety officer for the Far East, who, he said, has tried since the early 1990s to bring about new rules for general aviation. Other factors, Dwayne added, included efforts by the Transportation University, his flights to Providenya in the 1990s and the April 26 flight, which he called a "huge encouragement that it can be done."

"We've been so involved that we've been able to see this coming," Dwayne said. "The vision the Lord has given us is all based on His promise that the nations will hear the Gospel."

According to travel and aviation writer Joel Siegfried, "Boris and Natasha... can look forward to logging many hours in the sky, many of them at the controls of their own aircraft."

In the not-too-distant future, Dwayne hopes, that could be Pastor Boris and Missionary Natasha.

Part 6

THORNS
AND CROWNS

Seasons of Darkness, Echoes of Love

My ears had heard of you but now my eyes have seen you.
—Job 42:5

18. DWAYNE AND CAROLYN
The Refiner's Fire

... I didn't love her anymore.
                    —Dwayne King

I felt totally worthless.
                    —Carolyn King

I will refine them like silver and test them like gold.
They will call on my name and I will answer them.
                    —Zechariah 13:9

DORRIS STEVENSON had no doubts about the Kings' marriage. "The Lord knew exactly what He was doing when He put Carolyn with Dwayne. Dwayne knows and everyone else knows that Carolyn King is a jewel, who quietly sparkles in his crown. They both will receive crowns to cast at Jesus' feet."

Another longtime friend, Glenna Dufresne, had no doubts about the value of that marriage to her, her husband and others whose lives Dwayne and Carolyn touched during the years in Tok. She described the gifts the Kings brought to their ministry, and to each other.

Dwayne and Carolyn are very unique and special people to us. They are our spiritual parents. In all our dealings with them, it would have been easy to become followers of them and not of Jesus Christ, and yet, they never allowed it. Or God never allowed it. Dwayne is a charismatic person, drawing people to himself. And yet he is transparent, almost guileless. He is like a chameleon, taking on the culture of those around him, but never in a mimicking or ridiculing way. When he's with Alaska native people, he's an Alaska native—he even speaks with their accent. When he's with fishermen and mechanics, he's a fisherman and a mechanic. It makes him effective in that culture. He becomes accepted because he is so accepting.

... Carolyn is one of the most stable people that I know. Often in those early years, much fell on her shoulders. She kept the family going. She played the piano, often following Dwayne's lead. Singing ... always the harmony to his melody. It was a blessing to watch him move from being bored with her role, and what she represented, to desiring to be home and be rested and refreshed by her. I truly don't know what he would do without her. He'd never rest or eat right or take care of himself. She is truly as gifted and dynamic as he is—in every different way possible.

They are truly a couple, both needing the other to survive. Their ministry reflects the total commitment to, and calling of, God on both of their lives. They are not perfect ... Dwayne overcommits and is very forgetful... He's considered to be unreliable. He doesn't submit to any leadership. If there is a way to get around the rules, he will... Carolyn is reserved and often withdrawn. She never nags and never takes over. She's washed lots of hearing aids because she won't check shirt pockets before washing them. "I'm his wife, not his mother ... I'm not the Holy Spirit."

There was a time in each of their lives when flaws became chasms. In Alaska, Dwayne, a vessel of God's love, found himself empty. In Far East Russia, Carolyn, a child of God, felt like a helpless orphan. The couple who modeled Christ's love in dark places spent seasons in darkness themselves.

They described their losses and deliverance in uncharacteristic ways. Dwayne, the public speaker who rarely fears to be totally open, summed his up in a few short statements that expressed only what happened, not how. Carolyn, usually the private, quiet one, confronted hers by publicly questioning herself and God in Job-like detail. Both, true to themselves, turned their experiences into a tribute to God and a teaching time for themselves and others.

At the 1991 missions conference in Vestal, Dwayne thanked Twin Orchards—Carolyn's home church—for giving him his wife. He celebrated their growing love rooted in a common faith and call to duty. He traced their twenty-eight years of marriage from courtship rituals with other teens in the parsonage basement to a bond in which, he claimed,

Carolyn saved him from burnout and went "way, far above me in her faithfulness to God's Word, every day."

No one in the audience at Twin would have guessed what Dwayne was about to share.

Descents into Darkness

In the middle of his tribute to Carolyn, he made a startling admission: "It was about fifteen years [after] we were married, and I grew to an understanding that I didn't love her anymore ..."

> ... and I was a pastor and I was preaching about love, and I was preaching the Bible, and you were supporting us as missionaries, and people were praying for us, and all of the above, and I did not love my wife. A missionary on a mission—what a predicament, you see! And I really had to pray that God would give me love for this woman ... the Lord did that. And I have grown since that point in a real love affair with my wife.
>
> I didn't intend to say that tonight, but I wanted to tell you because I kind of bared my soul with you in this conference ... that's the kind of thing that happens in missionaries' lives. We're just like you. We are not super saints ... we struggle and go through the same problems and deal with sin just like you do. We're no different.
>
> So when you want to pray about your missionary, pray like you would for yourself.

Carolyn's crisis was triggered by their impending move to a place where she did not want to go, she wrote in her testimony delivered at the 2001 Eurasia Field Conference. The mission wife, who knew that she and others were of infinite worth to God, came to feel worthless.

> I knew after Dwayne made that first flight into Russia that we would be going. I fought it by ignoring the possibility. In '93 I had major surgery and was diagnosed with diabetes. It's as if the Lord was saying, "See, I've taken care of everything. For the first time in years you feel well." And in Oct. '93 we went. Then the struggle that was to become one cycle of depression after another, for years, began. I wrote in my journal, "Loneliest Christmas ever!" Life was *not* great and I certainly didn't want to stay here forever.
>
> ... Leaving every security I'd known, I felt like Max Lucado described, "out on a limb when I'd rather be hugging the tree." The only other choice was saying *"No"* to God. But years ago, inspired by another missionary wife, I had made a promise to the Lord. I would never

... cause my husband to say "No" to the Lord. I was also committed to never intentionally bringing shame to the name of the Lord.

Carolyn compared her situation to that of still another missionary "who expresses so well a lot of what I was feeling." In an article in the July-August 2001 issue of *Women of the Harvest* magazine, the missionary—identified only as "M.H. Central Asia" for security reasons—wrote:

> We lost ourselves. Some of us couldn't find our microwaves and others of us were trying to get cream of chicken soup out of a live chicken. We lost our adulthood, our meticulously organized schedules and many of us have almost lost our sanity!
> ... When I moved to Central Asia my walk with the Lord spiraled downward. How could that be? I am a missionary for goodness sake! ... This was unacceptable.

M.H. wrote that she prayed continually for knowledge. She finally realized that, despite subtle feelings of negativity, she loved her mission field. But Carolyn wrote:

> My problem was a little different—I *didn't* love the country. It was not the inconvenience—after all, I'd lived in Alaska for twenty-five years—but the stress of "red tape" and the loneliness... I didn't love learning the language and meeting new people—though I did like the people, and the service of the Russian church was very meaningful, even when I understood so little.

M.H. found the reason for her feelings of negativity—she felt superior to those around her—but again, it wasn't Carolyn's answer: "Those were definitely *not* my thoughts—in fact, I felt the Russians were so much better at evangelizing that there was really *no* point to our being here. I felt totally worthless." It was a stark contrast to the fulfillment of life in Glennallen.

> I had worked in the college bookstore for seven years and now was working in the library. Had just gotten my Bible degree... I was no longer just Dwayne King's wife (not that that was bad) but I had my own identity. Even though I was developing physical problems, again, life was great and I loved it there.

Where M.H.'s and Carolyn's experiences converged was in realizing what they had lost in their new countries. M.H. wrote:

I became an infant. Every day, so many *times* a day I needed help. I needed people to walk me down the street, to take me to the store, to get my visa. I had to ask someone how to flush the toilet in my own home. I am not an expert on anything. No one *ever* seeks my advice or appreciates my thoughts. I have *nothing* to offer. I am a learner. Twenty-four hours a day. Seven days a week.

Carolyn agreed. "*This* was my real problem—I had totally lost my identity and everything that gave me security. I was 50-plus and back in preschool... It's one thing to suffer through our own learning process, but the people around you are affected too. I was of no use to my teammates, which only added to my guilty feelings."

The two women's experiences also converged in the realization that restoration involved not doing, but being. M.H. wrote:

I spend all my time trying to make myself valuable, when my job here is to magnify Someone else. I had forgotten why I am here. Not to be valuable, but as a sacrifice, poured out on His altar because I love Him. I am not here to "make a difference," or even to survive, but to glorify God and enjoy Him forever ... I did not come here to be meaningful, useful or comfortable. I came because He asked me to.

Sitting in His Light
Carolyn pored over the Word and discovered, or rather rediscovered, a similar answer.

Psalms and the prophets were especially meaningful. These guys were not afraid to say what they felt. I read Ron Dunn's book, *When Heaven is Silent*, at least three times. God took me back through all the lessons I had learned twenty years ago ... I decided that if all He wanted me to do was twiddle my thumbs, that was okay. And my only role here [in Russia] was to make a safe place for my husband to come home to ... that's still my role... One of the greatest things I can do is free Dwayne to do what he needs to. Not that I don't still grumble when he's gone so much. And I still don't know for sure what's expected of a Director's wife, and it was comforting to find out at our Couples in Leadership Conference recently that nobody else knows either.

> I learned that what I *do* is far less important than what I *am* and that
> I belong to Him. Psalm 27 reads: *One thing I ask of the Lord, this is what*
> *I seek: that I may dwell in the house of the Lord all the days of my life, to*
> *gaze upon the beauty of the Lord... My heart says of you, "Seek his face."*

Citing author Cynthia Heald, Carolyn wrote that sitting at the feet of
Jesus might seem to the world like a waste of days, but was vital to her in
rediscovering who He is—and the first step toward serving Him.

> So what if the most-asked question is: "And what do *you* do over
> there?" My value lies in the fact that my Father has chosen me and loves
> me with an embrace so affirming and satisfying that even a glimpse of
> it takes my breath away. In Tok I learned to know the Lord as my gentle
> Shepherd. In Russia, twenty years later, He took my breath away with
> His incredible Father love. He became the father I had lost so long ago.
> Isaiah 30:15 says: *In repentance and rest is your salvation, in quiet-*
> *ness and trust is your strength ...* And in 32:17: *The fruit of righteousness*
> *will be peace; the effect of righteousness will be quietness and confi-*
> *dence forever.* In other words, God's work in me results in service for
> Him. Too often we try to do it the other way around. Serve Him without
> sitting with Him.
> Cynthia Heald writes: "... I will no longer try to show what great
> things I can do for Him, but will yield myself to Him so that He can show
> the world what great things He can do for me."
> Ministry is not about us—it's for *His* glory.

As Zechariah might say, Dwayne and Carolyn called on God's name
and He answered them. That cry and response, when they were passing
through their fires and at other times, had nothing to do with usefulness.
But as other testimonies will show, it made them useful in the lives of
many others who saw what God had done for them, and through them.

19. MANY VOICES: Lives that were Changed

As the Father has sent me, I am sending you.
—John 20:21

MANY PEOPLE REMEMBER how Dwayne changed their lives. As three of his children, Joel, Becky and Dave remember more than most. In a letter to his father, Joel remembered one of the ways Dwayne answered his questions: "Am I your beloved son?" and, "Do I have what it takes?"

> ... you had to go somewhere in one of the planes... You asked me if I wanted to go. It was going to be an all-day trip and I was thrilled. Just you and I. I was too young to see over the dash so I was sitting on a stack of sleeping bags... Once airborne and en route you said you wanted to take a nap and the controls were mine. You pointed to a peak in the mountain range ahead and told me to fly to it. Showed me how to keep the horizon on the cowling and watch the altitude. Said to wake you up when we got there. I remember looking over and seeing the eye closest to me closed ... You trusted me. Thinking back on it today, I am pretty sure the other eye was open ... when we got there and you "woke up" you were so proud of me and expressed it over and over again. Met the people you were going to see and you introduced me as your copilot. That has always stayed with me.

Years later, it was Joel's turn to use a plane to help others grow. He became involved in his church's efforts to heal men's hearts. Many of the study materials for the men's ministry described broken men abused by fathers who were far different from his, he wrote in his 2009 letter to Dwayne. At a weekend retreat later that year, his ministry tool was a Cessna 172.

Joel, of Duvall, Washington, said God puts desires in men's hearts that can awaken them to Christ—"for me, it's flying"—but sometimes the desire is buried. He helped those at the retreat find their lost desires by letting them fly the small plane: "I saw twelve men come alive this weekend!"

In the years between Joel's magic childhood flight and his adult ministry, Dwayne played a shaping role. "Over and over again," he wrote, his father affirmed his achievements. "You taught me to fish, hunt, raft, hike, camp... You taught me how to fix things." When necessary, his father also taught him to take ownership of his mistakes. "But above all things," Joel wrote,

> ... you showed me the importance of God in your life. In every thing you did, every thing you said, God was always the Number One most important thing... And that, right there, has taught me more than anything. I have never in my life seen a man more dedicated, consistent and true about their walk with God as you.

So it was no surprise that Dwayne's greatest joy was reserved for his son and daughter-in-law's biggest decision: "About three-and-a-half years ago when LaReina and I started truly walking with and for God, you pulled me aside and just said, 'I am so proud of you and LaReina.' It felt so good."

Joel told his father that of all the things he had taught him, "One of my favorites is that you taught me to fly." But it wasn't always an easy gift to accept, nor, later, was it easy to understand what God wanted him to do with it. Joel wrote:

> When it came time for me to be thinking of what I wanted to do with the rest of my life, flying was the last thing on my mind. Even though a lot of the time you were around was awesome with adventure, there was a lot of time you were gone flying or out at the hangar ... I blamed airplanes and flying for you being gone a lot. It took me a long time to come to terms with that.

Joel justified the absences by realizing his father was "doing God's work ... helping others," but he still wanted nothing to do with flying. However, time and events changed his attitude:

After two years of college and reality, the thought of flying was pretty appealing. When I came back that summer and you officially taught me to fly, you sparked a desire in me that ran incredibly deep. The times spent in the cockpit with you are some of my favorite memories.

Joel sought God's will—whether to use aviation in ministry, and if so, where? In Duvall or "some far off land?" On a Colorado hilltop behind a men's "boot camp" retreat, he heard an answer to the first question:

... God spoke to me very clearly. *I trained you for a mission and a purpose... You just weren't ready for my calling. You are ready now, my son. I want you to fly.* I then remembered a saying I had heard, "The glory of God is man fully alive," and then He added, *and you are fully alive when you are flying.*

At first, he wrote to Dwayne, God seemed to have a plan for him in Duvall. "There are so many broken, dead men (and women) right here among us," who might be reached in the same way his father had reached others. "You once told me that you have witnessed to more guys in the cockpit of an airplane and over an open cowling than anything else you have done." Having the use of one of Dwayne's planes, and buying another that Dwayne helped him find, reinforced Joel's leaning toward an aviation ministry at home. However, he added that his and LaReina's prayers about the next step could be leading to a third-world country.

"But through it all," Joel wrote, "there was something else God was trying to speak to me."

He shared with his father a concern that went deeper than decisions about What, Where, and When—a concern he had repressed, but which had to be resolved before any of the other decisions could be put into effect. The last hurdle was fear.

I remember ... hearing God say, *What are you so afraid of?* ... and my answer was, *I am afraid of what you might ask me to do. I am afraid of where you might ask me to go.*

The issue was resolved later, in August 2008, as Joel was sitting on an island in the Skykomish River. All God called on him to do was to *"Go* ... and I said *'Okay.'"*

"And as for you and the impact you have had on my life, I could never thank you enough," Joel told his father. "I just hope and pray that I can be the dad to my kids that you were to me."

Becky Sherman, an emergency room nurse in Ashland, Oregon, also has good memories, expressed in a somewhat different style: "The problem with asking Dwayne's kids to put thoughts down on paper is that, well, they're Dwayne's kids. We aren't organized and we are definitely not good with deadlines. It isn't our fault, it's a hereditary disorder."

She was able to surmount her disorder sufficiently to offer the following:

Things I learned from my father:
—It's easier to get forgiveness than permission.
—How to handle a drunk (it was great preparation for working in the ER).
—How to scrounge. It's only in the last few years that I find it's often better just to buy the thing new than spend hours cobbling together some item.
—Compassion (stinky people need love too).
—The world is full of very serious people who are very productive. These people are annoying but necessary. Try to learn to live with them, but never forget it is your mission to bless their lives by helping them lighten up. (Whether they want to or not.)
—It's OK to talk to strangers.
—Girls can do anything.
—Adventure has a purpose. Home is great but there is no place like a new place.
—How to wait. Always wait for [Dwayne] to stop talking to people. This is hard when you are 8.
—It's all in the telling. The most mundane event can be entertaining when told in the right (but possibly exaggerated) way.
—Act like you know what you're doing even if you don't.
—If you need to get from point A to point B, do it as quickly as possible. This way you will have more time for whatever the purpose of getting to point B is. It is easier to convince those with you regarding the urgency if you have waited until the last possible moment to leave for point B. The journey may be fun, but it is not the point.
—Do justly, love mercy, walk humbly.

What I would like to teach my father: It's OK to throw things away.

What I learned from my mother, who had to live with my father:
—Cook extra.
—Take time out from your children.
—How to exist with a difficult spouse. Send them to distant lands
   frequently.

It was difficult growing up competing with so many people for his attention, but I think I see that now as a blessing. I was exposed to so many
people from so many places, and I think that is what makes me always
wanting to be overseas, living in another culture. We no longer use the
term "cross-cultural" much, but it really shaped my whole world view.

Dave, like Becky, half-seriously blames a "procrastinating gene" for
his initial reluctance to share memories. Seriously, he explained, it took a
while before he was willing to plunge into trying to capture the essence
of a private relationship with a public legend who has impacted "so many
lives and souls."

... Or maybe it's because he is still here among us, still known to me as
the "Tasmanian devil" who hits the ground running ... stirring up dust
devils everywhere you turn—getting things done, getting people motivated and inspired to either pick up the pace or get out of the way. His
work is not done, so how can it be memorialized? I, for one, see the
changes, and their impact every day! It's almost as if my dad is a character from a movie, larger then life itself, but yet as real as, and consis-
tently authentic as, his arrival back on the ranch each spring.

It was not only Dwayne who shaped him, Dave added.

... There is no influence that I can think of that actually even comes in
a close second, except for my mother's. I've been told before, much
to my dismay, that I am an equal blend of my father and my mother.
Funny, though, how my father says, "You're like your mother," when
I've heard my mother say, "He's just like his father." They're total oppo-
sites—how can this be? However, as I get older, I see in myself the mix
of both. I think that in my youth, I somewhat resented my mother's quiet
reserve and embarrassingly realistic frankness. I was more attracted to
my father's exuberance for everything in life—his *Make-it-up-as-you-go*
aptitude, his *Git'er-done-now!* way of doing things, his *Get-permissions-
and-ask-forgiveness-later* perspective ... I have an understanding now,
that without my mom being the total opposite ... I really don't think [my

father] or I would be here today. For that, I owe both of them my deepest gratitude.

What some see as Dwayne's disorganization and lack of planning was, to Dave, often a virtue, freeing his father to take quick action or give total and loving support:

> "The unexpected was to be expected" is the way he taught me to fly when I was just a kid ... This started as early as I was able to reach the pedals of the little Piper [Cub model] we built as a family in the back yard. It's the same way he teaches new [KAC] recruits to think: Though you're ready to land, be prepared at all times to go around, because you never know what might come up at the last second.
>
> Some may say that Dwayne King is a loose cannon and not reliable because of his lack of proper planning and preparations... For me, because of his ability to adapt to situations that arise out of control and respond to them efficiently and effectively, he was, and still is, the most reliable man on the planet whenever I had a crisis in my life. From my earliest memories to this very day, whenever my flying machines were broken or bent, or I was heartbroken or spent, my dad would drop whatever he was doing to come to the rescue. Though he could not always count on me, I could count on him.

Dave has vivid memories of a disaster that brought out Dwayne's best qualities:

> ... my newly refurbished airplane I was flying on a very remote herring fishery in Kamishak Bay . . . was battered by a storm, sunk in the ocean and mangled by a rushed recovery. I was left hypothermic, heartbroken, desolate and without a livelihood. After hearing the news and responding immediately with the right parts and abilities, Dad showed up at the perfect moment. Within a few short days—long on hours—we cobbled that airplane back together just in time to make the next fishery in Togiak. In the first fifteen minutes after arriving on the fishing grounds . . . we caught enough fish to pay for the entire airplane and save the day. Without my father's love, reliability and talents, this never would have happened. My life is full of such events and blessings by this man I know as the best father a son can have.

Dwayne's influence appears undiminished in the third generation. Becky's older daughter, Aurora, wrote the following in 2007, when she was 11:

Flying

Ever since I was born I have done quite a bit of flying. Maybe it's because I was almost born in the back of an airplane. Over the years I have learned to steer a small plane and on my 16th birthday I will be allowed to solo. I have flown different kinds of small planes but my favorite model is a Cessna 150.

Sometimes, when I go flying with my grandpa we land on gravel bars of the Matanuska River. . . . My grandpa is a prankster and sometimes we quietly fly below a sightseeing point and buzz up around the stunned people. When I fly from my grandpa's house he lets me steer and navigate to Merrill Field, an airport in Anchorage for small planes. I navigate by the black highway twisting and turning with the cars below me. Sometimes I fly high and sometimes I fly low depending on where I'm at. I can't land or takeoff by myself yet because I'm still learning.

My cousin Jeremiah and I have made it a contest to see who will solo first! He is older than me by ten days but I have done more flying than him. We both like to fly with my grandpa in the back of a two-seater airplane. I like to fly among the high and majestic mountains looking for moose, sheep, reindeer, but mostly bear. I count the animals we see from the airplane and take pictures through the open door.

To me the best part of flying is being up so high. I love to look down and see people as tiny as ants or the blurs of cars in so many colors. I like watching the ground below as we zoom along.

To some people flying may seem hard, but I think I almost have it! It may be genetic, because my mom, dad, grandpa and all my mom's brothers fly. So I kind of have to be a pilot so that my family can live with me!

Becky reported the following conversation with Aurora's younger sister, 8-year-old Taiga:

Taiga's been asking why I was sitting here for so long. I told her I was reading this book about Grandpa.

Taiga: "Oh, is he famous?"

Me: "Well, kind of."

Taiga: "Well that makes me famous too, right? Make sure they say in the book that he has two granddaughters who are learning to fly."

Above: King family, 2010, at wedding of Debbie (standing left) and Dave (not in picture). Others standing, from left, are Aurora, Becky, Jeremiah (son of Jon King), LaReina and Joel. Seated, from left, are Taiga, Carolyn, Dwayne, Briana, Cathy King (wife of Jon, wearing sunglasses). Inset, from left, are Ian and Renee, children of Joel and LaReina; and Canyon, son of Jon. Below: Dave, piloting helicopter.

The lives of many others, some of whose comments follow, have also been changed by Dwayne. Some are famous, and some are unknown outside the circle of their own families and friends. All of them count Dwayne as a friend.

His influence has often been strong and direct, but sometimes subtle. Those touched by it range from strong Christians, made stronger by Dwayne, to those who have seen in him their first glimpse of a servant of God; from those whose lives have been transformed by his influence to those who sense, if only faintly, that he represents something desirable. Others have seen how he has changed those around them, and still others have changed him, as he has changed them.

One of those quoted, missionary pilot Roger Krenzin, is among those whose lives have been enriched by Dwayne despite having met him only briefly.

Rev. David King
Older brother (letter, 2007)

All it took for Dwayne to transform his brother's life was a long-distance telephone call.

Perhaps the most life-changing experience connected with my brother Dwayne was when he called from Far East Russia and asked me to come and help him. To make a long story short, I did and was never the same. Our call to serve with SEND International in Kiev is directly related to my brother and his passion for the peoples of the former Soviet Union. Thanks brother!

Lew Parks
Former co-worker, Gault Chevrolet (interview, 2007)

After working together in the early 1960s at Gault Chevrolet in Endicott, Lew and Dwayne went their separate ways—Lew to a career as a NASCAR and Indianapolis 500 mechanic, Dwayne to missions. Lew had known Dwayne as an intelligent young man, but one who was mainly interested in fast cars. When he learned years later that Dwayne had become a missionary, "I couldn't believe it!"

He saw Dwayne's slides of Russia and heard him speak at Twin Orchards. They chatted on later occasions, whenever Dwayne was visiting in the area, and Dwayne became one of the influences that made him look beyond the immediate here and now.

Lew had attended church as a teenager, but life was moving too fast then for him to pay much attention. Dwayne re-entered the scene as he was growing older, and realizing that life was becoming less controllable and predictable.

"He made me aware there's more to life than just what we see," Lew recalls. It was Dwayne's character, not just his words, that influenced him. "He was just one of those guys that are special. I was impressed with his direction. You could just trust him—not worry about him."

In the early 2000s, Dwayne spoke at Twin Orchards about his work in Russia and Kazakhstan. He said Lew came up to him afterwards and showed him his Indy 500 team ring, saying: "What you've got is much more valuable than this!"

On a Georgia highway around the same time period, Lew's avoidance of two breakdowns and a serious accident triggered thoughts that reflected Dwayne's influence. "The whole situation was out of my control—and I had a little help along the way," Lew recalls "If you're going too fast, you can miss a lot of things around you."

He later told Dwayne, "I have a few cherished friends, and you're one of them."

Years before their friendship developed, Lew unknowingly played a part in launching Dwayne's career. He was the previous owner of the 1948 Ford hot rod that transported Dwayne and his new bride to Texas, where Dwayne learned to fly. Lew had bought the car in 1957 in Honesdale, Pennsylvania, for $150, and traded it for Dwayne's notorious 1939 Cadillac LaSalle of Practical Bible Training School fame.

Rev. Paul Blasko
Friend (interview, 2005)

In *The Wizard of Oz*, a Kansas tornado whisks Dorothy away from her farm and sets her down in a strange place. Dwayne has a similar technique. He whisked Paul out of his comfort zone in upstate New York to the far side of the world to do things like leading Russian Bible college students on street-witnessing expeditions down Karl Marx Boulevard in Khabarovsk.

Dwayne's "great insight," said Paul, is knowing that if you can lure people—for whatever reason—to where they can see a need, "something good's going to come out of that. They're going to get more out of it than their motivation deserves." That's how Dwayne got him to teach and lecture in Far East Russia in 1998, zeroing in on the skills which, he knew, Paul had confidence and enjoyment in exercising.

"Dwayne lets a lot of people into his life," he added. "I was one, and the impact was significant. He taught me the value of being connected to people, to let what happens in the course of friendship develop. He also modeled for me an unusual work ethic and commitment to integrity... He never wanted to let down anyone who was counting on him—often at his own inconvenience or cost."

Dwayne also introduced his friend to Alaska, leading to Paul's wild-life photography and game dinner ministry that dominated his retirement. "My experience is typical. Dwayne's willingness to say 'Come along!' ultimately led to a ministry neither of us could predict at the time."

Elsie Livers
Widow of Fay Livers, boss and mentor in Texas (letter, 2006)

"He worked for my husband and was always the same sweet Christian, did his work cheerfully, and was like a son to my husband. He was always witnessing for Jesus. He strengthened our lives."

Dorris Stevenson
SEND/Alaska administrative secretary, 1980-1995 (letter, 2009)

"People were drawn to Dwayne like a moth to a flame. When flying, he was on the radio constantly, talking to everyone and anyone on the ground who would talk to him. When we landed, we saw folks drawn from the control towers or from inside hangars to greet and hug him.

"On one of our trips to Providenya ... we boarded a crowded bus. Within minutes, Dwayne spotted an old *babushka* in her head scarf, and he totally disregarded any cross-cultural training we'd been taught, and pushed his way up through the crowded aisle and loudly greeted her, and they exchanged big hugs.

"Dwayne would (and probably still does) slaughter the Russian grammar ... but he communicated, and the people loved him for that. And he could get away with it when others could not."

Dr. Alvin O. "Bud" Austin
Former president, LeTourneau University (letter, ca 2007)

"I have learned to be more spontaneous in my personal witness just by observing Dwayne. He is a doer, always saying 'yes' to every opportunity to engage, to witness, to try something new. He has unlimited energy ...

not always easy to focus. His wife and kids say he has Attention Deficit Disorder ... he moves from one project to another and often finds himself up against time restraints he cannot meet. I think my organizational ability and analytical style help Dwayne stop, assess, and put together a meaningful plan to help him put more structure to his actions. We balance each other out on many fronts."

Rev. Gennady Abramov
Former chief Baptist pastor, Far East Russia (interview, 2005)

"Dwayne had a very strong effect on my life... He taught me to accept others just as they are, and to work with them ... he accepted me just as I was." Dwayne's "good relations" with Carolyn, Gennady added, were a model for him and his wife, Vera.

"He was a brave man. A real man ... a very trustful man. A simple man. An open man."

Gennady, in turn, taught Dwayne an even deeper level of trust—which he needed on one occasion, when officials tried to expel him from Russia and Gennady vouched for him. "Here, only God and prayer could help," Gennady recalls. "He learned to trust God more. He just believed me, and trusted in God."

Lena Sidenko
Interpreter and secretary (interview, 2005)

Lena became a Christian in 1990, and her first husband left her two years later. "It was a difficult time for me," said the Khabarovsk woman who became Dwayne's key helper in much of his Far East work. "I didn't trust men. But [Dwayne] showed me there are different kinds of men," she said, crediting him with strengthening her spiritual outlook.

He was reliable, she said with a laugh—not for his administrative or theoretical skills, but for qualities of the heart: "... loving, caring, faithful, trustworthy, compassionate. He's unique. He's a hands-on guy," she added, expressing amazement at his language progress. Despite his bad grammar, she said, Russians understand him "because it's from his heart."

Dwayne's words of encouragement—and correction, when needed—were also from the heart, and served as a model for her: "I use this with others. If we love each other, we have to tell some things we don't like."

"He's a very adventurous person. You will never be bored with him."

Rev. Yuri Sipko
Immediate past president, Russian Baptist Union (letter, 2007)

"Dwayne has a heart filled with love to Russian people. I saw many times how he was able to waken the same feelings in the hearts of American people. During my stay in the United States in February 2003, I saw myself how he was speaking with one of [the] college students. She was weeping and there were tears in her eyes while she was speaking to Dwayne. When we asked him what was the problem with her, the answer was she made a decision to be a missionary and go to Russia.

"Dwayne is a good preacher... We observed at the meeting with hunters [local church game dinner] how he was able to lead people and attract their attention.

"At the same time, Dwayne is a very modest person. I remember in March 2002 he was our guest at the Baptist Union Congress. There were many foreign speakers ... but Dwayne was not among them ... I asked him why he did not ask to be included ... the answer was: 'I did not dare. I was sitting among the delegates and I was enjoying the atmosphere of love and gladness.' I know Dwayne as a person who is ready to sacrifice for his ministry. I was impressed to learn that he ... is using a house on wheels in order to be mobile and travel across the United States.

"I know he had a problem with his health but it never affected his ministry. Dwayne is a good husband. We know how he loves his wife and his children. We hope to see him again and again in Russia."

Oleg and Tanya Vasin
Russian missionaries (letter from Tanya, late 1990s)

"Dear Dwayne, our friend and brother!
"... Since college time you've been an example of a pastor for us, and taught us how to love God and people.
"... When I worked as a choir director in Khabarovsk you also always encouraged me... We remember our first Summer Missions Program team from America. You were driving the van, tired, didn't sleep during the night. But you gave us instructions and encouraged us. When Oleg was in the hospital, you visited him there. You just simply supported us with your trust and love during [a] difficult time for us.
"... We remember your ministry here in Far East Russia. And the fact that you left is a pain for us. We love you very much and pray for you, and cry. Our desire—that you won't get disappointed about Russian people.

"Please pray for us. The church is growing and there is much work to do and many needs.

"With love, the Vasins family"

Oleg Vasin

Nicolai and Tatiana Koshelupov
Friends (letter from Tatiana, 2006)

"Our first introduction to Dwayne King occurred on December of 1993 in [the] city of Khabarovsk . . . in the apartment that Dwayne and Caroline were renting... It was either Thanksgiving or Christmas dinner with 'real' turkey, which was brought from America by [SEND missionaries] Rex and Lori [Durham]. We were introduced to Dwayne and his family by our new mutual friend Gennady Abramov... Just then, my husband and I were not members of any church or believers in God.

"Our first impression of Dwayne was: cheerful, kind, open-hearted, candid, trustworthy and intellectual individual.

"Acquaintance with Dwayne changed our spiritual outlook on church and the meaning of Christian life. In addition, it modified our view about people [who are] called believers and their purpose of serving God.

"The first example of an effective missionary that comes to our mind is Dwayne King. God blesses him with wisdom and gives him possibilities to reach out and witness to people about His love and salvation. Dwayne's effectiveness comes from obeying the Lord and taking every opportunity to serve Him."

Win and Gracia Stiefel
Alaska friends and Siberian missionaries (letter, 2009)

Win and Gracia Stiefel joined Dwayne's congregation in Tok, Alaska, in the 1970s, and later became SEND missionaries to Siberia. Whenever they returned to Russia after home service,

> Dwayne would meet us at the airport and we'd usually have a few days before our flight to Yakutsk [Siberia]. We'd go with Dwayne on his trips to various camps, villages and individuals. We could see how much the people loved him and looked forward to his visits. Many were going through many stresses because of officials against Christians, etc. Dwayne would encourage them and pray with them and soon there would be smiles and laughter. We also saw how the [Russian] Baptist leadership regarded Dwayne. Several years later we met Dwayne in Moscow and met some more pastors and leaders, and they all respected and loved him.

Durland "Dur" Vining
Friend and mission supporter (reminiscence, 2002)

Dwayne was only one of the kings, but an important one, in Dur's life. His fascination with kingship began in childhood—he was excited by the label on the silk lining of his father's fine English derby: *Hatters to His Majesty the King*.

"... what a privilege ... to be able to say you were working for the King," recalls Dur, a longtime friend from Vestal. His fascination was later reinforced by a tale of two youngsters who, when questioned by a policeman for wandering too close to the fence around Buckingham Palace, replied, "We're nobody—but our father is the King!"

This resonated with Dur, who later traveled with Dwayne in Far East Russia and hand-crafted wooden communion sets for congregations there.

> And so it is with the job of producing communion sets ... The work was set out for me by a king—Dwayne King. The Russians who got the end product are kings in my mind, having "ruled over" such things as ridicule, ostracism, prison and martyrdom through the practice of the very

Gospel that was forbidden them. Most importantly, the work was placed in my heart by the *King of Kings*.

Don and Ann Lewis
Friends and mission team leaders (interview, 2006)

Dwayne's favorite Russian phrase was "Pi-ekalee!" (Let's go!) and when Don and Ann heard it, nothing was the same.

"There wasn't much he didn't change. I went from a farmer boy to a missionary boy," Don said. He and Ann were looking forward to comfortable retirement in upstate New York when Dwayne got hold of them. They were already in God's service as local church leaders, but his influence "sure turned us around, mission-wise," Ann recalls. "Our lives became very full."

Dwayne first persuaded them to come to Alaska and help with mission preparations before signing them up for Russia—"He must have evaluated us a little bit," Don recalls. The main thing Dwayne taught them, Ann said, was, "Be ready and willing, and God will make you able." Their experience as construction team leaders, publicly articulating their faith before Russian believers, resulted in at least one big change in Ann's soft-spoken husband.

"Don never spoke to groups, even under threat of death," Ann said. "That all changed!"

Herbert Paul
Friend (interview, 2010)

About thirty-five years ago, a young Athabaskan man heard something that made hope taste better than whiskey. Christ was the message, and Dwayne was the messenger.

Without it, Herbert recalls, "I'd be long gone into eternity."

He repaired planes for the Air Force in Vietnam and fought fires throughout Alaska for the Bureau of Land Management. Despite arthritis in his knees and ankles, Herbert still does some hunting and fishing and cuts his own wood for his home in Tanacross. He's 70 now. But in the 1970s, numbed with alcohol and freezing on the winter streets of Tok, or tapping for help on the Kings' bedroom window in the darkness of summer nights, it didn't seem likely that he would reach 40.

He was among the villagers in the Upper Tanana River Valley whose lives Dwayne helped save, physically and eternally.

I'm pretty sure I wouldn't be around if it weren't for Dwayne. The Bible says, *go into the world and present the Gospel.* That's what he did. He was the bearer of good news, salvation in Christ Jesus. A lot of people don't understand they're lost. I learned through him to understand what the Bible is all about.

I quit drinking a long time ago. I didn't have a problem leaving it... When you turn to God, you have the peace of God. You don't need that stuff to feel high. It's all God's work. Dwayne's someone God uses to change lives. I'm sure God used him a lot in my life.

Dwayne buried Herbert's father, David, a lay Episcopalian minister, and helped his son stay alive. He described Herbert as his friend, "a child of God who defeated alcohol and knows the Lord." Herbert calls Dwayne "my brother in Christ. He changed the lives of others, too."

Roger A. Krenzin
Second-generation missionary pilot (letter, 2010)

"Dwayne's life has shown me the depth and width of his commitment to reaching the world with the Gospel, and has encouraged and challenged me to continue using my life and God-given gifts and abilities likewise."

J.C. Harder
Dwayne's first flight instructor (letter, 2010)

"It is not unusual to see, either winter or summer, Dwayne crawling into a Super Cub or some other airplane at 5:30 in the morning to take a friend up to the glacier to view the beautiful creation, or to spot some wild game or give some flight instruction.

"I have been trying to teach Dwayne how to say 'No,' but since I haven't learned myself, it is a lost cause. If Dwayne thinks he can use an airplane to introduce someone to the Lord, he's on his way to the cockpit."

20. MEASURING A LEGACY
To God be the Glory

You know, there's only three things that are eternal. Only three.
God, God's Word, and people.

—Dwayne King,
1991 missions conference

O victory in Jesus, my Savior forever,
He sought me and bought me with His redeeming blood;
He loved me ere I knew Him, and all my love is due Him,
He plunged me to victory, beneath the cleansing flood.
— "Victory in Jesus" (E.M. Bartlett),
Dwayne's favorite song

THE CHALLENGE of writing the biography of a living man is that he's a moving target, as is the changing world in which he lives. Even an up-to-date presentation is an image frozen in time, obsolete by definition as time moves on.

Some temporary updating is possible. Kingdom Air Corps is growing—in March 2010 Dwayne excitedly told supporters, "The Russians are coming!" The five new flight students would include several who, in April, cheered while he and a Russian copilot took off from a muddy airstrip near Khabarovsk. The students saw in that short flight the coming realization of a long dream. As foreign mission groups continue to be expelled from Russia, reflecting a growing chill that began only a few years after the Soviet Union dissolved two decades ago, Dwayne sees the Russian trainees as the first of many who will become increasingly important in flying the Gospel to remote parts of Siberia and Russia's Far East. The recent relaxation of Russian aviation rules promises to bring that dream closer.

But overall, Dwayne's biography depends less than others on a connection with historic events. His story is less about what he did yesterday or will do tomorrow to open Russia's skies, and more about who he is and what he has always done to open individual human hearts. This is because he long ago yielded his life to what he understands as God's changeless purpose: redemption, one heart at a time.

This chapter is therefore not a final summary of events, but a celebration of the gifts and achievements he has brought, and still brings, to that purpose.

A Work of Love

At the 1991 missions conference, Dwayne—an obsessive car-cleaner despite his acceptance of rough living conditions—summed up God's purpose and human needs with a unique illustration that could be called "talking trash."

> We were just up in Maine—in every little town and village, I see in big letters, "Redemption Center." I love it! I'm thinking, *This is where people come to get saved.* But it isn't. I become disappointed when I see ... *garbage.* Bottles and cans and jars and paper. It's where people bring their *garbage* to be redeemed. But I think about that—what a beautiful illustration! Where we need to bring our garbage, and get it turned into something good. They take those things, and they melt them down and they burn them, or they process them and make something good out of something worthless. That's redemption. That's what God is doing in your life and in my life.

Calling himself and others at the missions conference "key links" in God's purpose, he offered a seeming contradiction: He urged listeners to sacrifice their personal plans to God's, but at the same time said that ministry is "not a difficult thing." The contradiction is resolved, he indicated, in the joy of service that comes from sharing the knowledge of what redemption means to one's self and others.

> When we really have upon our hearts—as a driving, motivating force—the purpose of Almighty God, it's exhilarating... It really gets us going and keeps us going, because we see and understand what God is up

to worldwide. And we see ourselves as an important link in God's chain of accomplishing His purpose.

... When you are driven with the same purpose that God had when He sent His son Jesus to die for a lost world ... when you look into the eyes and rub shoulders with the people alongside of you at work, and you hear about the people in a foreign country—foreign to our imagination, foreign to our thought and our experience—it's not difficult to go [on mission service] when you have the heart of God and you identify with the purpose of God ...

God is about His business of working through you to bring [others] to a saving knowledge of Jesus Christ... When we really understand the character of Almighty God, we will be motivated, we will be encouraged to give our all for Him.

Dwayne does not share an older view that some particular person will be lost because some other particular person did not witness to him or her. "God simply asks His children to go ... That is a command"—a command which, if ignored, brings loss of the blessings of service. His understanding of his own part in the process leads in a clear, bright line to relationships with people.

His personality is well suited to demonstrating redemption as a work of love. Once, while cleaning guns at his home in Alaska after a hunt with some visitors, he said quietly: *"They're not believers. I'm being gentle with them."* His voice was warm and excited—not like a judge, bent on reforming wrongdoers, but like the winner of a huge prize, eager to share it with two cherished friends.

In Khabarovsk, recalls friend Dur Vining, Dwayne was making ice cream on the tiny balcony of his apartment when a woman doing laundry a few floors up accidentally dropped a sock. When she came downstairs to retrieve it, Dwayne gave her a cup of fresh-made ice cream.

"He didn't have to do that. He's a friend-maker," said Dur. "I think Alaska was his training ground. Russia is where he bloomed. SEND told him to repeat it in Kazahkstan."

Another longtime friend, former LeTourneau President Bud Austin, cites Dwayne's gift of establishing strong, bonding relationships:

His instant smile and deep-hearted laugh will break down any barriers instantly. Open, friendly and interested in each person ... one cannot help but love him instantly. My son spent half a day with him and now resonates when I mention Dwayne.

The gift is effective, Bud adds, because of the transparent emotional reality that authenticates Dwayne's words and reproduces his passion in others:

> He lives to share God with others—it comes out of his pores. He is effective because he loves Jesus. He would say ... "If you know Him, you will love Him; if you love Him, you will serve Him; if you don't serve Him, you must not know Him." As I travel the world ... I've met numerous missionaries, pastors and Christian lay people who have said, "Dwayne led me to the Lord" or "Dwayne inspired me to ministry."

Remembering details, as well as establishing relationships, enhances Dwayne's credibility. Interpreter Lena Sidenko admits her former boss was no great administrator, but adds, "People in Russia love him very much. The relationship is more important than work. I was impressed that he knew all the missionaries and pastors in Far East Russia, and their wives and children."

Respecting the details is at least as important as knowing them. Here's missionary Gracia Stiefel's take:

> I think what has made Dwayne successful working with other cultures is his ability to listen and not put forth his own agenda... Some missionaries came to Alaskan villages and Russia with their own agenda and ideas. They saw things they didn't like in the host culture, and were determined to change the people and the way they did things. And as Americans, they wanted the changes to come fast. However, Dwayne learned as much as he could about the culture, and showed respect, and tried his best to learn the language... While in Alaska he tried to learn greetings and phrases in the difficult Athabaskan language, and again the people loved him. He had a knack for being at ease in well-to-do settings with leaders, and also to be at ease in situations of extreme poverty with the poor and neglected. He was patient with people, and didn't expect them to do or think like him.

Leander Rempel, Dwayne's former boss and mentor in Alaska, has no hesitation in terming him "outstanding" in every category of missionary work—church planting, evangelizing, recruiting and fund-raising—for one reason: "His love for people." The love, according to mission team leaders Don and Ann Lewis, is believable.

"People can see into Dwayne's heart right away. There's nothing false," says Don.

"What you see is what you get," says Ann.

Dwayne's daring and love of speed prepared him well for the mission path. He understands that time is short, the task huge and the stakes eternal, making his path a running track. Colleagues use words like "visionary," "starter," "pioneer," "field-opener" and—sometimes behind his back—"Energizer Bunny."

"He is at his best in a starter, pioneering role, where his entrepreneurial gifts can be freely used. He exudes faith and a spirit of trusting God for the impossible," says Frank Severn, SEND director emeritus. "I believe his greatest legacy will be his spearheading our work in Russia and Kazahkstan."

"I have never met anyone who is a better recruiter," says Carl Kresge, former SEND Eurasia co-director. If Dwayne hasn't always been the "obstetrician" in delivering new Christians, says his friend, Rev. Paul Blasko, "he's sure altered the landscape to make it easier for other people to do that. He blesses the socks off everyone he works with." Russian Pastor Gennady Abramov credits Dwayne with a "huge role" in launching the work of both native and foreign missionaries in Far East Russia.

"He lit the torch and opened the way to working with the [Russian] Baptist Union," says former SEND planner Robert "Bob" Provost.

Dwayne doesn't let the age of potential missionaries stand in the way of his recruiting efforts.

"Russia still needs us. You've got a few more trips and a few more miles in you," he told a crowd of aging, short-term volunteers at a Davis College mission reunion in 2009. At the other end of the age continuum, according to Elsie Livers, a friend from the LeTourneau years, "He is bringing many young Christians to Jesus and to the mission field."

Biblical comparisons are inevitable.

Elsie compares him to the Apostle Paul, saying, "Dwayne will go anywhere or do anything, or even endanger his life to spread the Gospel."

"Dwayne reminds me of Joshua and Caleb," says Frank Severn. "He sees the promises of God and the great possibilities of advancing the Gospel as much greater than the obstacles that stand in the way."

Leander Rempel thinks of the young King David. "Dwayne has the same ability to instill in others the loyalty and excitement to follow him to the ends of the earth."

A "King" of Song and Laughter

On March 21, 2010, in Vestal, Dwayne stood before a small Sunday school class in his home church, Cal Tab, and addressed serious issues:

Support for missions. Pilot training. A meeting, scheduled the next day in Moscow with high-level evangelical leaders, to discuss (among other things) the future of Russian believers threatened by erosions of religious freedom.

"Here we are," he told his longtime friends, mostly middle-aged and elderly worshipers, "creakin', squeakin', and leakin'!'"

His willingness to fly under the radar of dignified pomposity and mock his generation's—and thus his own—aging joints, digestions and bladders endears him to friends and strangers alike, clearing the way for them to take his serious issues seriously. If merry hearts and witty sayings are celebrated by the writer of Proverbs and Jesus Himself, who is Dwayne to disagree?

One might expect a determined missionary confronting a lost world to sound more dramatic and eloquent—and Dwayne does, when necessary. But overall, his style is not like Aragorn's somber exhortation to the warriors of Gondor before the Black Gate, surrounded by the grim hosts of Mordor in *The Lord of the Rings*. It's more like Col. Henry Blake of *M*A*S*H*, or the possibly apocryphal Marine or Israeli noncom who, with his squad pinned down by heavy fire, says: "They've got us surrounded—the poor b......s!"

Some memories of Dwayne's humor and spontaneity—and friendliness toward strangers whom others might want to avoid—are recounted by Carl Kresge and another longtime friend, Marla McCrorie, Paul and Joann Blasko's daughter. When Carl was visiting in Alaska:

> Dwayne took me on a fishing trip for silver salmon. I caught about a twelve-pounder first. Just minutes before we left the river, Dwayne caught a good-sized one as well. He informed me that his fish was bigger than mine ... we had pictures taken side by side, with each of us holding our fish. It took me three or four minutes before I realized that Dwayne was intentionally holding his fish slightly closer to the camera ... to make it look like the bigger fish! You gotta watch this guy! Truth be told, my fish was slightly bigger than Dwayne's!
>
> One of my girls' fondest memories of Dwayne is sitting around our living room in Khabarovsk during team meetings and singing. Dwayne is not one to sing quietly or sitting still. We all remember his enthusiastic leading of "Victory in Jesus," especially his gestures on the chorus.

Marla cites the same song, and adds:

> Dwayne has given Christians of several cultures a fresh love of singing in church. This reminds me of 2 Chronicles 20:22, where Jehoshaphat

sent singers out at the head of the army: *As they began to sing and praise, the men ... who were invading Judah ... were defeated.* If people are singing first, then everything else follows.

Most people avoid proximity or eye contact with drunks, especially ones they don't know, particularly in foreign countries. Not Dwayne, says Carl.

... we spent the day with our Russian friends at the beach, teaching them how to play American football. When we returned to Dwayne's house, he got out of the van with bare, sandy feet, and his jeans rolled up to his knees. A couple of drunks were sitting on the bench in front of his apartment and, being Dwayne, he stopped and talked with them.

Dwayne's sense of humor sometimes gets him into trouble.

On an Aeroflot plane, gum left on the seatbelt by a previous passenger stuck to Carl's pants, and a flight attendant insisted on trying to remove it. "Dwayne couldn't resist the opportunity, and took a picture of what he considered a very humorous event," Carl recalls. "He promptly got chewed out by the flight attendant, who didn't appreciate this American gathering photographic evidence of a less-than-satisfactory flight experience on their Russian airline!"

But according to Carl, the value of contact outweighs gaffes. "Several times I have been with Dwayne on a plane or in an airport, or out in public someplace, and seen him strike up a conversation with a total stranger ... And often, Dwayne would turn those conversations into opportunities to say a word for Christ."

Carolyn usually leaves the humor to Dwayne. But in her realization that he has, and will, spend all of his being in saying that word for Christ, she found something to smile at in an irreverent description of finality: *Life is not a journey to the grave with the intention of arriving safely in a well-preserved body, but rather skidding in broadside, thoroughly used up, totally worn out, and proclaiming, "Wow! What a ride!"*

Time for Everyone—One at a Time

According to a printout titled "Dwayne/Carolyn King's Schedule," a recent fifteen-day visit to the Binghamton area listed twenty-three blocks of time containing thirty-one separate events at six churches and two schools. Worship, eat, lecture, sing, PowerPoint, listen, preach, pray, repeat same numerous times, at every conceivable faith-related institution, church group, age group, fellowship, performance, brotherhood, sisterhood, etc. etc.

But according to Carl Kresge,

> Whenever I spent the day with Dwayne, traveling around on errands, meeting various people, etc., I'd always have to figure it would take twice as long as expected, since Dwayne would always stop and talk with someone, whether a stranger on a street or an acquaintance or a long-lost buddy. He could never resist a chance to talk with someone; and it seemed like we could never go for more than a few hours without him bumping into someone who knew him.

... And according to Dwayne, "Plan for years in advance, but live each day as if nothing will go as planned."
... And according to J.C. Harder, his former flight instructor, "He takes time for each person he meets. The person is more important than the project." For Dwayne, the person *is* the project. As he explained at the 1991 missions conference, he just does what he understands God wants him to do, and God doesn't appear to be interested in anything that takes precedence over human souls.

> You know, there's only three things that are eternal. Only three. God, God's word, and people. And when we stop to think about the effort, the time, the energy, the money, the drive and the motivation that we put into so many things ... so much energy that we put into doing this and doing that, and going here and going there, and the plans that we've set forth—they don't include God's purpose ...
> We need to sit down. We need to be quiet. We need to think... We have a lot of things that we want to accomplish in an hour from now. Or tomorrow or whenever. But He says, *Sit back, think and remember. I am God and there is no other. I am God and there is none like me.*
> Who is God to you? The impact of what we become in this life is determined by what we think about the character of Almighty God. Who is He to you? Not *who is He to this world?* Not *who is He to this church?* Not *who was He back then?* But, *Who is He to me?*
> ... God is up to redemption. God is up to bringing people to Himself.
> ... Growing in the Christian life ... is the process by which we conform more and more to the image of Jesus Christ. What is the image of Jesus Christ? *As the Father has sent Me, even so send I you.* See, He came for a purpose.

In serving that purpose, good judgment is also more important than any project or schedule—for which J.C., Kostya Rudoy and I are grateful. In 2006 we were rolling down the runway in Soldotna, Alaska, bound for Kingdom Air Corps after a busy day of collecting information for the demonstration flight to Khabarovsk. Dwayne, who was piloting, sensed a balky cylinder. He aborted the takeoff and made a temporary repair.

Time lost: about three hours. Advantage gained: live to follow God another day—and reach more people.

The Sky Isn't the Limit

Some say Dwayne's main legacy is the advancement of mission aviation.

"I guess he could be compared to Elijah, who rode a whirlwind, accompanied by chariots of fire, out of this world," says Leander Rempel. "If it were possible to pilot a chariot of fire and a whirlwind, Dwayne would do it. He certainly has flown every conceivable aircraft he could get his hands on." But, he adds, "I don't think you can isolate an area and say that is his most important accomplishment."

J.C. Harder puts Dwayne's passion into perspective. "He loves aviation as a tool to introduce people to the Lord. People know that as much as he loves aviation, he loves them more." He loves them more because he loves God above all, and he loves what God loves—which demands all he has. In *Let the Nations Be Glad*, one of Dwayne's major inspirations, author John Piper says:

> God is calling us above all else to be the kind of people whose theme and passion is the supremacy of God in all of life. No one will be able to rise to the magnificence of the missionary cause who does not feel the magnificence of Christ. There will be no big world vision without a big God. There will be no passion to draw others into our worship where there is no passion for worship.
>
> God is pursuing with omnipotent passion a worldwide purpose of gathering joyful worshipers for himself from every tribe and tongue and people and nation. He has an inexhaustible enthusiasm for the supremacy of his name among the nations. Therefore, let us bring our affections into line with his, and, for the sake of his name, let us renounce the quest for worldly comforts and join his global purpose. If we do this, God's omnipotent commitment to his name will be over us like a banner, and we will not lose ...

Asking about Dwayne's legacy in terms of achievements ranked by importance or number invites the same answer Jesus gave when Peter also asked about something specific: ... *what is that to thee? Follow thou me.* (John 21:22 KJV) For Dwayne, simply obeying that command has been his biggest achievement, making the others possible.

Astonishing as it seems, he once doubted that he was being obedient at all. "I don't know if I ever led anyone to Christ," he confided to Paul Blasko in Khabarovsk during a moment of discouragement. Paul reassured him that by reaching into the lives of others, he had probably caused them to make decisions he was unaware of. "Because they loved Dwayne," he recalls, "they fell in love with Whom he represented."

Although, in Paul's view, Dwayne is best at encouraging Christians, he rarely misses an opportunity to witness to unbelievers. "He never grabs them by the throat. He leaves room for God to work." Some of the people Dwayne approached were in very early stages of spiritual awareness. "If they didn't respond to the Gospel the first time," Paul said, "he sure got them interested in hearing it a second time!"

Paul describes what he calls his friend's greatest accomplishment in Russia: "He's modeled for his colleagues what it means to serve the church. That's the antithesis of lording it over the church." Dwayne's recruitment of both career and short-term missionaries, he adds, "has multiplied him many times over."

"His legacy is himself," Leander asserts. Dwayne would probably concede as much, but only—as he has insisted—if God gets the glory. In fact, he'd be just as happy to pass unnoticed. He recently said he was glad that many Russian Christians no longer know him. "It's not my name-sake—it's God's."

A quote Dwayne loves, by motivational speaker Mac Anderson, goes as follows:

> *Excellence is the result of caring more than others think is wise, risking more than others think is safe, dreaming more than others think is practical, and expecting more than others think is possible.*

By itself, the definition says nothing about the object of all that dreaming, caring and daring. It could be excellence in computer games or hotdog-eating contests. It's probably a popular mantra at graduations and sales meetings. Context helps. Where Dwayne first saw it was on a wall-mounted plaque at SOAR International Ministries in Soldotna. He had visited SOAR in August 2006, seeking help in planning the flight to Khabarovsk he hoped would stimulate general aviation in Russia, leading in time to opening the skies to the spread of the Gospel. Dwayne has made it clear that this is what he wants to be excellent at—doing his part in bringing about God's ultimate purpose as John Piper describes it:

> ... It is our unspeakable privilege to be caught up with [God] in the greatest movement in history—the ingathering of the elect from every tribe and language and people and nation until the full number of the Gentiles comes in and all Israel is saved and the Son of Man descends with power and great glory as King of kings and Lord of lords and the earth is full of the knowledge of his glory as the waters cover the sea forever and ever. Then the supremacy of Christ will be manifest to all, and he will deliver the kingdom to God the Father, and God will be all in all.

The life of His servant testifies to joyous obedience to the command to help fulfill that purpose. The excellence of Dwayne's effort is already known by many who have been able to thank him and follow in his footsteps, and in the hearts of numberless others whose gratitude is known only to themselves and God. It will be known fully to Dwayne when he hears it from the Control Tower after the last landing.

TO THE READER

⌒

IF YOU ARE a believer seeking God's will for your life, and if Dwayne's story has moved you, you might be a potential missionary. Consider asking God if this would be the best way for you to magnify His glory: living out for others the love He has given you.

Many churches, schools and other Christian organizations offer mission opportunities ranging from one-week volunteer projects to lifelong careers. Those who can't go can still partner in the work of the Kingdom by praying, giving, and telling the mission story.

If you're near to belief but still unsure if Christ offers you anything, now or eternally, think about what you've just read. Dwayne's life, and the lives he has touched, show the joy, adventure and peace enjoyed by those who go beyond mere intellectual assent to Christ's life. Making a decision to trust Christ, as Dwayne did when he was 11, brings empowerment to live in His light.

Missions have changed the lives and strengthened the faith of many lukewarm believers, illustrating the biblical truth that God moves closer to those who move closer to Him. It's a journey open to anyone.

If you're not a believer, you still, apparently, had enough interest in Dwayne's story to read this far. So you might want to know whether He who has first claim on Dwayne's life also has a claim on yours. Without going into theological detail, it's as simple as admitting you need a Savior and accepting Christ's gifts: forgiveness, the power to live as He wants you to live, and a relationship of love and worship that lasts forever. If you have trustworthy Christian friends who believe and live the whole Word of God, they'll be happy to explain who Christ was and is, and why He alone can give you these gifts.

The same God who filled Dwayne's life with adventure and purpose can enter your life and, through you, the lives of others.

ABOUT THE AUTHOR

M ARK WINHELD was born in 1941 in Philadelphia and spent his early childhood in Manhattan. He played in Central Park and gawked at dinosaurs in the Museum of Natural History while his dad, an Army doctor, treated GIs in New Guinea. The family later moved to suburban Philly, where Mark attended Lower Merion High School and lusted after artistic fame, soccer stardom, popular female classmates, triumph over bullies, and proficiency as a writer.

Only writing survived the predictable fate (a decent burial) that overtook the other adolescent fantasies.

Mark graduated from Antioch College in Ohio and received an M.A. in anthropology from the University of Arizona. From 1969 until retiring in 1998, he reported for daily newspapers in South Dakota, Ohio and upstate New York, and won several awards.

He and his wife Mary Lou, a former nurse and high school teacher, have three children, four grandchildren and a fluctuating number of dogs and cats. He enjoys traditional archery and playing the guitar and harmonica, but his family has been fortunate enough not to have to depend on his skill at those disciplines for food or entertainment.

Pivotal influences include Russian-Jewish ancestry and parents who gave him a love of literature and a passion for social justice. His mother and father also gave him a sense of history underlain by World War II, the central event of their generation, and the Civil Rights movement, a central event in his. Youthful hitchhiking journeys, wilderness adventures and unskilled labor jobs showed him that the beauty of the earth and the heroism of ordinary people are more than sentimental abstractions.

The master influence, faith in Christ, entered around 1990. This added an eternal dimension to everything that had shaped his life up to then, and from then on. Mission trips to Far East Russia to help build evangelical churches made him appreciate his roots with new vividness. A few brushes with mortality transformed his conviction of God's love from conceptual to personal.

Catalyzed by belief and enabled by the skills of journalism, *"Open the Sky"* and his previous book—*Light: A "Jewish Cowboy's" Journey*—reflect his growing focus on the mostly joyous adventure of discovering where God leads, in his own and others' lives.

CPSIA information can be obtained at www.ICGtesting.com
Printed in the USA
LVOW040115191212

312337LV00004B/230/P